On Classical Economics

ON CLASSICAL ECONOMICS

THOMAS SOWELL

YALE UNIVERSITY PRESS   NEW HAVEN & LONDON

Printed in the United States of America.

Library of Congress Cataloging-in-Publication Data

Sowell, Thomas, 1930–
On classical economics / Thomas Sowell.
p. cm.
Includes bibliographical references and index.
ISBN-13: 978-0-300-11316-7 (alk. paper)
ISBN-10: 0-300-11316-1 (alk. paper)
1. Classical school of economics. 2. Economics—History. I. Title.
HB94.S69 2006

330.15'3—dc22   2005026877

A catalogue record for this book is available from the British Library.

The paper in this book meets the guidelines for permanence and durability of the Committee on
Production Guidelines for Book Longevity of the Council on Library Resources.

10 9 8 7 6 5 4 3 2 1

CONTENTS

Preface   *vii*

Acknowledgements   *ix*

Social Philosophy of Classical Economists   1

Classical Macroeconomics   22

Classical Microeconomics   48

Classical Methodology   79

Sismondi: A Neglected Pioneer   104

The Enigma of John Stuart Mill   129

The Mysteries of Marxian Economics   155

Thoughts on the History of Economics   187

Notes   *203*

Index   *285*

PREFACE

The history of an intellectual discipline is more than a collection of facts. The history of economics has relevance and implications well beyond the boundaries of the profession. Brilliant and profound minds struggled for years with economic complexities, and with each other, before evolving principles and tools of analysis that can now be taught in a few meetings of an introductory economics class. When David Ricardo wrote to his friend Thomas Malthus in 1814, "I sometimes suspect that we do not attach the same meaning to the word demand," he was not only correct, he was putting his finger on a complex subject behind a simple word, and an ambiguity that would not be resolved by economists until decades after he and Malthus had both passed from the scene.

Retracing the footsteps of giants not only makes us witnesses to the intellectual clashes of the past, it adds depth to our understanding of the ideas that resulted from it all and which are still with us today. The history of economics can shed light on the history of ideas in general, and much that we can learn from that history about the dynamics of controversies and the emergence of paradigms applies to other fields and to our own times, as well as to the past. We can also learn how many misconceptions of the past exist today and how easy it is to be mistaken about people and ideas, past and present. This is especially so when we make the mistake of reading the ideas, concerns, and agendas of the present back into the past, instead of seeing the thoughts and thinkers of the past in their own context.

Most of the essays that follow first appeared in print over a span of more than four decades while the essays on John Stuart Mill and Karl Marx were written expressly for this book. So was the final essay on the history of economic thought, as a look back on a lifetime of research in the field that first attracted me to economics.

Brought together now, these essays present a sketch of one of the long stages through which economics went before emerging as the discipline we know today. I can only hope that these essays bring as much pleasure and sense of understanding to the reader as the research and writing of them did for me.

Thomas Sowell
The Hoover Institution
Stanford University

ACKNOWLEDGEMENTS

The article on Sismondi is reprinted from the Spring 1972 issue of *History of Political Economy*, whose permission to copyright it is hereby acknowledged. Permission to reprint the first four essays was granted by Princeton University Press, which first published them in 1974 as *Classical Economics Reconsidered*. Acknowledgement must also be made to Brandeis University and the University of California at Los Angeles for grants which allowed me to do the research for the article on Sismondi. Colleagues at UCLA who made valuable comments on the first four essays included Professors William R. Allen and Earl Thompson, as well as a then graduate student, Gerald P. O'Driscoll, who has since gone on to a distinguished career. Last, but by no means least, the support of the Hoover Institution is gratefully acknowledged for enabling me to do the research and writing of the remaining essays, as well as much other work in my quarter century at this outstanding institution. A special debt must also be acknowledged to my assistants Na Liu, who prepared the computer files from which this book was typeset, and Elizabeth Costa, whose meticulous work ferreted out errors, inconsistencies, and unclear statements that had escaped the attention of the author, reviewers, and copy-editors. Any remaining errors are of course my own responsibility.

Social Philosophy of Classical Economists

The classical period in the development of economics is an important chapter in intellectual history, with general implications for the evolution of concepts, the dynamics of controversy, and basic problems of methodology. Yet too often the insights of that era are lost behind a veil of myths and stereotypes about classical economics that have arisen in later eras. Many people outside — and even inside — the economics profession think of the classical economists in terms of social conservatism, blind faith in the market, denials of depression, and dismal prognoses of subsistence wages. This image has become as common as it is grossly inaccurate.

Vague and shifting terms have become so common in discussions of the classical economists that any reconsideration of them must begin with such basic questions as who they were, what these particular individuals had in common that causes them to share a common label, and what their role was in the intellectual and social history of their time. The main substantive propositions of classical economics still require enumeration, definition, and analysis, despite — and to some extent, because of — the voluminous interpretive literature which has accumulated over the years. The criticisms of the classical economists, by their contemporaries and by modern interpreters, must also be considered in order to understand their role and their relevance to modern economics and to intellectual history generally.

THE MEANING OF CLASSICAL ECONOMICS

Who was "classical"? Definitions range from that of Karl Marx, who coined the term, to that of John Maynard Keynes, who gave it its broadest meaning. For Marx, classical economics began with Sir William Petty and ended with Ricardo in England, and covered the period from Boisguillebert to Sismondi in France[1] — in both countries, spanning the period from the turn of the eighteenth century to the second decade of the nineteenth century.

The distinguishing feature of classical economics, as seen by Marx, was its emphasis on human relationships in the economic process — "economic sociology" in modern terms — as contrasted with "vulgar economics," which emphasized economic phenomena narrowly defined.[2] The classical economists had, of course, also dealt with economic phenomena in the narrow, impersonal sense — as did Marx himself — but, according to Marx, only as part of an explanation of more general social relationships. Marx's criticism of the classical economists, in this regard, was that they did not clearly *separate* the two kinds of inquiries on different levels of abstraction[3] (as he did in the three volumes of *Capital*).[4] Clearly Marx conceived of the classical economists as forerunners of Marxian economics, as suggested by the title of his mammoth history of economic thought: *Theories of Surplus Value*.

The Keynesian definition of classical economics was no less tendentious and egocentric. It included all of the post-Ricardian economists who had not repudiated Say's Law.[5] This led him to include among the "classical" works writings only a few years old at the time his *General Theory* appeared — writings whose doctrines appeared to a leading contemporary to be "quite as strange and novel as the doctrines of Mr. Keynes himself."[6] Moreover, there were serious questions raised from the outset as to whether *any* identifiable set of economists had ever believed the things attributed by Keynes to the "classical economists" as he defined them. Certainly no major economist from David Hume to the present has ever claimed (or suggested) that the velocity of circulation of money remains constant through all phases of the business cycle, which Keynes treated as a major classical doctrine to be refuted.[7] Indeed, most of the classical and neoclassical economists were quite explicit that it did not.[8]

Since the two classic definitions of classical economics, by Marx and by Keynes, are both so idiosyncratic, some other basis must be sought for the general usage of the term. There is something honorific, as well as indicative of certain doctrines and approaches, in the term "classical" economics. It connotes the giants of the field — Adam Smith and Ricardo, but not Harriet Martineau or Jane Marcet, who popularized the same doctrines and who may have directly reached a wider audience than the more illustrious economists. In economics, as elsewhere, "classical" usually implies something that has established an authoritative tradition which serves as a point of departure for later developments in the same field. In this sense, Adam Smith can be said to have founded classical economics, even if many (or all) of his concepts and theories can be found scattered through the works of numerous predecessors who left no disciples and founded no enduring school.

Since the authoritative tradition that built upon *The Wealth of Nations* underwent a major change with the marginalist revolution of the 1870s, the end points of classical economics can be reasonably well established, about a hundred years apart. Within that span, there were three men who were clearly classical in every sense: Adam Smith, David Ricardo, and John Stuart Mill. There were others as fully part of the same tradition, though not of equal stature, James Mill and J.R. McCulloch being the best representatives of this group. There were still others who contributed key concepts to classical economics without sharing all of its methods and conclusions: J.B. Say, whose law was embedded in classical tradition, but who opposed the classical theory of value; T.R. Malthus, whose population theory held a central position in classical economics, but who was a leading dissenter on the value theory and on Say's Law; and Sir Edward West, who shared with Malthus the development of the law of diminishing returns and the "Ricardian" rent theory,[9] but who did not join in the general development of classical economics.

There were other economists who did not make contributions of this magnitude, but who shared with Say and Malthus the characteristic of being classical in some respects but not in others: Robert Torrens, Nassau Senior, and Karl Marx being prominent among these. In short, the classical economists were not a sharply defined set of economists, but a certain small solid core shading off into a larger penumbra, which was an essential part of the overall phenomenon, since classical economics includes fundamental ideas which did not originate with those who were classical economists in all respects.

The criticisms of classical economics by contemporaries and by later interpreters can be divided into (1) criticisms of the philosophy underlying classical approaches and conclusions, and (2) criticisms of the substantive economic analysis which constitutes classical economics. The philosophic criticisms include criticisms of methodology as well as criticisms of social values and the general classical moral and behavioral theories. The positive economic propositions criticized included all the major propositions of classical economics: the labor theory of value, Say's Law, the Malthusian population theory, and the quantity theory of money.

THE "CONSERVATISM" OF THE
CLASSICAL ECONOMISTS

The classical economists are often depicted as defenders of the status quo, apologists for the socioeconomic powers (and practices) that be, and as believers in a "natural harmony" which makes deliberate intervention in the economy unnecessary and detrimental. Sometimes they are excused because the "simpler" conditions of their time were more in accord with their theories than are the "complexities" of our time. Of course, there is not a shred of evidence that eighteenth-century or nineteenth-century society was any simpler than present day society, though undoubtedly our *knowledge* of the complexities of other ages is often primitive and shallow. Moreover, the notion that laissez-faire economics originated in a laissez-faire world[10] is grotesque.

Transfer versus Production of Wealth

Mercantilism was still the dominant theory and practice when Adam Smith's *The Wealth of Nations* appeared in 1776, though it was an orthodoxy already under attack theoretically and beginning to crumble in practice. The mercantilists still promoted and supported an enormous array of detailed economic controls designed to produce an export surplus, largely at the expense of the lower classes, by keeping labor cheap so as to be able to undersell foreigners in the international market while still permitting substantial profits for domestic merchants and manufacturers. Adam Smith opposed the mercantilists, not simply on policy, but on such basic concepts as the meaning of "wealth" and the meaning of "nation."

The mercantilists conceived of wealth in *competitive* terms, as something taken by one from another, an inherently differential gain, like winning a race.[11] It was *only* "the demand of strangers" which could increase the wealth of a nation, according to mercantilist doctrine.[12] Wealth being gold, which is obtainable by an export surplus, riches "are forbid to all countries which have neither mines, or foreign trade."[13] It is only "the treasure which is brought to the Realm by the ballance of our foreign trade" which constitutes the amount "by which we are enriched."[14] The government was repeatedly invoked to advance the economic interests of society "at the expense of other societies."[15] The cardinal rule of mercantilism was "to sell more to strangers yearly than we consume of theirs in value."[16] By the same token, a nation must try to produce at home, instead of buying abroad "things which now we fetch from strangers to our great impoverishing."[17]

From the mercantilist point of view, not only an export surplus but also the repression of wages, the promotion of imperialism and even slavery could be seen as natural corollaries to the pursuit of wealth by the propertied classes which constituted the nation. With the nation conceived of as only part of its population, it was possible to speak of "a whole nation fed and provided for gratuitously"[18] under slavery.

Adam Smith's conception of the nation was implicit in his statement that "no society can be flourishing and happy, of which the far greater part of the members are poor and miserable."[19] This seems so obvious today only because society or the nation is implicitly conceived of as coextensive with its population — a view by no means universally accepted by Smith's contemporaries in Europe or in America. Even a century later, John Stuart Mill could say, "When they say country, read aristocracy, and you will never be far from the truth."[20]

Wealth, according to Smith, et. al.

For Smith and later classical economists, wealth was conceived of not as a stock of money but as a flow of goods — "real income" in modern terminology.[21] Smith rejected the view "which represents national wealth as consisting in the abundance, and national poverty in the scarcity, of gold and silver."[22] More fundamentally, Smith and the classical school stressed the *creation* of wealth, rather than its *transfer*. International trade was seen as a source of mutual benefit, rather than of differential gain, since it led to a larger and cheaper aggregate output among the trading partners.[23] Both imperialism and slavery were regarded as *losing* ventures by Smith, for they inhibited the creation of wealth while concentrating on its appropriation.

The classical economists saw the gains from imperialism going to a small class of wealthy businessmen and colonial officials to be greatly outweighed by the costs paid by the taxpayers to maintain an empire. Adam Smith declared that "great fleets and armies . . . acquire nothing which can compensate the expense of maintaining them."[24] The interference of the mother country with the colonies' economies inhibited the latter's economic development,[25] but without a corresponding gain to the mother country, except in terms of national glory. The loss of one was not the gain of the other, for the aggregate output between them was reduced below what it would otherwise be. *The Wealth of Nations* closed with the observation "it is surely time that Great Britain should free herself from the expense of defending those provinces in time of war, and of supporting any part of their civil or military establishments in time of peace, and endeavor to accommodate her future views and designs to the real mediocrity of her circumstances."[26]

Adam Smith could not have felt that this rational advice would be heeded, for he had observed earlier:

> No nation ever voluntarily gave up the dominion of any province, how troublesome soever it might be to govern it, and how small soever the revenue which it afforded might be in proportion to the expense which it occasioned. Such sacrifices, though they might frequently be agreeable to the interest, are always mortifying to the pride of every nation, and what is perhaps of still greater consequence, they are always contrary to the private interest of the governing part of it, who would thereby be deprived of the disposal of many places of trust and profit, of many opportunities of acquiring wealth and distinction, which the possession of the most turbulent, and to the great body of the people, the most unprofitable province seldom fails to afford.[27]

Similar reasoning later led James Mill to regard the British Empire as an elaborate government make-work project, "a vast system of outdoor relief for the upper classes."[28] Ricardo saw theoretical possibilities for a nation as a whole to benefit economically at the expense of its colonies,[29] but did not argue that this had in fact happened generally.

Slavery was attacked not only in moral terms but in economic terms by the classical economists. Its key economic weakness was the <u>absence of the incentive of self-interest by the worker</u>. Although the maintenance costs of slaves were lower than the rate of pay of free workers, the labor costs of getting a given amount of work done with slaves was often higher, Smith claimed.[30] Though "work done by slaves . . . appears to cost only their maintenance" he said, it is "in the end the dearest of any."[31] It was man's "pride," which "makes him love to domineer," rather than the economics of the situation, which explained the persistence of slavery for Smith.[32]

Ricardo did not analyze the economics of slavery, though he did express his shame at being part of a nation that permitted it.[33] John Stuart Mill argued morally against slavery[34] and, as an economist, followed the classical tradition by pronouncing it "inefficient and unproductive," due to its limited incentives.[35] Mill, however, was not nearly as confident as Smith had been that slavery was so unprofitable to the individual slave owner that only psychological reasons could explain its persistence. Mill sharply separated the question of the profitability of slavery to slave owners from the larger question of the economic effect of slavery on "the community,"[36] which was considered largely negative.

The most thorough application of classical economic analysis to slavery was *The Slave Power* by John Elliot Cairnes, a disciple of Mill and often considered the last of the classical economists. Cairnes systematically traced the economic and social consequences of slavery, including (1) the exhaustion of the soil by a work force whose incentives were insufficient to produce a varied knowledge and application of agricultural techniques,[37] (2) the desperate need for territorial expansion by a slaveholding community, to replace its own successively exhausted soils,[38] and (3) the external cost of slavery in generating attitudes inimical to economic progress in the general free population.[39] His was the most systematic application to slavery of the classical approach, which viewed the creation of wealth as central, in contrast to the mercantilistic emphasis on its appropriation or transfer.[40]

Political Classes

In addition to opposing such major contemporary institutions as imperialism and slavery, the classical economists attacked the dominant social classes of the time: the landed aristocracy, the rising capitalists, and the political powers that be. A recurring theme in *The Wealth of Nations* was "the clamour and sophistry of merchants and manufacturers,"[41] whose "mean rapacity" and "monopolizing spirit"[42] led them "on many occasions" to "deceive and even to oppress the public."[43] These were people who "seldom meet together, even for merriment and diversion, but the conversation ends in a conspiracy against the public, or in some contrivance to raise prices."[44] In contrast to the exalted role of "the statesman" in mercantilist literature,[45] Adam Smith referred to "that insidious and crafty animal, vulgarly called a statesman or politician, whose councils are directed to the momentary fluctuation of affairs."[46] Political leaders were not only careless of the public's long-run interests but extravagant with its tax money, according to Smith:

> It is the highest impertinence and presumption, therefore, in kings and ministers, to pretend to watch over the economy of private people, and to restrain their expense, either by sumptuary laws, or by prohibiting the importation of foreign luxuries. They are themselves always, and without any exception, the greatest spendthrifts in the society. Let them look well after their own expense, and they may safely trust private people with theirs. If their own extravagance does not ruin the state, that of their subjects never will.[47]

Landlords were regarded by Smith as well meaning on the whole, though easily taken in by businessmen,[48] but landlords were passive beneficiaries of progress[49] and "love to reap where they never sowed."[50] If the landlord got off relatively lightly in Smith, he was the chief villain of the Ricardian school. Landlords grew richer "in their sleep, without working, risking or economizing,"[51] according to John Stuart Mill, their income being the price exacted for their "consent" for the use of land, a consent made necessary solely "by the arrangements of society,"[52] a legalized "tribute"[53] paid to someone who is "merely a sinecurist" quartered on the land.[54] The great political crusade of the Ricardians was the repeal of the Corn Laws, which kept wheat prices artificially high to benefit the landed interests.

Capitalists were considered more useful, but no more appealing, at least not to John Stuart Mill, who said: "I confess I am not charmed with the ideal of life held out by those who think that the normal state of human beings is that of struggling to get on; that the trampling, crushing, elbowing, and treading on each other's heels, which form the existing type of social life, are the most desirable lot of humankind, or anything but the disagreeable symptoms of one of the phases of industrial progress."[55]

One of the most ill-founded charges against the classical economists is that they believed in a natural "harmony of interests" among the various social classes. Certainly the classical economists did not regard social classes as subjectively harmonious nor the political rulers as a harmonizing influence. The laissez-faire doctrine of the classical economists was based on the hope and belief that *conflict* — economic competition — within a suitable institutional framework would lead to the best allocation of resources. It was not "benevolence" but "their own interest" which caused people to serve each other, according to Smith.[56]

The famous "contradiction" between the "sympathy" which was central to Adam Smith's *The Theory of Moral Sentiments* in 1759 and the "self-interest" which was central to his *The Wealth of Nations* in 1776 is more apparent than real. It is one thing to explain how we derive our moral sentiments and quite another to explain economic behavior, which is only partially affected by moral sentiments. The shift of topics between the two books was not a change of mind. *The Theory of Moral Sentiments* itself had regarded beneficence as "less essential to society than justice," without which society "must in a moment crumble into atoms."[57] It was the artificial maintenance of some system of justice — *indirectly* derived from sympathy — and not any "natural harmony" among men which made possible the existence of society, even "without any mutual love and affection . . . by a mercenary exchange of good offices according to an agreed evaluation."[58]

The supposed "harmony of interests" in Adam Smith has often been interpreted to mean that the optimum situation for society is simply the aggregation of individual optimum situations — ignoring mutual interdependence and committing the fallacy of composition. But Smith never advanced such a doctrine, and his famous reference to an "invisible hand" which leads the individual self-seeker "to promote an end which was no part of his intention,"[59] suggests that he did distinguish individual benefit from social benefit conceptually, advancing a *behavioral theory* that the former promoted the latter (by its effect on resource allocation), not a conceptual *identity* that simply defined the latter as the summation of the former. Private and social economic interests coincided in an uncontrolled market "in ordinary cases,"[60] not by definition. In cases where externalities were involved, Smith was prepared to agree even to "a manifest violation" of natural liberty when "the natural liberty of a few individuals" endangered society at large — not only in such things as fire regulations but also in certain banking regulations as well.[61]

The emphasis of the Ricardian school on the distribution of income by social class certainly was not one which exemplified any "harmony of interests." In Ricardo, as in Smith, the landlord gained in the long run at the expense of capitalists and workers,[62] and, in addition, wages and profits — in Ricardo's peculiar definitions — always moved inversely to one another.[63] John Stuart Mill found the distribution of income anything but harmonious, "the largest portions" going to "those who have never worked at all, the next largest to those whose work is almost nominal, and so in a descending scale, the remuneration dwindling as the work grows harder and more disagreeable, until the most fatiguing and exhausting bodily labour cannot count with certainty on being able to earn the necessaries of life."[64]

Even J.B. Say, sometimes depicted as an apologist for the status quo, was in fact quite critical of existing conditions:

... in countries said to be in a flourishing condition, how many human beings can be enumerated, in a situation to partake of such enjoyments? One out of a hundred thousand at most; and out of a thousand, perhaps not one who may be permitted to enjoy what is called a comfortable independence. The haggardness of poverty is everywhere seen contrasted with the sleekness of wealth, the extorted labour of some compensating for the idleness of others, wretched hovels by the side of stately colonnades, the rags of indigence blended with the ensigns of opulence; in a word, the most useless profusion in the midst of the most urgent wants.

Persons, who under a vicious order of things have obtained a competent share of social enjoyments, are never in want of arguments to justify to the eye of reason such a state of society; for what may not admit of apology when exhibited in but one point of view? If the same individuals were to-morrow required to cast anew the lots assigning them a place in society, they would find many things to object to.[65]

To say that the classical economists were not advocates of "natural harmony" doctrines is not to deny that such doctrines flourished in the classical period or that classical theories were used by popularizers of such doctrines. Bastiat's *Harmonies économiques* in 1850 was perhaps the most famous, though by no means the sole, example of this genre. Richard Cobden, Jane Marcet, Harriet Martineau, and numerous others preached social harmony, as to some extent did T.R. Malthus, who had one foot in the classical tradition and one foot outside. The classical economists cannot be blamed for the uses made of their doctrines, and in at least one case — John Stuart Mill reviewing Harriet Martineau — there was a public repudiation of these social apologetics.[66] Indeed, one of the distinguishing features of classical economics, which Marx contrasted with later "vulgar economics," was that the classical economists had openly discussed "the economic bases of the different classes" and their "ever-growing antagonism."[67]

The Market

Although the classical economists favored the conduct of economic activity through market processes rather than political processes, it should not be supposed that they found the market perfect. The classical economists recognized the existence of monopolies, and in fact used the term "monopoly" very broadly to include many forms of market imperfection or inelastic supply, as in the "monopoly" of land.[68]

Adam Smith saw the effect of a monopoly as "keeping the market constantly understocked"[69] and reducing the efficiency of management, which requires highly competitive markets to force everyone to be efficient in "self-defense."[70] Monopolies cause "the whole annual produce of the land and labour" to be "less than they would otherwise be"[71] because they "derange more or less the natural distribution of the stock of society."[72] In addition, Smith recognized the external social costs of the division of labor, which demoralized the worker who performed simple, repetitive tasks, and advocated publicly subsidized schooling — not to be general in England for another century — to offset this.[73] Ricardo (and his contemporary disciples) formally analyzed a model of perfect competition, though noting in *ad hoc* fashion the existence of monopoly, defined as inelastic supply.[74] John Stuart Mill went beyond the simple dichotomy of competition and monopoly to suggest modifications of traditional competitive results due to social mores, even in markets not structurally non-competitive.[75] The classical economists were not rigidly opposed to all government intervention in the market. Smith's "natural liberty" and laissez-faire principle was never a dogma.[76] The classical economists not only accepted certain intervention in the market, they suggested some themselves. Adam Smith wanted highway toll charges to be so arranged that the luxuries of the rich would subsidize the shipment of the necessities of the poor.[77] He also wanted a tax system which would be somewhat progressive and redistributive,[78] based on the ability-to-pay principle.[79] John Stuart Mill advocated public subsidy of emigration by the poor.[80]

While classical economists neither asserted the perfection of the market nor denied any possible beneficial role to government intervention in the economy, they were steadfast in their *general* policy of laissez-faire, in part precisely because of the *dis*harmony of interests and the dangers to the public when organized private groups influenced government economic policy. Adam Smith said:

> . . . the monopoly which our manufacturers have obtained . . . has so much increased the number of some particular tribes of them, that, like an overgrown standing army, they have become formidable to the government, and upon many occasions intimidate the legislature. The member of Parliament who supports every proposal for strengthening this monopoly, is sure to acquire not only the reputation of understanding trade, but great popularity and influence with an order of men whose numbers and wealth render them of great importance. If he opposes them, on the contrary, and still more if he has authority enough to be able to thwart them, neither the most acknowledged probity, nor the highest rank, nor the greatest public services, can protect him from the most infamous abuse and detraction, from personal insults, nor sometimes from real danger, arising from the insolent outrage of furious and disappointed monopolists.[81]

To Smith, government intervention in the economy was conceived of as intervention on behalf of the wealthy and powerful — as it was overwhelmingly in his day, and as it still is to a greater extent than popularly assumed, even today.

By the time of John Stuart Mill, it was at least widely believed that government intervention in the economy on behalf of the poor was a real prospect, so that Mill criticized "impatient reformers, thinking it easier to get possession of the government than of the intellects and dispositions of the public," such reformers being "under a constant temptation" to expand "the province of government."[82]   Mill declared that laissez-faire "should be the general practice" and "every departure from it, unless required by some great good, is a certain evil."[83]   This was not only because governments tended to be inefficient,[84] but because democratic government readily becomes a vehicle by which intolerant majorities can impose their standards and tastes on individuals,[85] and because the spread of government economic activity was also the spread of its extra-legal influence,[86] including its ideological influence on education[87] and its seductive opportunities for important jobs.[88]

The classical economists were profoundly mistrustful of all governments.   Ricardo considered it "salutary" that government action should be constrained by a certain "dread of insurrection,"[89] though he had no desire to see actual insurrection and promoted reform as "the most efficacious preventative of Revolution."[90]

Wars

In addition to attacking the most powerful classes, institutions, and philosophies of their time, the classical economists opposed the contemporary wars in which their countries were engaged or were being urged to engage.   Smith's *The Wealth of Nations* appeared in the year of the American Declaration of Independence from Great Britain, and his analysis of that conflict led him to suggest either a negotiated peace or a unilateral withdrawal by his own country.[91]   During the Napoleonic Wars, James Mill urged a negotiated peace,[92] though powerful forces were in favor of a policy of fighting on to total victory, as of course Britain did.   The elder Mill declared that "war is the greatest calamity with which a nation can be visited."[93]   In a later era, John Stuart Mill was to say of a British military leader and hero, "every feather in his cap has cost the nation more than he and his whole lineage would fetch if they were sold for lumber."[94]   J.B. Say expressed similar disgust with the "military fanaticism" of Napoleon.[95]

The classical economists were less naive than some modern opponents of war. Wars were not seen as simply the work of evil men who imposed them on "the people," but as popularly supported adventures. Adam Smith said:

> In great empires the people who live in the capital, and in the provinces remote from the scene of action, feel, many of them, scarce any inconveniency from the war; but enjoy, at their ease, the amusement of reading in the newspapers the exploits of their own fleets and armies. To them this amusement compensates the small difference between the taxes which they pay on account of the war, and those which they had been accustomed to pay in time of peace. They are commonly dissatisfied with the return of peace, which puts an end to their amusement, and to a thousand visionary hopes of conquest and national glory, from a longer continuance of the war.[96]

Smith urged that wars not be financed by government deficits but by pay-as-you-go taxation, so that the full economic cost should be clearly visible and personally felt by everyone.[97] Were this policy followed, wars "would in general be more speedily concluded and less wantonly undertaken," he said.[98] Ricardo opposed the creation of a special fund to retire the national debt on grounds that it was sure to be diverted to military adventures: "While ministers have this fund virtually at their disposal they will on the slightest occasion be disposed for war. To keep them peaceable you must keep them poor."[99]

The classical economists were not pacifists,[100] but were simply critical of the wars of their time and of the recklessness with which wars had been undertaken throughout history. Opposition to war in general is much easier than opposition to the particular current wars supported by one's fellow countrymen, but the classical economists boldly opposed both.

THE PRACTICAL BEHAVIOR OF
THE CLASSICAL ECONOMISTS

The classical economists were men of affairs as well as theorists, and their actual behavior in the struggles of their times provides additional evidence on their underlying values and convictions.

One fact stands out clearly: the classical economists were not activated by personal self-interest in the things they advocated. Adam Smith, who achieved financial security from an annuity paid for tutoring a young nobleman on a tour of the continent, declared this method of acquiring an education "absurd" in *The Wealth of Nations.* [101]   He also denounced the indolence, irresponsibility, and log-rolling in his own profession as an academician. [102]   Contrary to prevailing practice, he insisted on returning students' fees when he had to be absent. [103]   Ricardo's economics and his speeches in Parliament attacked the landed interests more severely than any other, though he was himself a large landholder. This pattern was typical of Ricardo's whole career:

> When a Bank proprietor, he argued strenuously and warmly against the inordinate gains of that body; he defended the cause of the fund-holders when he had ceased to be one; he was accused of an attempt to ruin the landed interest after he became a large landed proprietor; and while a member of Parliament, he advocated the cause of reform, which, if adopted, would have deprived him of his seat. [104]

Personal pecuniary self-interest was by no means a dominating characteristic of the classical economists themselves. Adam Smith gave away "large sums" in secret acts of charity, "much beyond what would have been expected from his fortune."[105] Ricardo also secretly offered and gave aid to friends in financial distress.[106] Henry Thornton, the leading monetary theorist of the classical period, provided the money for Hannah More's schools for the poor for 25 years,[107] and before his marriage gave away six-sevenths of his annual income to charity.[108] Nassau Senior, holder of the first chair in political economy at Oxford, went into teaching at a salary no more than one-fifth what he had been earning in non-academic pursuits.[109] John Stuart Mill "gave money freely," sometimes to organized charities and sometimes to poor people he simply encountered on the streets.[110]

Malthus, who usually defended landlords, was no landlord himself. Malthus was a far more conservative figure than Adam Smith or the Ricardians. So were Lauderdale and Chalmers, who, together with Malthus, were the major figures in the British school of dissenters from Say's Law. If Malthus is to be regarded as classical, then he must be held responsible for a highly conservative image which was generalized to those more centrally classical economists who took very different positions from him on most social and political issues. It is doubtful whether the general public carefully distinguished the different schools of economists, since political economy was a new phenomenon in itself, and educated opinion in the early nineteenth century tended to be divided for and against the whole field. Certainly such popular writers as William Cobbett lumped Ricardo, Malthus, and others together for a general condemnation, and his approach could not have been unique, for Walter Bagehot observed that "no real Englishman in his secret soul was ever sorry for the death of a political economist."[111]

One of the crusades of the classical period was the drive to repeal the Combination Laws which had effectively outlawed labor unions as conspiracies. Adam Smith had alluded to the partiality of such laws, which left working men at the mercy of "combinations" of employers who are in "a sort of tacit, but constant and uniform combination, not to raise the wages of labour."[112] Francis Place, a Benthamite in politics and in economics a disciple of Ricardo and James Mill, spearheaded the

drive.[113] He was aided by McCulloch,[114] who was encouraged
by Ricardo, who termed such laws "unjust and oppressive to the
working classes."[115]   James Mill joined "heartily" in Francis
Place's drive for schools for the poor,[116] and John Stuart Mill, as
a young man, was arrested with Place for handing out birth
control leaflets in a working-class neighborhood.[117]   Even
Malthus supported child labor laws.[118]

The central figures in classical economics promoted or
supported many specific reforms in their own times, most of
these reforms being aimed at aiding the working class or the poor
generally.   However, some reforms with similar aims were
opposed by the classical economists, as conflicting with specific
classical doctrines — notably the Malthusian population theory.
Moreover, some classical economists or disciples were more
reform-oriented than others — as was true among their
non-classical contemporaries, such as Nassau Senior.[119] There
was, in short, no rigid doctrinaire position on social policy in
general or on the specific issues of the day.

SUMMARY AND IMPLICATIONS

The classical economists can hardly be considered
conservative in terms of a favorable predisposition toward
existing institutions or the dominant social classes.   Adam
Smith's attacks on both were sweeping, and the Ricardians
were active in attacking not only economic anachronisms (the
Corn Laws, prohibitions against trade unions, and other
mercantilistic regulations) but were also active — as
Benthamites[120] — in attacks on political relics and abuses.[121]

The rise of more radical critics, schools, and movements
with the development of industrial capitalism made the
classical economists seem more conservative. Moreover, the
rallying cry, *laissez-faire*! was, in the new context, no longer
simply an attack on institutional favoritism to the upper classes.
It was now usable as a defense of new vested interests who were
imposing important external costs on society by unsanitary

working and living conditions, child labor, pollution, etc. The classical economists themselves were not inclined to use their doctrines in this way, and in fact favored some legislation aimed at the abuses of industrialism and urbanism.[122] However, they were constrained to some extent by their general tradition of laissez-faire as well as by the implications of their economic theories. The Malthusian population theory made all kinds of income-transfer policies appear futile as a means of helping the poor, and raised the specter of all of society being dragged down to the poverty level if they attempted directly to raise the poor above it.[123] Say's Law, together with the comparative statics, long-run equilibrium analysis of the Ricardians, made unemployment a transitory phenomenon growing out of passing maladjustments and government interferences. Theories of aggregate disequilibrium and wage inflexibilities were both rejected by the Ricardians.[124]

Whether the conservative elements in a given school of thought arise from predisposition or from the implications of certain analysis may matter little from some points of view. But it matters considerably in assessing claims that ideas in general (or economic theories in particular) are rationalizations of socially determined predispositions,[125] which can be treated as "modern" or "outmoded" instead of being analyzed in terms of their logical and empirical validity.

The really savage comments of the classical economists were all directed toward the powers that be. Their criticisms of more radical thinkers tended to be more in sorrow than in anger. Ricardo's references to Robert Owen were laudatory as to his intentions and character,[126] and he had similarly high regard for the character of Sismondi,[127] though he rejected the specific analyses and policies of both men. John Stuart Mill's analyses of socialist thought were very similar in this respect.[128] Even as conservative an economist as Malthus never impugned the motives of such revolutionary thinkers as Godwin and Condorcet.

One of the curious facts about the classical economists is that most of them were members of minority groups —

minorities not simply in some numerical sense, but in ways that were socially relevant. Being a Scotsman was not an incidental fact in the England of Adam Smith's day, as he discovered in his youth from his fellow students and the Oxford University administration.[129]   In later life he wrote back to Oxford to complain about continuing discrimination against Scottish students, and on another occasion he warned his friend and compatriot David Hume that "the whole wise English nation... will love to mortify a Scotchman."[130]   James and John Stuart Mill, and J.R. McCulloch, were also of Scottish ancestry. David Ricardo was of Jewish ancestry and Jean-Baptiste Say was descended from Huguenots who had fled France during religious persecutions.   Whatever their varying personal fortunes might be, these men were never full-fledged members of the establishment.

Classical   Macroeconomics

Classical economics was much more than a miscellaneous collection of theories and doctrines. Its particular theories and policy prescriptions revolved around a single central concern: economic growth.   Unlike modern growth theory, classical economists were not primarily concerned with the adjustments of the economy to the growth process, but with how such a process could be generated and sustained. The full title of Adam Smith's classic included the nature and *causes* of the wealth of nations.[1]

Even the static Ricardian model was concerned, as a practical matter, with the progress of the economy toward the stationary state, and with what this implied for the functional distribution of income "in different stages of society."[2] The static concept of Say's Law became so entangled in growth theory as to confuse the issues involved in the "general glut" controversy and to cause that controversy to continue needlessly for years. Even such verbal disputes as that revolving around the difference between "productive" and "unproductive" labor (or consumption) turned on growth problems — in this case, the growth-promoting ("productive") labor, spending, or consumption being distinguished from the non-growth-promoting ("unproductive") counterpart by the indirect criterion of product materiality rather than the direct criterion of accumulability.   Education, for example, can be accumulated, even though it is not physical matter. Classical microeconomics revolved as much around economic growth as did classical macroeconomics. Ricardian rent theory and Malthusian population theory, though based on behavior in specific markets (agriculture and labor), dealt with the growth of the economy as a whole.

This concern for promoting growth had a very serious practical basis. Smith argued that it was not in the wealthiest, but in the fastest growing, countries that wages were highest.[3] Only the maintenance of growth kept wages above the subsistence level.

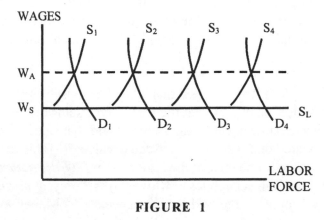

FIGURE 1

The whole classical school — including some who were heretical on other points — accepted the proposition that the long-run supply curve (S_L) of labor was infinitely elastic at some conventional subsistence level. The short-run supply curves (S_1, S_2, S_3, S_4), were rising, since additional labor could be obtained from a given population only by offering higher wages to get more hours from existing workers and/or attract entry into the labor force. Therefore, an ever-increasing demand for labor (D_1, D_2, D_3, D_4) was needed to keep the actual wages (W_A) above the subsistence wages (W_S). If the "stationary state" of Ricardo were ever reached in reality, wages would fall to subsistence. Therefore the maintenance of the on-going growth process was essential for the well-being of the bulk of society. The same preoccupation dominated the dissenters from the classical tradition, as well as the classical economists themselves.

SAY'S LAW

There has been considerable controversy as to whether Say's Law was in fact the product of J.B. Say or of James Mill.

Substantial elements of it had, in fact, appeared earlier in *The Wealth of Nations* (1776). A still earlier version — in some ways better rounded than that of the classical period — existed in *L'Ordre naturel* (1767) by the physiocrat Mercier de la Rivière, whose writings were known to Say, Mill, and Adam Smith.[4]

Origins

Mercier de la Rivière stated that all buyers must be sellers and all sellers must be buyers, that the respective "sums of these two operations must be equal to each other," and that sales "even in money" were "only exchanges of equal values."[5] This *ex post* identity was only one facet of the argument in *L'Ordre naturel,* as in later classical economics. Money was "only a *means of exchange*" not to be confused with "true wealth."[6] Money was an "intermediary standard,"[7] and a distraction which "only threw ideas into such confusion" that the basic barter was overlooked.[8]

Although the equality of supply and demand was sometimes expressed as an *ex post* identity of purchases and sales, it was essentially a behavioral theory of an *ex ante* equality of supply and demand. One must be a seller in order to be a buyer,[9] for sales which one "proposes to make" can continually take place only insofar as one has spent the proceeds of other sales, the various transactions "alternately" providing each other with markets.[10] The correct proportions between supply and demand "will be established by themselves" through the workings of the market, since it is "impossible" that changes in demand and supply will not bring on changes of value which re-establish equilibrium.[11] According to Mercier de la Rivière, "equilibrium can only be deranged accidentally";[12] it will "maintain itself always and *necessarily*, provided that we do nothing to disturb it."[13]

The equality of supply and demand, or of the opposite flows of goods and money, did not mean for Mercier de la Rivière that aggregate output could not change. "Consumption" — which meant aggregate demand as a whole (including investment), in the physiocrats as in the classical economists — "has no known limits,"[14] but at any given time it may be insufficient to cause the

total current output to be reproduced. Consumption was the
measure of *reproduction* (Y_{t+1}),[15] for "production which remains
unconsumed" would "degenerate" in utility and value and
"subsequently advances would cease to be made" for their
production.[16] By "consumed" was not meant merely that the
market was cleared, for consumption meant demand at
cost-covering prices:[17]

> When we say that consumption is the proportional
> measure of reproduction, it must be understood to mean
> a consumption which returns a profit to those whose
> labor and expenses will reproduce the output; a
> consumption which was of no use to them would
> certainly not cause them to labor and to spend in order to
> renew the things which were absorbed.[18]

J.B. Say was openly contemptuous of Mercier de la Rivière's
"tiresome trash,"[19] despite (or because of?) his clear anticipation
of Say's Law. By interpreting consumption in the narrow sense
of consumer demand and by reading the classical emphasis on
growth into this argument, Say and Mill were able to represent
L'Ordre naturel as claiming that spending for consumer goods
promoted growth more than spending for investment goods.[20]
Later interpreters have made the physiocrats predecessors of such
economic dissenters as Sismondi and Malthus (and, ultimately,
Keynes),[21] but they were equally predecessors of classical
orthodoxy.[22] Looked at another way, the physiocrats made Say's
Law and equilibrium income theory mutually compatible, as they
were *not* to be regarded for most of the next 200 years.

Adam Smith separated aggregate demand into investment
and consumer goods components. He argued that savings or
"parsimony" was "the immediate cause of the increase of
capital," and conversely the increase of capital was the inevitable
effect of savings: "What is annually saved is as regularly
consumed as what is annually spent, and nearly in the same time

too."[23] Money "will not be allowed to lie idle."[24] There is only a transactions demand for money. It "can serve no other purpose besides purchasing goods," and it is desired "not for its own sake" but for the sake of what people can purchase with it.[25] Therefore, "though a particular merchant, with an abundance of goods in his warehouse, may sometimes be ruined by not being able to sell them in time, a nation or country is not liable to the same accident."[26] Though here was the essence of Say's Law, Smith did not have the dogmatism of some later classical writers. His doctrines on money were true "in the long-run" and he acknowledged that "goods do not always draw money so readily as money draws goods," that money "is not always obtainable with equal readiness" for goods.[27] But there was no elaboration of such qualifying statements or their implications.

Say's Law, as it emerged during the classical period, was a cluster of related propositions contributed and refined by a number of individuals. Some of these propositions were fully accepted by the dissenting economists of the "general glut" school and some were partially or completely rejected by them. Some have come down through history and others have quietly disappeared along the way. A present-day analysis of Say's Law and of the controversies revolving around it cannot proceed as if the earlier economists were necessarily arguing about the modern doctrine that carries the same name. Say's Law in classical economics involved six major propositions:

1. The total factor payments received for producing a given volume (or value) of output are necessarily sufficient to purchase that volume (or value) of output.[28]

2. There is no loss of purchasing power anywhere in the economy, for people save only to the extent of their desire to invest and do not hold money beyond their transactions needs during the current period.[29]

3. Investment is only an internal transfer, not a net reduction, of aggregate demand.[30] The

same amount that could have been spent by the thrifty consumer will be spent by the capitalists and/or the workers in the investment goods sector.[31]

4. In real terms, supply equals demand *ex ante*, since each individual produces only because of, and to the extent of, his demand for other goods. [32] (Sometimes this doctrine was supported by demonstrating that supply equals demand *ex post*.)[33]

5. A higher rate of savings will cause a higher rate of subsequent growth in aggregate output.[34]

6. Disequilibrium in the economy can exist only because the internal proportions of output differ from consumers' preferred mix — *not* because output is excessive in the aggregate.[35]

In short, this implied that there was no such thing as an equilibrium level of national income.

The first three propositions were never in dispute among any of the recognized economists of the classical period, orthodox or dissenting. These propositions served to refute popular fears that the rapidly growing output and sharp depressions of that period implied that some absolute limit to economic growth had been reached. The general glut economists were as zealous in refuting these popular notions as were the supporters of Say's Law.[36] With the exception of Malthus, they were also as zealous as the orthodox economists in emphasizing the "real" variables in the economy and treating money as only a "veil" which obscured the workings of the economy without affecting end-results.[37]

The last three propositions were the focus of controversy. The fundamental disagreement was over the classical denial of an equilibrium aggregate output (number 6). Sismondi developed a theory of aggregate output equilibrium determined by a balancing of the declining utility of additional output and of the rising disutility of labor. This was analyzed on the individual level through Robinson Crusoe models,[38] and extended to the economy by analogy[39] — with the important note that the complexities of a modern economy made individual miscalculations inevitable, and therefore an aggregate balance problematical.[40]

A very similar theory of equilibrium income reappeared in Malthus' *Principles of Political Economy* a year after Sismondi's *Nouveaux Principes*, though developed by Malthus directly on the economy level and emphasizing the possibilities of a mistaken, excessive volume of savings. According to Malthus, a transitory increment of savings and investment may fail to yield an "adequate" return to investors, so that there is "first an unnatural demand for labour, and then a necessary and sudden diminution of such demand" as disappointed investors disinvest, so as to "throw the rising generation out of employment."[41]

With Say and especially the Ricardians, Say's Law took on the meaning that there was no such thing as an equilibrium level of aggregate output. The classical economists were never guilty of the absurdity of denying the existence of depressions, unemployment, or unsold goods, as sometimes claimed.[42] They recognized such phenomena as effects of production that was internally out of proportion as far as product mix was concerned, but *not* excessive in the aggregate. In John Stuart Mill's words, "production is not excessive, but merely ill-assorted."[43] To Ricardo, "it is at all times the bad adaptation of the commodities produced to the wants of mankind which is the specific evil, and not the abundance of commodities."[44] "Men err in their productions," he said, "there is no deficiency of demand."[45]

Lesser lights pushed this doctrine to its logical conclusion: Equilibrium could be restored by increasing the output of those products undersupplied relative to others — that is by an increase of aggregate output. According to McCulloch, a glut of the market was "not a consequence of production being too much increased, but of its being too little increased." The remedy: "Increase it more."[46] Sismondi accurately summed up the differences between the supporters of Say's Law and the proponents of equilibrium income or "general glut" theories when he said:

> You have produced too much, say some. You have not produced enough, say the others. Equilibrium will be re-established, peace and prosperity will be created again, only when you have consumed all this surplus of merchandise which remains unsold on the market, and when you have regulated your production thereafter by the demand of the buyers. Equilibrium will be re-created, say the others, provided that you redouble the efforts to accumulate as well as to produce. You are mistaken when you believe that our markets are glutted. Our stores are only half filled; let us similarly fill the other half, and these new riches, exchanged against the others, will revive commerce.[47]

The issue — whether aggregate supply always equals aggregate demand — turned on ambiguities in the concept of "demand" as well as in the concept of "cost" underlying supply. For the Ricardians, "demand" was simply the quantity demanded.[48] For Sismondi and Malthus, "demand" meant the quantity demanded at cost-covering prices, where "cost" was the *ex ante* supply price, not simply the *ex post* factor payments, "not what it has cost now, but what it would cost hereafter."[49] Differences between expectations *ex ante* and results *ex post* permitted aggregate supply to differ from aggregate demand, even with no leakages from the circular flow. None of the major general glut theorists — Sismondi, Malthus, Lauderdale, or Chalmers — based his theory on leakages from the circular flow, and all except Malthus went to considerable pains to disassociate themselves from those who did.[50] Malthus felt that too much attention had already been devoted to correcting "the absurd notions of the mercantile classes."[51]

Statics versus Dynamics

In contrast to Ricardian comparative statics, the proponents of equilibrium income or general glut theories reasoned in dynamic terms. Sismondi originated period analysis in his *Richesse commerciale* in 1803, where arithmetic examples and algebraic equations showed a model in which the output of one year was 2.5 times the wages fund of the previous year, in countries with various kinds of international trade balances.[52] Malthus' verbal models were equally dynamic, though not so clearly period analysis. The Ricardians' refutation of the doctrine that some levels of aggregate output could be above the equilibrium — a "general glut" — relied heavily on comparative statics. They showed that "after the readjustment has been affected,"[53] "after the lapse of such a period as would permit... transfer to new businesses," [54] "after an inconsiderable interval,"[55] there can be no "lasting"[56] or "permanent"[57] glut, for people will not "continue" to produce unprofitably,[58] so that the situation will be automatically "rectified" [59] and "infallibly produce its own remedy."[60]

Such statements brought fierce denunciations from contemporary critics that it was "quite useless to repeat, like a parrot, that things have a tendency to find their own level,"[61] and that "this tendency, in the natural course of things, to cure a glut or scarcity, is no more a proof that such evils have never existed, than the tendency of the healing processes of nature to cure some disorders without assistance from man, is a proof that such disorders have not existed." [62] Modern interpreters have overlooked the blind persistence with which the Ricardians translated others' dynamic analyses into comparative statics terms, and have assumed that the general glut controversy was a controversy over permanent secular stagnation [63] rather than cyclical fluctuations and over the concept of an equilibrium income. As Malthus said, "the question of a glut is exclusively whether it may be general, as well as particular, and not whether it may be permanent as well as temporary."[64]

Eventually Ricardo grudgingly yielded somewhat to Malthus' ideas in the dynamic sense that was so alien to his approach.[65] The real conversion was that of Jean-Baptiste Say himself. In the fifth edition of his *Traité d'économie politique* (1826) he openly disavowed the doctrine that there were no short-run limits to production, and in his correspondence of this period he repudiated the Ricardians and their "syllogisms," "obscure metaphysics," "abstract principles," and "vain subtleties." He admitted to Malthus that Say's Law was "subject to some restrictions"[66] and to Sismondi that the fifth edition of his *Traité* contained a "concession" to the latter's theory of equilibrium income.[67] In the *Traité* itself, Say now observed that "it is only with abstract quantities that there are infinite progressions" while "we are studying practical political economy here."[68] He then argued in Sismondian fashion:

> Beyond a certain point, the difficulties which accompany production, and which are in general overcome by productive services, grow at an increasing rate and soon surpass the satisfaction which can result from the use made of the product. Thenceforth a useful thing may certainly be created, but its utility will not be worth what it cost, and it will not fulfill the essential condition of a product, which is to at least equal in value its costs of production.[69]

Say's later textbook, *Cours complet d'économie politique pratique*, first published in 1828–29, followed the chapter on Say's Law with a chapter on "the limits of production,"[70] which repeated the same general reasoning.[71] Unfortunately, neither this work nor that part of his correspondence has ever been translated into English, nor has the fifth edition of his *Traité*. Moreover, Say's "recantation" on this point made no visible impression on the British classical school.

John Stuart Mill's role in the development of Say's Law was an unusual one. On the one hand, his *Principles of Political Economy* (1848) repeated the same arguments and misinterpretations that had existed at the outset of the general glut controversy, nearly 30 years earlier. Throughout Mill's writings, Sismondi, Malthus, and their allies were depicted as believers in secular stagnation;[72] their dynamic analysis was answered in comparative statics terms,[73] and supply was said to equal demand "by the metaphysical necessity of the case,"[74] possessing "all the certainty of a mathematical demonstration" because it depended upon "the very meaning of the words, demand and supply"[75] rather than being contingent on the validity of a particular theory of behavior.

On the other hand, once having disposed of the heretics and their supposed doctrine, Mill discussed the real substance of the issue more clearly and thoroughly than any other classical economist. Mill was, in fact, the first of the classical economists to explore directly the possibility of a demand for money beyond the transactions demand. In his *Essays on Some Unsettled Questions of Political Economy*, he said:

> Although he who sells, really sells only to buy, he needs not buy at the same moment when he sells; and he does not therefore necessarily add to the *immediate* demand for one commodity when he adds to the supply of another. The buying and selling being now separated, it may very well occur, that there may be, at some given time, a very general inclination to sell with as little delay as possible, accompanied with an equally general inclination to defer all purchases as long as possible.[76]

He was still more explicit in his *Principles*: "I have already described the state of the markets for commodities which accompanies what is termed a commercial crisis. At such times there is really an excess of all commodities above the money demand: in other words, there is an under-supply of money."[77] *Ad hoc* suggestions of deficient money demand had been made by Say and Torrens, and implied by Adam Smith, and a deficiency of demand had been dubbed synonymous with excess output by G.P. Scrope.[78]

Mill also set forth a theory of oversaving very similar to that of Malthus, Lauderdale, and Chalmers:

> . . . unless a considerable portion of the annual increase of capital were either periodically destroyed, or exported for foreign investment, the country would speedily attain to the point at which further accumulation would cease, or at least spontaneously slacken, so as no longer to overpass the march of invention in the arts which produce the necessaries of life. In such a state of things as this, a sudden addition to the capital of the country, unaccompanied by any increase of productive power, would be of but transitory duration; since, by depressing profits and interest, it would either diminish by a corresponding amount the savings which would be made from income in the year or two following, or it would cause an equivalent amount to be sent abroad, or to be wasted in rash speculations.[79]

The doctrine that savings promote growth was a prime target of the dissenters, from Lauderdale in 1804 through Chalmers in 1832. All dealt with the dynamic effects of a transitory increment of savings beyond what would be forthcoming at the *ex post* rate of return. All recognized that technological improvements tend to increase the equilibrium volume of profitable investment over time, but argued that at any *given* time, under given conditions of technology and taste, there was a limit to sustainable investment.[80] Sismondi summed up this viewpoint when he said that "a nation which cannot make progress should not make savings."[81]

The classical rejoinders either (1) implicitly assumed that "savings" meant equilibrium increments of savings or (2) pointed out the transience of the situation created. Not all the classical economists followed Adam Smith in promoting savings as a growth-producing factor. Ricardo disavowed any intention to advocate growth-promoting policies in general,[82] though Say and

James Mill were such advocates.[83] Much of the general glut controversy revolved around this now-discarded growth feature of Say's Law. Neither side claimed that saving and investment would remain in disequilibrium in an unregulated market, but the general glut theorists assumed that government fiscal activities sometimes artificially increased savings and investment beyond a sustainable level.[84] They were not discussing "voluntary parsimony," as James Mill noted,[85] so this aspect of the controversy had little in common with modern post-Keynesian controversy, other than the use of similar words.

The doctrine that supply equals demand *ex ante* was sometimes supported by showing that supply equals demand *ex post*. McCulloch pointed out that there cannot "be any *selling* without an equal *buying*."[86] Torrens said that supply and demand were "correlative and convertible" terms while James Mill said that "annual purchases and sales" will "always balance."[87] John Stuart Mill and J.B. Say also had tautological versions.[88] This is not to claim that the whole argument was purely tautological. It was simply defended this way on occasion under polemical stress.

MONETARY THEORY

Several factors add to the difficulty of understanding classical monetary theory or present plausible bases for misinterpretations:

1. The anti-mercantilist origins of classical economics were a continuing verbal influence producing sweeping statements about the unimportance of money — even in the midst of explanations of its effects on real variables.

2. Ricardian comparative statics and concentration on long-run equilibrium assumed away many transitional monetary

phenomena, especially in Ricardo's *Principles of Political Economy and Taxation* — though his polemical pamphlets and correspondence dealt with such problems, even if sometimes somewhat grudgingly.

3. The tendency of the classical economists — and their contemporary opponents — to conceive of causation in sequential terms (rather than in terms of reciprocal interaction or mutual determination)[89] meant that money was sometimes treated as causally neutral when a given series of events was considered to *originate* with a change in some real variable, even though the resulting monetary phenomena were important features of the adjustment process.

4. Keynes' well-known polemical interpretations of classical monetary theory make it difficult to read classical statements with fresh eyes or in the context in which they were originally made.

Many classical monetary doctrines can be traced to *The Wealth of Nations*, whose consuming purpose of refuting mercantilism caused many statements to be made within the framework of a mercantilism-versus-laissez-faire controversy which could not stand alone outside such a framework. Apparently these statements were not meant to stand alone outside such a framework, for other statements were made apparently contradicting them.

As already noted,[90] the mercantilists tended to conceive of wealth as a stock of money or gold, rather than as a flow of real goods and services. Smith and the classical school not only denied that money was wealth[91] or capital[92] but asserted that money was wanted solely for transactions needs — "money can serve no other purpose besides purchasing goods"[93] — and that it did not affect such real variables as the rate of interest,[94] which depended upon the return on real capital.[95] The recipient of money wants it "only for the purpose of employing that money again immediately"[96] in some other transaction, for purchasing "forthwith"[97] something else, according to Say and his followers.[98]

The opponents of Say's Law were no less zealous in promoting the same monetary doctrines. According to Sismondi, money is "immediately" respent,[99] for to allow "useless stagnation" of money would mean "lost interest."[100] Whether money income is consumed or saved, "it is equally spent in either way,"[101] according to Chalmers, so that there was no change in aggregate demand. Sismondi, Chalmers, and Lauderdale deliberately developed their economic analysis "without speaking of money,"[102] without the complications of "overgrown financial arrangements,"[103] for money was "not necessary" to the real phenomena in question, and served only to "obscure the character of the proceeding without essentially changing it."[104] Money was only a "veil" to the general glut theorists as well as to the supporters of Say's Law. The lone apparent exception to this was Malthus, who *mentioned* money as a neglected element,[105] but who did not explore monetary phenomena or incorporate it into his analysis any more than the others did.

What is significant is whether either group meant this in the unqualified way in which it was sometimes expressed. For the same Adam Smith who asserted that "money can serve no other purpose besides purchasing goods," said on the same page that "goods do not always draw money so readily as money draws goods," though "in the long-run" they attract each other. The same J.B. Say who referred to "immediate" respending also referred to idle balances accumulating beyond transactions needs during a depression; the same Sismondi who asserted that money was "immediately" respent also traced the effects of credit contraction in a crisis.[106] Chalmers even referred to capitalists' demand for money wealth as such, aside from any transactions which might be contemplated.[107]

Part of the apparent ambivalence of classical economics in monetary theory was due to implicit shifts between long-run and short-run perspectives, and in part to shifts between arguments against mercantilism (and/or its popular remnants) and general analyses of monetary phenomena. The effect of the money supply on the interest rate illustrates both kinds of shifts. Hume, Smith, Ricardo, and J.S. Mill all denied that the quantity of money affected the interest rate[108] — in the comparative statics sense that once a given amount of money (or gold) had been absorbed into the economy and prices had adjusted accordingly, there was no reason to expect the final equilibrium interest rate to be any different from what it had been initially. They stated that during the transition period, however, the interest rate would tend to be lowered,[109] idle resources activated,[110] and real wealth increased.[111]

Conversely, if there is a contraction of money or credit, then during the transition, there may be "the most disastrous consequences"[112] domestically as well as disturbances in the equilibrium of imports and exports.[113] A strong *precautionary* demand for money may develop,[114] raising the rate of interest.[115] The rate of interest is affected in the short run by changes in the demand for money,[116] as well as by changes in the supply of money.[117]

The leading monetary work of the classical period, Henry Thornton's *Paper Credit of Great Britain* (1802) carefully noted the "immediate" and "temporary" reactions to monetary changes,[118] pointing out that adjustments are "certainly not instantaneous,"[119] and that money may be "hoarded" during a period of "alarm."[120] He also noted "the fresh industry which is excited" during an increase of the money supply.[121] He distinguished these dynamic changes from the effects to be expected after a changed quantity of money "shall have been for some time stationary" and producing its "full effect." In this long-run equilibrium sense, the interest rate is unaffected by the quantity of money,[122] for in the long run it is only a "progressive augmentation" of money "and not the magnitude of its existing amount" which can lower interest rates.[123]

Thornton's careful separation of short-run transitional effects from long-run equilibrium effects contrasts sharply with Ricardo's repeated interpretation of *others'* doctrines in his own comparative statics terms — a feature of Ricardian monetary controversy as well as of Ricardian controversy on Say's Law and general gluts. Even though Jeremy Bentham had explicitly declared it "essential to begin by making a distinction between *immediate* causes and the more or less *remote* causes,"[124] Ricardo's criticism of Bentham's monetary theory was in strictly comparative statics terms — and in these terms Ricardo could not see how "an increase of money will call forth an additional amount of commodities,"[125] though he noted in passing that a momentary effect of this kind might be possible through wage lag and increased profitability,[126] that other "temporary" effects might occur,[127] but in general he assumed that Bentham simply "confounds the terms riches and money."[128] A similar pattern was apparent in Ricardo's polemics with Malthus and Thornton on international money movements.[129]

Perhaps the most familiar features of classical monetary theory were (1) the "quantity theory of money" and (2) the belief that money was a "veil" obscuring but not changing real variables. The real question is the substantive meanings of these two propositions, for in their pure, unqualified senses these two doctrines are incorrect individually, mutually contradictory, and inconsistent with the actual views of the classical economists.

The dominant monetary theory during the classical period was of course the quantity theory of money — but a very different theory in substance from what might be expected from the Keynesian interpretation of it. The idea that the price level usually moves in the same direction as, and at similar rates to, the quantity of money goes back much further than classical economics. The idea that the price level is *rigidly* linked to the quantity of money by a velocity of circulation which remains constant through all transitional adjustment processes cannot be found in any classical, neoclassical, or modern proponent of the quantity theory of money. Changes in the velocity of circulation — short run and/or long run — were analyzed by David Hume, Adam Smith, Henry Thornton, T.R. Malthus, David Ricardo, Nassau Senior, John Stuart Mill, Alfred Marshall, Knut Wicksell, Irving Fisher, and Milton Friedman.[130] A fixed velocity of money was a straw man attacked by Keynes.[131]

The quantity theorists have postulated a relatively stable velocity over long periods of time, though with some secular trends due to evolving methods of economizing in the use of money. Short-run changes in velocity were thought of as more abrupt, and potentially catastrophic in their effects on real variables, but as predictable in theory and foreseeable in practice. Moreover, such changes did not offset changes in the quantity of money, but tended to reinforce them. A rapidly increasing quantity of money tended to reduce money holdings because of fears of its future decline in purchasing power, thereby speeding up the velocity of circulation and causing the price level to rise somewhat more rapidly than the quantity of money. Conversely, a rapidly declining quantity of money tended to produce loss of "confidence" and promoted additional precautionary money holdings, causing deflation to be accentuated.

The actual mechanisms tending to create the conditions described by the quantity theory of money were spelled out only in part during the classical period. However, there was recognition by the classical economists that the general price level rose when there were general shortages of goods at the existing prices. Similarly, there was a general price decline when more goods were supplied than demanded at existing prices. John Stuart Mill was the first major classical economist to equate an excess demand for money with an excess supply of goods, though George Poulett Scrope had done so earlier,[132] and suggestions of such a relationship are found in Robert Torrens[133] and in J.B. Say.[134] Indeed, such a relationship is implied in the many classical denials of a demand for money beyond the demand for it for transactions purposes during the current period. The *neo*classical economists were more explicit in pointing out the inconsistency between the assertion that aggregate supply always equals aggregate demand for goods ("Say's Identity") and the quantity theory of money, which requires the possibility that aggregate supply may differ from aggregate demand, in order to change price levels.[135]

The demand for money was analyzed by the classical economists in much more detail than might be expected from individuals who sometimes wrote as if the only demand for money was a transactions demand and who strenuously denied hoarding. Here, as in other areas of monetary theory, the fullest, most incisive, and most respected [136] analysis during the classical period was that of Henry Thornton. He recognized that during "times of alarm" there is a "disposition to hoard,"[137] that a scarcity of money for some is due to larger than usual cash balances being held by others, causing "a more slow circulation" of money in general.[138]

Ricardo also recognized that "alarm" could cause people to "hoard" money, [139] that money could be demanded for speculative purposes.[140] John Stuart Mill likewise said that during "a commercial crisis" the individual's demand "is specifically for money, not for commodities or capital,"[141] i.e., not simply a transactions demand. Robert Torrens pointed out that the usual relationship between the rate of interest did not hold at such times, that "the interest of money may rise while the profits of stock fall to nothing."[142] The demand exceeds the supply of money during a glut brought on by disproportionality, for while the increased money income of the underproducers equalled the reduced money income of the overproducers (in accordance with Say's Law), the willingness of the former to lend to the latter could be lessened: "The multiplied failures in agriculture, manufacturers, and trade, would strike a panic into the holders of floating capital, and they would refuse to grant accommodation upon securities, which in more prosperous times they would be disposed to consider unobjectionable."[143]

While McCulloch flatly denied that "gluts" were due to "a permanent deficiency of money," he nevertheless agreed that "sudden and extensive changes" in the money supply could cause "great derangement" of the economy and "may thus occasion a glut of the market, not only in the country which is the seat of the revulsion, but also in those countries whence she has been accustomed to draw any considerable portion of her supplies."[144]

The supply curve of money was conceived of quite differently by the classical economists than by modern economists. Instead of an infinitely inelastic money supply determined by monetary authorities, there was an infinitely elastic supply of gold at a national price level equal to that of other nations. The purchasing power of bullion was rendered equal internationally,[145] through either direct gold shipments or through paper transactions that tended to produce the same purchasing power parity. Where there was a paper currency, international price levels need not be equalized but the international purchasing power of gold still tended to be equalized — which meant that, with an inflated paper currency, the bullion price of gold would tend to exceed its value as minted money or its nominal value in paper currency.[146] Various governmental restrictions might prevent these tendencies from manifesting themselves openly, but the pressures generated would work themselves out in other ways, such as the disappearance of gold coins from circulation or international smuggling.

Many of the monetary controversies which raged during the classical period turned on empirical questions as to the past and present behavior of the money supply — defined variously, then as now — and as to the consequences to expect from various policies proposed. Purely theoretical controversy in the monetary field was not a feature of classical economics, though such purely theoretical discussions did occur on a considerable scale in classical value theory and in other areas. The classical economists, with their general distrust of government, tended to regard a paper currency as the road to inflation, but favored paper money in principle, if properly regulated, as a means of replacing gold with a far less expensive device for doing the same work.[147]

Contrary to Keynesian interpretation, the classical economists did *not* assume infinite price flexibility. No such assumption was explicit in the writings of the classical economists, and their repeated acknowledgements of important short-run changes in real variables due to monetary changes implicitly denied perfect price flexibility. As noted above, the classical economists agreed that an increased money supply could, under some short-run conditions, lower the interest rate, bring fuller utilization of capacity, and thereby increase real output. Ricardo also acknowledged that money wage rates might lag behind rising prices, causing a short-run reduction of real wage rates and a corresponding increase of the profit rate, and therefore of the rate of savings and investment.[148] This was the so-called forced savings doctrine, also subscribed to by Malthus, Thornton, and Torrens,[149] among others. Correspondingly, a suddenly decreased money supply could be "disastrous" according to Ricardo,[150] and J.B. Say argued that idle money was in fact a cause of a contemporary depression.[151] Ricardo resisted the idea of downward wage rigidity which was part of the Malthusian system,[152] but he cited examples of it himself.[153] Thornton distinguished the effect of *low* prices from the effect of *falling* prices, arguing that low prices as a permanent equilibrium condition would not cause unemployment, but that a temporary fall in prices, "probably with no correspondent fall in the rate of wages," would cause unemployment and reduced national output.[154]

FISCAL POLICY

The incidence of various forms of taxation by social class and the allocational implications of these taxes were a major microeconomic concern of Ricardo and the Ricardians. Indeed, Ricardo regarded economic principles as directly useful "only" when "it directs Government to right measures in taxation."[155] This was because laissez-faire was a sufficient policy (or lack of policy) elsewhere. The unavoidable necessity of financing government activities made taxation inevitable, and raised the question of how to neutralize the effects of taxes on allocation and distribution. Adam Smith was similarly concerned with the effects of taxation, though not so preoccupied with it as the Ricardians. While the classical economists gave somewhat more attention to the microeconomic aspects of government fiscal operations than to their macroeconomic aspects, they nevertheless had important things to say on the consequences of government fiscal activities on aggregate demand, the capital stock, and employment. The dissenting economists — notably Lauderdale — had even more to say on such macroeconomic questions.

The classical economists opposed deficit spending and advocated paying off the national debt, though not for any of the naive reasons which post-Keynesian economists have concentrated on refuting. The modern doctrine that "we owe it to ourselves" was apparently current in Adam Smith's time, for *The Wealth of Nations* set out to refute the notion that revenue is merely "transferred" without the nation as a whole being "a farthing the poorer."[156] Smith argued that this was factually incorrect, since "a very considerable share in our public funds" was held by foreigners. More fundamentally, Smith and the later classical economists saw the losses from the national debt as resulting from the behavioral responses it produced in the market. Smith saw the heavier taxation made necessary by the existence of a large national debt as a serious disincentive to efficient production at home and a reason for some capital to move abroad.[157] Here Smith did not seem to consider the disincentive effects of alternative means of financing the same governmental expenditures, and in fact he apparently thought that the total expenditure would be less if the government had to go to the people for more taxes instead.

Ricardo likewise opposed deficit spending because it "tends to make us less thrifty — to blind us to our real situation."[158] "In the point of economy, there is no real difference" between tax finance and bond finance, if everyone behaved with perfect rationality, despite those who "have some vague notion" that debt "would be paid by posterity."[159] He asked, "Where is the difference" if a man leaves a given fortune to his heir charged with a given tax, or leaves a fortune free of tax, but smaller by the capitalized value of the total tax payments due.[160] Ricardo, like Smith, feared an export of capital when investors became fearful of the effects of a large national debt.[161] Like Smith he was concerned that the political advantages of deficit spending would increase the total amount spent and increase the danger of "wantonly" — both men used the same word — becoming engaged in war.[162] He added: "There cannot be a greater security for the continuance of peace than the imposing on ministers the necessity of applying to the people for taxes to support a war."[163]

The biggest challenge to classical fiscal policy came from Lord Lauderdale and was connected with his general challenge to Say's Law. Lauderdale made the argument that we owe it to ourselves,[164] that "a transfer of any given sum from the one to the other could never diminish the collective wealth of the whole,"[165] and rejected analogies between public and private debt, so long as the former was an internal debt.[166] This part of his argument represented a revision of classical assumptions rather than a basic theoretical difference. The theoretical differences between Lauderdale and the classical traditions arose during their discussions of the theory of a sinking fund. The so-called sinking fund to retire the national debt, which Smith and Ricardo had denounced as illusory,[167] and as a temptation to increased spending[168] was attacked by Lauderdale in terms of its expected effect if honestly carried out.

According to the theory behind the sinking fund, a series of budgetary surpluses would be invested by the government and the interest and principal used ultimately to retire the national debt. Lauderdale argued that budgetary surpluses would in effect convert consumption expenditures into investment expenditures — "It effects the *creation* and not merely the *transfer* of capital"[169] — thereby raising the question whether there was any limit to profitable investment.

By taxing income which would otherwise have been spent (wholly or partially) on consumption, and devoting it to investment, the sinking fund scheme was one which would produce "forced accumulation, by the authority of the government,"[170] beyond the point where voluntary investment would have been forthcoming at the prevailing rate of return. The involuntary nature of this additional investment was repeatedly stressed by Lauderdale.[171] Even James Mill, in criticizing Lauderdale, acknowledged that the latter was not discussing "voluntary parsimony."[172] In the long run, of course, the same total investment (public plus private) might exist, as the private investors disinvest when the increased supply of capital forces the rate of return below their supply price. Lauderdale did not explicitly discuss this possibility, though his reference to "suddenly" changing demand patterns[173] and to the "rapidity" of forced investment, as well as his general context, suggests a short-run problem. Certainly there was no suggestion of secular stagnation in Lauderdale,[174] who accepted as indisputable that aggregate supply and aggregate demand tended to equality if left to themselves.[175]

Since Lauderdale was as convinced as Smith or Ricardo that the theory of the sinking fund would never be carried out in practice, the real thrust of his argument was directed against the classical view that there is no limit to the amount of capital. Lauderdale was the first to explore the short-run limits to sustainable investment — given declining returns to successive units of capital[176] — and, though his views were ignored or distorted by the Ricardians with their emphasis on comparative statics, the substance of his argument reappeared in its entirety in John Stuart Mill.[177]

The contrast between the wartime prosperity in Britain during the struggle against Napoleon and the postwar depression brought on a number of re-evaluations of the effect of government spending on aggregate demand. The classical doctrine that government spending was only a transfer of spending, rather than a net increment, was challenged by William Blake in 1823. He argued that sometimes liquid funds which were unavailable for private investment at the going rate of return were nevertheless available for the purchase of government bonds at the same rate of return, since the lenders "prefer the security of government to that of private borrowers," [178] so that deficit spending represented a net increment of money demand, rather than a simple transfer. Although Blake disclaimed any attempt to show permanent growth rate increases through fiscal policy,[179] he was attacked by Ricardo, James Mill, and John Stuart Mill in essentially long-run comparative statics terms.[180] Later the younger Mill appropriated (without credit) Blake's assumption of idle capital and idle liquid hoards in the economy in his *Essays on Some Unsettled Questions in Political Economy.*[181]

SUMMARY AND IMPLICATIONS

The preoccupation of classical economics with questions of economic growth influenced their whole development and presentation of macroeconomics. Say's Law answered those who feared that economic growth had reached, or was approaching, some ultimate limit to what the economy could profitably absorb. The central point of Say's Law was that no such limit existed, "otherwise how could it be possible that there should now be bought and sold in France five or six times as many commodities as in the miserable reign of Charles VI?" [182] The dissenters from Say's Law — Sismondi, Lauderdale, Malthus, and others — never challenged the basic proposition that markets could always be cleared or that secular growth was unlimited. They challenged another growth-related idea — that increased quantities of savings necessarily increased the growth rate. For the general glut theorists there was an equilibrium level of savings and output, beyond which declining earnings forced a retrenchment, even though at some future date, under improved technology, a larger amount of savings and/or output would be sustainable.

The role of money was also seen within a growth-related

framework. A greater or smaller quantity of money made no long-run difference to the growth of real output, contrary to the mercantilists, and this was sufficient reason for the classical economists to call it a "veil" which obscures without changing reality. The continuing campaign against popular mercantilist notions led to some strong words on the neutrality of money, which were inconsistent with many classical acknow-ledgements of the short-run effects of money on the behavior of real variables. The possible short-run effects of fiscal policy on aggregate output were ignored or denied by shifting to a long-run perspective in which economic growth was unaffected by transfers. Short-run situations in which the government's supply of investment (Lauderdale) or demand for goods (Blake) represented more than a transfer were denied by assuming that such demand could *only* be a transfer.

While the classical economists were never at their best in interpreting other viewpoints, their understanding of economic phenomena was much more sophisticated than their interpreters have allowed. Despite a penchant for dogmatic assertions, the classical economists had the saving grace of inconsistency which allowed them to recognize exceptions and modifications, and even to quietly incorporate some of the views of heretics, once orthodoxy had been vindicated.

Classical Microeconomics

Classical allocation and distribution theory, like classical macroeconomics, reflected a preoccupation with secular growth. Despite the classical economists' many static concepts and theories, the dominating concerns to which these theories were applied were not wholly or primarily short-run problems. The *analytical law* of diminishing returns, as a static concept, was only a point of departure for discussing *historical* diminishing returns and its implications. The Ricardian scheme of functional distribution under static equilibrium was used as a basis for discussing Ricardo's real concern, the changes in distributional patterns over time[1] with economic growth and development. The short run was largely the province of dissenters during the classical period.

Classical microeconomics was as much dominated by the law of diminishing returns as classical macroeconomics was by Say's Law. Diminishing returns was not only important to the theory of rent, but was also an implicit assumption of the Malthusian population theory, and was essential in the theory of wage and profit movements over time. Classical value theory was the basic building block of the whole classical system as it was developed and presented, but the substantive theories of that system can be presented without the so-called labor theory of value. After consideration of the substance of classical microeconomics, without reference to classical value theory, it will be easier to see the reasons for the various formulations of value theory in the classical period.

DIMINISHING RETURNS

With the law of diminishing returns, as with Say's Law, modern refinements have produced an analytical principle far less ambiguous than that enunciated and disputed in the classical period. Again, as with Say's Law, this analytical clarification can be a source of historical confusion when the modern doctrine is read back into the earlier economists as the object of their discussions and debates. Classical diminishing returns meant three different things:

1. Agricultural output increased at a decreasing rate as inferior land was taken under cultivation. This was simply a tautology, since "inferior" land was inferior precisely with respect to its ability to convert inputs into output.
2. Equal successive increments of variable input added to a fixed input produced declining increments of output at a given level of technology. This approximates the modern, static, law of diminishing returns.
3. Historically, equal successive increments of labor and capital with fixed availability of arable land had produced and/or will produce declining increments of output, despite the usual technological improvements. This was the doctrine that was crucial for classical policy.

The classical economists usually did not keep their ideas on diminishing returns very distinct, but shifted from one concept to another in the middle of their analyses with relative ease and unconcern. Sometimes they treated the law of diminishing returns as referring to a declining average product,[2] sometimes to a declining marginal product,[3] sometimes to a diminishing return with given technology,[4] and sometimes to a diminished return despite technological advance.[5] Diminishing returns were thought to apply peculiarly to agriculture, while manufacturing was thought to show either constant or increasing returns. Here again there was an ambiguity: Manufacturing was sometimes said to have increasing returns to scale,[6] and sometimes to have increasing returns over time.[7] However, Ricardo and McCulloch also noted that the law of diminishing returns and the determination of price by rising marginal cost may apply more generally — outside agriculture as well as within it.[8]

What was quite clear to the classical economists was the crucial importance of diminishing returns for their whole analytical system. John Stuart Mill said: "This general law of agricultural industry is the most important proposition in political economy. Were the law different, nearly all the phenomena of the production and distribution of wealth would be other than they are."[9]

Rent

Few concepts in classical economics were defined so clearly and directly as Ricardian rent: "Rent is that portion of the produce of the earth which is paid to the landlord for the use of the original and indestructible properties of the soil."[10] Yet this definition was immediately modified by Ricardo himself. Whether a payment was made to the landlord or not did not matter. With fixed leases or a tax on rent (or a society with different institutional arrangements), more or less than the rent might go to the landlord, without changing any allocational conclusions.[11] Moreover, not only the original properties of the soil but any permanent improvements yielded rent.[12] Finally, rent could apply outside agriculture.[13] Ricardo's less often quoted definition of rent was more consistently adhered to, and was closer to the modern doctrine: " . . . rent is always the difference between the produce obtained by the employment of two equal quantities of capital and labour."[14]

It was a common expository device of the Ricardians and their popularizers to depict a successive recourse to poorer and poorer land to meet rising food needs. The poorest land cultivated at any given time would be that land whose proceeds would just cover the cost of production, including "normal profits," with nothing left over for rent. The difference between output on such no-rent land and that on superior land was rent.

However, neither varying fertility nor no-rent land was necessary or sufficient for diminishing returns or rent. The assumptions of the West-Malthus-Ricardo analysis can be illustrated on a table showing output with various labor inputs on different grades of land:

	One Worker	Two Workers	Three Workers	Four Workers
Land A	10	18	24	28
Land B	9	16	21	24
Land C	8	14	18	20
Land D	7	12	15	16

Declining increments of output with increased variable inputs — reading across — were sufficient for diminishing returns and rent. If *all* land were *A*-quality land, both diminishing returns and rent would exist. If the price of agricultural produce were sufficient to cause two workers to be employed on land *A*, then the incremental return to the second worker — 8 units — must be yielding normal earnings. Therefore the return to the first worker — 10 units — must yield above normal earnings or rent. Similarly, if three are employed, the second worker's marginal product must include two units of rent and that of the first worker four units. Declining increments as poorer land was used — reading down the columns — was a prominent symptom rather than an essential feature of diminishing returns or rent.

Critics who questioned whether historical land progress patterns were those of the model, or whether there really existed any no-rent land, were wide of the mark. Smith, West, Malthus, and the Ricardians all recognized that the convenience of locations also affected rent,[15] and West remarked that *many* circumstances "may disturb the operation of the principle"[16] of progress to poorer soils. More importantly, recourse to poorer land merely indicated that the law of diminishing returns was *already* operating on better land.[17] If one worker is used on land *B* to produce 9 units of output, it is because the 10 units produced by the first worker on land *A* could not be duplicated by a second worker on land *A*. It "proves that additional work cannot be bestowed with the same advantage as before on the old land."[18]

As for no-rent land, its existence or nonexistence "is of no importance" for the principle, according to Ricardo, "for it is the same thing" if marginal increments of the variable input "yield only the return of stock with its normal profits,"[19] anything more than this being rent. In the table above, if an incremental output of 4 units per worker input yielded "ordinary profits," then four workers would be employed on land *A*, three workers on land *B* and *C*, and two workers on land *D*. Each quality of land would yield rent, equal to the difference between its yield at the no-rent *intensive* margin and the yield of its intramarginal increments of variable input. Rent would thus be 4 units on *D*, 6 on *C*, 9 on *B*, and 12 on *A*. Even if "there is never any *land* taken into cultivation" which does not yield rent, "it would be true, nevertheless, that there is always some *agricultural capital* which pays no rent," [20] John Stuart Mill pointed out, and the intramarginal returns above this measures the Ricardian rent on land.

The Ricardians clearly and consistently emphasized that rent was determined by price but was not itself a determinant of price. Price was determined by the rising cost of production at the margin. Lower cost units of output within the margin had no affect on price but sold for the same price as that already determined by higher cost units, thereby yielding a surplus return or rent. Ricardo was highly critical of Adam Smith, who sometimes depicted rent as price determined and sometimes as price determining.[21] However, what might appear at first as a simple case of confusion in Smith was in fact an indication of a deeper insight than the Ricardians', combined with a less rigorous use of terms.

The Ricardian model dealt with *one* agricultural commodity for simplicity. Smith's analysis took into account the alternative uses of the land, and treated the rent of land in one use as the necessary supply price of that same land for alternative uses.[22] In Smith's analysis, rent could even become part of the price of fish, when it was necessary to bid shore land away from its alternative uses in order to go fishing.[23] Sometimes Smith referred to the fact that rent was a "component part"[24] of price in a manner that might suggest that rent, profits, wages, etc., were independently determined and collectively determined price. Ricardo, in fact, interpreted Smith in this way.[25] However, Smith was as clear as the later classical economists that rent was in general price determined rather than price determining:

> Rent, it is to be observed, therefore, enters into the composition of the price of commodities in a different way from wages and profit. High or low wages and profit, are the causes of high or low price; high or low rent is the effect of it. It is because high or low wages and profit must be paid, in order to bring a particular commodity to market, that its price is high or low. But it is because its price is high or low; a great deal more, or very little more, or no more, than what is sufficient to pay those wages and profit, that it affords a high rent, or a low rent, or no rent at all.[26]

John Stuart Mill recognized that the economic concept of rent and the principles on which it was regulated applied outside agriculture as well as within it. Such cases "are more frequent in the transactions of industry than is commonly supposed."[27] These included patents, "superior talents for business,"[28] and in fact all economic advantages "whether natural or acquired, whether personal or the result of social arrangements,"[29] which enable one producer to make a commodity more cheaply than its cost at the price-determining margin.

Rent had important policy implications, not only to the Ricardians, but also to later and more radical groups. The historical extension of the margin of cultivation, accompanied by historically diminishing returns, implied an increasing share of rent in the national output, making landlords the passive beneficiaries of progress. The "Ricardian" rent model had its origin in the controversies over the restrictive laws which kept out foreign wheat — the so-called Corn Laws, with "corn" being used generically at the time to refer to cereal grains.[*] Free importation of food and technological progress were means of reducing the need for more intensive or more extensive cultivation at higher cost, thereby reducing (or retarding the increase of) agricultural rent. Because Ricardian rent was not a factor supply price, it could be taxed or controlled without adverse effects on resource allocation and national output.[30] Ricardo and J.S. Mill recognized the great practical problems of separating pure rent from observable rental payments, which included returns on agricultural investments — investments which would not be maintained if their returns were reduced. McCulloch even doubted whether pure agricultural rent was a significant part of total agricultural rental payments, much less of the national output.[31] However, the moral indignation generated by this unearned income made it a central feature of Henry George's later "single tax" (on rent) movement and of George Bernard Shaw's Fabian socialism.[32]

Profits

Diminishing returns in agriculture were central not only to the classical theory of agricultural rent but also to the classical theory of industrial profits. Here again, historical diminishing returns over time were more important than the analytical

---

[*]   When Europeans discovered maize being grown by the indigenous population in the Western Hemisphere, it was referred to as "Indian corn," leading to the American usage of the term "corn" to refer to what Europeans call "maize."

principle of diminishing returns under static conditions. Cost functions in manufacturing were considered to be different from cost functions in agriculture, not only in their shape but also in the way they shifted over time. Marginal costs in agriculture were assumed not only to be rising, but to be rising too sharply to be offset by any expected downward shift caused by improved technology. In manufacturing, cost functions were assumed to be either constant or downward sloping, and to be shifting downward more rapidly over time as well, in response to technological and organizational improvements.[33]

While real costs of production, in terms of factor inputs, were considered to be declining over time in manufacturing, the cost of hiring the major factor of production — labor — was rising, due to the rising marginal cost of food. The net result was a secular decline in profits. A higher proportion of the total labor time of society would be required to produce the workers' own subsistence, leaving less time remaining to produce the real income of property owners — profit and rent. Since rent would claim an increasing share of output as diminishing returns forced more intensive and more extensive cultivation, the residual share of profit must fall.

In the Ricardian model, real wages remained at some culturally determined "subsistence" level, but the number of man-hours required to produce this given subsistence increased over time, due to historically diminishing returns in agriculture. Ricardo did not in fact believe that wages remained at subsistence (a stationary population wage),[34] but more "realistic" assumptions — a rising standard of living, for example — would not have changed his conclusions but only reinforced them. Ultimately the declining rate of return on capital would reduce net investment to zero — the stationary state.[35]

If historical returns in agriculture were either constant or rising, then "the profits of stock must constantly rise in the progress of improvement."[36] This was not what was observed: "But the profits of stock are known to fall in the progress of improvement, and, therefore, neither of the first two suppositions is the fact, and labour in agriculture must, in the progress of improvement, become actually less productive."[37]

To move from the analytical principle of diminishing returns in a static model to the practical doctrine of historically diminishing returns throughout the economy in the real world would require two additional assumptions: (1) technological improvements in agriculture would not be sufficient to offset static diminishing returns, and (2) technological improvements in manufacturing would not be sufficient to offset the rising costs of labor due to diminishing returns in agriculture.

West and Ricardo both attacked Adam Smith's theory that secular declines in profit resulted from a growth of capital and the effect of competition in the factor market.[38] Smith had argued from declining profits in a particular industry, as investment in that industry increased, to declining profits in the economy as a whole as investment increased throughout the economy.[39] West and Ricardo pointed out that an increase in capital, output, and population would not change the *rate* of profit,[40] as distinguished from the accumulated quantity of profit. Ricardo claimed that Smith never discusses "the increasing difficulty of providing food for the additional number of labourers which the additional capital will employ."[41] Smith, however, did refer to a situation in which "the profits on stock gradually diminish" because after "the most fertile and best situated lands have been all occupied, less profit can be made by the cultivation of what is inferior both in soil and situation."[42]

Although Smith, West, and the Ricardian school (including, in this case, Karl Marx) attempted to explain a historical decline in the profit rate, there is a serious question whether there was in fact anything to explain — whether the profit rate had really declined. The interest rate had been observed to be historically declining, and the classical economists assumed some general relationship between the rate of profit and the rate of interest.[43] However, a declining risk premium as better markets developed over time may have reduced the observable gross interest rate, even though the pure interest rate and the pure rate of profit were unchanged.[44]

Population

The law of diminishing returns was implicit in the Malthusian population theory, but seventeen years passed before this implication of Malthus' *Essay on Population* in 1798 was made explicit in *The Nature and Progress of Rent* in 1815. The famous arithmetic and geometric ratios (of food and population growth, respectively) are not a statement of the law of diminishing returns. They are among the great ambiguities of Malthusian thought and — since ambiguities can be difficult to refute — one of the great sources of its enduring influence. At least three different interpretations are possible for Malthus' theory of differential growth rates between food and population:

1. The theoretically possible growth rate of population is greater than the theoretically possible growth rate of food.
2. The actual growth rate of population has been (or will be) greater than the actual growth rate of food.
3. The theoretically possible growth rate of population is greater than what the actual growth rate of food has been or will be.

Once stated in this way, the first two propositions practically collapse of their own weight. Man's food consists of plants and animals, which almost all reproduce in a shorter period of time and with more numerous offspring than man. Their theoretical growth potential is of a higher geometric order than man's. If actual rather than theoretical growth rates are compared, then historically per capita food consumption has in general increased over the centuries — prior to Malthus and since Malthus — which means that food has historically been increasing faster than population.

The third proposition, though more defensible, is less meaningful by itself. Any number of earlier writers had noted man's potential for reproducing at a rate in excess of observed rates of increase in the food supply. They typically assumed that either (1) this potential would not be fully utilized, or (2) the food supply would increase faster in the future than in the past, either as a result of agricultural improvements or the additional labor inputs resulting from the population growth itself. Malthus rejected both of these assumptions. Population "invariably" increases "when there are the means of subsistence," according to Malthus.[45] Historically diminishing returns in agriculture precluded sufficient food growth to overcome population growth (See Figure 2, below).

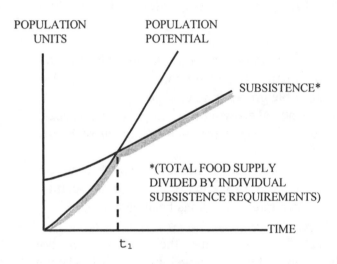

FIGURE 2

In the Malthusian tableau, the "unchecked" population growth potential was greater than the population for which there was sufficient food. Before some point in time (t_1), it was possible for population to actually grow at its potential rate, since there was sufficient food for a greater number of people than existed. Once that point was reached and the number of people equaled the number for which there was subsistence, actual increases of population (gray line) thereafter would necessarily follow the growth of the food supply. This was the empirical meaning of the Malthusian population principle, for Malthus assumed that the point t_1 had long been passed: " ... the period when the number of men surpassed their means of subsistence has long since arrived . . . has existed ever since we have had any histories of mankind, does exist at present, and will forever continue to exist."[46]

Given this clear-cut empirical proposition — that population and food grow at the *same* observable rates — it would be difficult to understand the fierce controversies which raged for decades among Malthus' contemporaries and which have been periodically revived for more than a century after his death. What was in principle an empirically resolvable question became in practice a doctrine to be salvaged by verbal shifts as the evidence piled up against it.

Two qualifications accompanied the Malthusian population theory from the outset. Firstly, since population grew with a lag in response to favorable living conditions (food, medical care, healthy environment, etc.) and declined with a lag as such conditions deteriorated, food and population growth could be temporarily out of phase in the short run, but one could not remain above the other for any long-run period sufficient to produce a new generation whose size was adjusted to the new circumstances. There could be "oscillations"[47] around the predicted trend line, though no change in the line itself. Secondly, the unrestrained increase of population to fill out all space provided by the available subsistence was held to be a characteristic of the lower or working classes *not* shared in the higher reaches of society.[48]

Although Malthus often referred to "human nature" and to "the laws of nature," his substantive analysis was in terms of differential behavior patterns in contemporary society. His openly avowed object was to vindicate such society from charges that poverty was due to institutions rather than to inherent natural causes. Malthus had little hope of solving the problem of poverty,[49] but he had hopes that his doctrine would solve the moral and political problem of assigning blame for that poverty:

> . . . it is evident that every man in the lower classes of
> society who became acquainted with these truths, would
> be disposed to bear the distress in which he might be
> involved with more patience; would feel less discontent
> and irritation at the government and the higher classes of
> society, on account of his poverty . . . . The mere
> knowledge of these truths, even if they did not operate
> sufficiently to produce any marked change in the
> prudential habits of the poor with regard to marriage,
> would still have a most beneficial effect on their conduct
> in a political light.[50]

While other classical economists did not share Malthus'
extreme conservatism, they defended his population theory as
an essential element of their system. Whatever the motivation,
the defenses of the Malthusian population theory as an
empirical proposition were (and are) a travesty of logic. From
the fact that population is *limited* by the means of subsistence (a
truism), Malthus deduced that population is *regulated* by the
means of subsistence (an empirical proposition),[51] but when
confronted by evidence that food was in fact growing faster than
population he fell back on the potential differences, on the
statement that population was somehow always "pressing" on
the food supply and was "ready" to grow faster than food
"whether population was *actually* increasing faster than food,
or food faster than population."[52]

Sismondi, Senior, and Whately all pointed out that Malthus'
use of the word "tendency" often confused an abstract
potentiality with a historical trend or a statistical probability.[53]
Malthus refused to be pinned down to any specific meaning. To
Malthus "saying that population had a *tendency* to increase
faster than food" was not "denying that it might practically at
times increase slower."[54] What he "intended to convey" was
"that population was always ready, and inclined to increase

faster than food, if the checks which repressed it were removed."[55] But he brushed aside Sismondi's objection that he was comparing an abstract potentiality of *A* with concrete data on *B*.

In his *Principles of Political Economy* (1820), Malthus agreed that higher incomes among workers might lead to either of "two very different results" — increase of population or "improvements in the modes of subsistence"[56] — that is, subsistence might grow faster than the population or at the same rate as population. Such statements continued to coexist with other statements about "the tendency in population fully to keep pace with the means of subsistence,"[57] and statements that "the average rate of the *actual* increase of population" must be one "obeying the same laws as the increase of food"[58] — without which he had no empirical proposition at all.

By the time that John Stuart Mill's *Principles* was published in 1848, a substantial body of data and of blatantly obvious observations made it clear that subsistence had been increasing faster than the population for some time. This caused some economists to reject or abandon the Malthusian theory. But the support of Mill's great treatise revived it and gave it a new lease on life, despite Mill's own damaging admission:

> Subsistence and employment in England have never increased more rapidly than in the last 40 years, but every census since 1821 showed a smaller proportional increase of population than that of the period preceding; and the produce of French agriculture and industry is increasing in a progressive ratio, while the population exhibits in every quinquennial census, a smaller proportion of births to the population.[59]

This did not prevent Mill from supporting the Malthusian population theory both as a theory of potential growth rates — the "power of increase" and the "capacity of multiplication" of population being the phrases used by Mill[60] — and as a theory of actual behavior in which "improvements in the condition of the labouring classes" give only "a temporary means" of prosperity, "speedily filled up by an increase in their numbers."[61] The objections of critics to shifting Malthusian concepts which evaded empirical confrontation were brushed aside by Mill as corrections of "mere language" which did not change the real problem, that population pressed "too" closely on the means of subsistence, bearing "too" great a ratio to capital,[62] that there was not "enough" improvement in living standards.[63] In his treatise *A System of Logic*, Mill declared, "where there is a more abundant production there may be a greater population without any increase of poverty, or even with a diminution of it."[64] In short, no matter what happened, it would be considered to be consistent with the Malthusian overpopulation theory. The theory had been emptied of empirical meaning, though not of insinuations or connotations.

Malthus' ultimate triumph was in *identifying* poverty with "over"-population, so that to deny the latter was considered synonymous with denying the former, and continues to be, in the eyes of many.　He set a pattern by relying heavily on extrapolations and truisms that serve as impregnable refuges during critical attacks and as bases for empirical sorties at other times. Malthus' heavy emphasis on empiricism in all areas of economics did not imply a systematic *testing* of empirically verifiable hypotheses by facts. He regarded his population theory as "incontrovertible,"[65] so that history would "elucidate the manner"[66] of its operation, rather than reveal *whether* it was empirically correct. The massive empirical material added to the second edition of the *Essays on Population* was intended to be used to "examine the effects of one great cause"[67] — the population principle — rather than to test that principle itself. No matter what the population might be, it was consistent with his principle: "The natural tendency to increase is everywhere so great that it will generally be easy to account for the height at which the population is found in any country."[68]

Modern apologists for Malthus have argued that technological progress in the West has "postponed" the

Malthusian result, while exploding population growth in the poorer or "underdeveloped" countries vindicates his prediction. But if population growth is regulated by the food supply or by the potential cost of production in agriculture, then it is precisely the West which should have the more rapidly increasing population. In Figure 2, the food supply curve should be rising more rapidly over time, with population correspondingly higher. Moreover, it is even questionable whether "over"-population in any meaningful sense is associated with national poverty, given that there are affluent nations, poor nations, and medium-income nations which have heavy population density, and thin population density. It is of course true that any nation will have higher per capita income with fewer people, assuming (implicitly) that its output does not decline in proportion. But this is a statement about the rules of arithmetic rather than about any empirical reality.

VALUE

Although value theory may be in some sense basic or logically prior to other aspects of microeconomics, classical value theory is more readily understood after some acquaintance with the substance and purpose of classical economics in general.

For example, the classical economists ignored a substantial body of earlier and contemporary economic literature which stressed the role of utility and demand in value theory, and gave almost exclusive emphasis to cost of production or labor. This is understandable, *given* the classical assumption of statically constant cost functions in manufacturing, so that no changes in demand could change value. As shown in Figure 3, $P_1 = AC$, regardless of demand (D_1, D_2, D_3).

The demand for (the utility of) the product might be insufficient to cover its cost of production, in which case this particular product would not be produced in the long run. Such unproduced products were outside the purview of classical

economics. Smith *defined* effective demand to mean only that
quantity demanded (Q_1, Q_2, Q_3) at a price sufficient to at least
cover production costs.[69] Utility and demand were therefore
necessary, but not sufficient, to determine value. The actual
level of value was determined by "the" cost of production.
Only in cases where a monopolist maximized price, selling only
one unit, would the utility determine the price. Utility in this
context did not mean marginal utility but the highest average
utility — the utility of having the commodity at all. And in this
sense utility was "only the limit of value,"[70] not a determinant
of value.

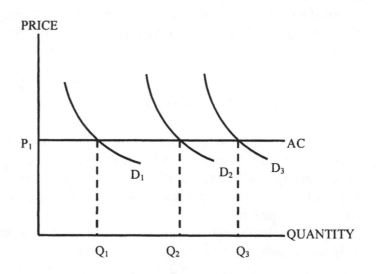

FIGURE 3

Measures of Value

Classical value theory dealt not only with narrow questions of price determination in particular markets but also with such broader questions as the functional distribution of income over time, the measurement of aggregate output, and changing relative prices between agricultural and manufactured goods over time. In short, classical "value" concepts ranged beyond problems of individual product price determination to problems of *measuring* or valuing output for various purposes. One such purpose was that of providing an index of welfare.

Unlike the mercantilists, who measured the prosperity of a nation by its accumulated stock of gold, Adam Smith measured national prosperity by its annual flow of per capita income[71] — to be maximized by efficient production at home and free trade abroad. As a welfare index, output was to be measured by how much labor it could command: "What every thing is really worth to the man who has acquired it, and who wants to dispose of it or exchange it for something else, is the toil and trouble which it can save to himself, and which it can impose on other people."[72]

At a given time, under given technology, an index of the amount of "other men's labour" is the same as an index of "the produce of other men's labour,"[73] and from this Smith drifted into using the terms synonymously over time and without regard to changing technology. However, more fundamentally, Smith saw the utility of goods to be indicated by the disutility of labor to which their consumers will submit to obtain them:

> Equal quantities of labor, at all times and places, may be said to be of equal value to the labourer. In his ordinary state of health, strength and spirits; in the ordinary degree of his skill and dexterity, he must always lay down the same portion of his ease, his liberty and his happiness. The price which he pays must always be the same, whatever may be the quantity of goods which he receives in return for it. Of these, indeed, it may sometimes purchase a greater and

sometimes a smaller quantity; but it is their value which varies, not that of the labour which purchases them. At all times and places that is dear which is difficult to come at, or which it costs much labour to acquire and that cheap which is to be had easily, or with very little labour. Labour alone, therefore, never varying in its own value, is alone the ultimate and real standard by which the value of all commodities can at all times and places be estimated and compared. It is their real price; money is their nominal price only.[74]

This defines a *measure* of value, but it is not a *theory* of value. No substantive proposition in *The Wealth of Nations* would be different if Smith had chosen a different index of welfare. Indeed, Smith chose a different measure of value in a "popular sense" on the same page and alternated between the two usages throughout the book. His "real" sometimes meant the quantity of labor command represented and sometimes the volume of physical output.[75]

Similarly, Ricardo's quest for an "invariable measure of value" was a search for a product whose cost structure was such that changes in *other* products' costs of production over time could be directly determined by observing how they exchanged with the invariable standard,[76] much as the length or weight of an object could be directly measured by a ruler or scale, without reference to the whole range of other objects having length and weight. Such a measure of value would show, for example, that agricultural goods were rising in value (cost) over time, while manufactured goods were falling. As John Stuart Mill observed, "Under the name of a measure of value," some economists had developed what "would be more properly termed a measure of cost of production."[77] For the Ricardians this was true. More generally, it was a measure of whatever was considered important in a policy area.

For example, Malthus' measure of value was a measure of "labour command" [78] — in keeping with his emphasis on macroeconomic unemployment problems. For Malthus, "the power of commanding a given quantity of labour of a given character, together with the will to advance it, represents a given demand."[79] When the output of a given period failed to command enough labor to reproduce the same output in subsequent periods, aggregate demand was said to be deficient. Goods are overproduced when "they are selling at a price which will not repurchase the quantity of labour employed in producing them."[80]

One of the great problems in understanding Marxian value is that it is entirely a *measure* of value rather than a *theory* of value. Marx had what he himself called a "definition of value,"[81] a "concept of value,"[82] and "value as defined."[83] He was flabbergasted at critics' "nonsense" about "proving" his concept,[84] and found it sufficient for his purposes that the allocation and distribution of labor time was a vital phenomenon in the economy.[85]

Malthus, Ricardo, and Mill all recognized that any specific, empirical measure of value was arbitrary,[86] and ultimately had to be justified by its usefulness rather than its logic alone. This was implicit also in Marx's justifications — not proofs — of his value concept. This did not prevent lengthy controversies between Ricardo and Malthus as to the best measure of value, for their general systems were oriented toward different questions — Ricardo tracing the functional distribution of income over time and its implications (the stationary state, for example), and Malthus concerning himself with the short-run behavior of aggregate output and employment.

The classical economists admitted that there was no perfect empirical embodiment of the concept of an invariable measure of value. Samuel Bailey went beyond this to assert that it was *conceptually* as well as empirically impossible to have such a thing. Bailey's *Critical Dissertation on the Nature, Measures, and Causes of Value* (1825) insisted repeatedly that the nature of value was wholly relative, so that it was "contradictory" to speak of "an invariable standard of value amidst universal fluctuation,"[87] for no goods could even conceivably remain constant in value as all other goods varied. He recognized that what the Ricardians were seeking, under the label of a "measure" of value, was in fact "to determine in which commodity any changes of value have originated."[88] This was not, for him, a measure of value in any sense analogous to measuring weight. The third part of Bailey's title — the *causes* of value — dealt with the theory of value, which he was the first to clearly separate from the other two features of classical value with which it was usually confused.

Theory of Value

However much the classical economists differed among themselves as to the best measure of value, they were substantially united on the theory of value. The cost of production determined the value of those goods with which classical economics was preoccupied — competitively sold commodities produced at constant cost. Commodities produced at increasing cost sold at their respective marginal costs.[89] Commodities sold in non-competitive markets and commodities in fixed supply sold at prices determined by supply and demand.[90] Samuel Bailey pointed out that all apparent differences among his contemporaries on this point were merely differences in the use of words.[91] John Stuart Mill also stated this to be the substantive theory of *all* economists — "from Ricardo down"[92] — on the subject.

Supply and demand was, in one sense, a general mechanism through which any particular determinant of value operated. It was consistent with utility, cost of production, and other theories of price determination. "You say supply and demand regulates value," Ricardo wrote to Malthus. "This, I think, is saying nothing,"[93] since it is equally compatible with one theory or another. In another sense, however, price determination by supply and demand meant that there was no other specific principle at work — the competitive market was not operating as required by general theory — and prices were whatever the market happened to make them. In this sense, J.S. Mill could say that supply and demand determined prices "in cases where cost of production is inoperative," [94] depicting supply-and-demand and cost-of-production as mutually exclusive and jointly exhaustive,[95] even though elsewhere he depicted supply and demand as an all-encompassing pheno-menon through which all particular determinants of value produced their concrete results: "nothing else has any influence whatever, except in as far as it may be calculated to affect either the demand or the supply."[96]

In short, Ricardian economics regarded supply and demand as a causally neutral mechanism — like neutral money — through which *other* variables determined value. Supply and demand independently determine the value only where the other determinants (cost of production, utility) were rendered ineffective by non-competitive market structures or fixed supply.

The terms "supply" and "demand," as used by Ricardo and John Stuart Mill, referred exclusively to *quantities* supplied and demanded.[97] As Ricardo wrote to Malthus:

> I sometimes suspect that we do not attach the same meaning to the word demand. If corn rises in price, you perhaps attribute it to a greater demand, — I should call it a greater competition. The demand cannot I think be said to increase if the quantity consumed be diminished, altho much more money may be required to purchase the smaller than the larger quantity. If it were to be asked what the demand was for port wine in England in the years 1813 and 1814, and it were to be answered that in the first year she had imported 5000 pipes and in the next 4500 should we not all agree that the demand was greater in 1813, yet it might be true that double the quantity of money was paid for the 4500 pipes.[98]

While Ricardo would say that demand had declined from 1813 to 1814, Malthus would say — with modern economics — that demand had increased (Figure 4).

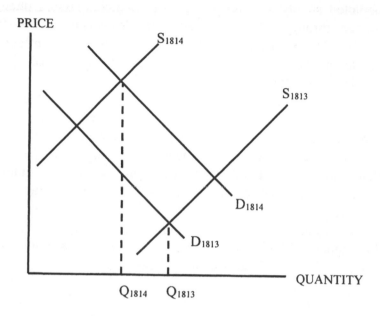

FIGURE 4

Definitions, as such, are neither "right" nor "wrong," but conflicting definitions made it difficult for these contemporaries to understand each other, or for classical statements about demand to be understood by later interpreters steeped in a different concept. Malthus, by contrast, presented the earliest *schedule* concept of supply and demand. He distinguished the "extent" (quantity) of the demand from the "intensity" of demand (height of the demand curve): " . . . it is not in the sense of mere extent of consumption that demand raises prices, because it is almost always when prices are the lowest, that the extent of demand and consumption is the greatest."[99] The "intensity" of demand was defined as "the sacrifice which the demanders are able and willing to make in order to satisfy their wants. It is this species of demand alone which, compared with the supply, determines prices and values."[100] The meaning of an increased demand in these terms was clear:

> Now this willingness, on the part of some of the demanders, to make a greater sacrifice than before, in order to satisfy their wants, is what I have called a greater intensity of demand. As no increase of price can possibly take place, unless the commodity be of such a nature as to excite in a certain number of purchasers this species of demand, and as this species of demand must always be implied whenever we speak of demand and supply as determining prices.[101]

Samuel Bailey phrased Malthus' theory even more directly in modern terms: "A disposition to give more for the quantity actually taken, or to buy more at the same rate"[102] — a shift outward of the demand schedule. Supply was similarly regarded by Malthus in schedule terms, as the "conditions of the supply,"[103] meaning the cost of production.[104] Malthus saw the traditional classical cost-of-production theory of value as only a special case of supply and demand theory, the more general theory being applicable to both short-run ("market") and long-run ("natural") prices, and to monopolized as well as competitively produced commodities.[105]

Utility and Schedule Concepts

While the cost of production theory of value dominated British classical economics, the competing utility theory of value existed in continental Europe even before Adam Smith, though it would be nearly a century after *The Wealth of Nations* before the utility theory would be so formulated as to supplant the cost of production theory of value among economists in general. Adam Smith offered as his refutation of the utility theory the contrast between water and diamonds:

> Nothing is more useful than water: but it will purchase scarce anything; scarce anything can be had in exchange for it. A diamond, on the contrary, has scarce any value in use; but a very great quantity of other goods may frequently be had in exchange for it.[106]

Modern economists would see the key to this paradox as being a distinction between total, average, and marginal utility. To be totally deprived of water would of course be worse than to be totally deprived of diamonds, and anyone faced with such a choice would of course prefer to spend what was necessary to ensure a continuing supply of water. Only after the amount of water available more than amply supplied basic requirements would further increments of water become much less valued than an increment of diamonds. Before utility theories of value could replace cost of production theories of value, utility had to be seen as subjective and variable, with the marginal utility then determining price. The beginnings of this can be seen in *An Outline of the Science of Political Economy* by Nassau W. Senior in 1836:

> Not only are there limits to the pleasure which commodities of any given kind can afford, but the pleasure diminishes in a rapidly increasing ratio long before those limits are reached. Two articles of the same kind will seldom afford twice the pleasure of one, and still less will ten give five times the pleasure of two.[107]

Many of the same economists who challenged classical orthodoxy on Say's Law also challenged the classical theory of value as determined by production costs, notably labor costs. A number of important features of the Sismondi-Malthus macroeconomic analysis are difficult to express without schedule concepts to distinguish an increase in quantity along a given function and an upward shift of the function itself. For example, an increase in "demand" was for both Sismondi[108] and Malthus an increased willingness to make a "sacrifice"[109] to obtain a desired good. An increased *quantity demanded*, as during a period of overproduction, was not for them an increase in demand.[110] They also distinguished between increased investment at a given level of technology — where it "is in the nature of all such means of employing capital to become less and less advantageous"[111] — and increased investment in response to technological advance;[112] in short, they distinguished a downward movement along the marginal product of capital curve and a shift outward of that curve. This idea had, of course, also appeared earlier in Lauderdale. Malthus further distinguished increased saving out of a given income and increased saving out of an increased income.[113] While condemning "excess saving" as a quantity, Malthus nevertheless wished to raise the savings function in order to promote substantial growth.[114]

Malthus' conception of demand was not only in schedule terms but was in essence based on utility. J.B. Say has generally been credited with being the leading early pioneer in the development of the utility theory of value. However, he was characteristically shifting in his concept of utility, so that it sometimes represented the economic agent's own subjective evaluation and sometimes Say's idea of what was "really" useful.[115] Malthus' "estimation" corresponds more closely with the modern concept of utility, since it depends entirely on the economic agent's own subjective feelings.[116] Malthus objected to the *word* "utility" and to its ambiguous usage in Say's theory of value,[117] but was by no means opposed to the utility theory of value in substance. Rather, he added a needed clarification of its meaning as wholly subjective. Malthus also derived macroeconomic conclusions similar to those of Sismondi: "Unless the estimation in which an object is held, or the value which an individual or the society places on it when obtained, adequately compensates the sacrifice which has been made to obtain it, such wealth will not be produced in future."[118]

Value therefore had two meanings for Malthus, or could be viewed in two ways: (1) the exchange-ratio between goods, and/or (2) the estimation in which a single good was held, relative to the disutility of obtaining it.[119] He rejected the idea of value as solely relating one commodity to another, since "in a country where there were only deer, and no beavers or other products to compare them with," the esteem in which deer were held could nevertheless be indicated by the fact that "any man would willingly walk fifty miles in order to get one."[120] In short, "if the real value of a commodity be considered as synonymous with the estimation in which it is held, such value must be measured by the quantity of labour which it will command."[121] This enabled him to introduce the concept of the value of *aggregate* output — "the value of the whole produce"[122] — which was to prove important in his discussion of general gluts and which was to puzzle and exasperate his critics.[123]

Obviously values defined as exchange ratios cannot rise or fall as a whole — a truism which Malthus repeatedly acknowledged.[124] But to "confine the term value" to "the mere relation of one commodity to another" would be "to render it pre-eminently futile and useless,"[125] at least for his purposes. While an increased quantity of output normally tended to represent an increased "value" or labor command, this was not so during a period of overproduction or glut when "a mere abundance of commodities" would not be capable of "employing the same number of workmen"[126] that produced it. At such times "the produce of a country estimated in the labour which it will command falls in value."[127] There is thus an "insufficiency of demand"[128] without any leakage from the circular flow. A general glut in these terms is a simple extension of a partial glut: " . . . it is quite obvious that this mass of commodities, compared with the labour with which it is to be exchanged, may fall in value from a glut just as any one commodity falls in value from an excess of supply."[129]

Disproportionality (the cause of temporary depressions in the Ricardian system)[130] is unnecessary for Malthus' denial of the proposition that an increased quantity supplied will necessarily entail an increased quantity demanded:

> It is asserted that effectual demand is nothing more than the offering of one commodity in exchange for another, which has cost the same quantity of labour. But is this all that is necessary to effectual demand? Though each commodity may have cost the same quantity of labour in its production, and they may be exactly equivalent to each other in exchange, yet why may not both be so plentiful as not to command more labour, than they have cost, that is, to yield no profit, and in this case would the demand for them be effectual? Would it be such as to encourage their continued production? Unquestionably not. Their relationship to each other may not have changed; but their relation to the wants of society, and their relation to labour, may have experienced a most important change.[131]

The macroeconomic implications of the utility theory of value were accepted even by Jean-Baptiste Say in his later writings. In his textbook of 1828–29, *Cours complet d'économie politique pratique*, he wrote, "products in general can be multiplied and purchased by one another until a limit is reached which no one knows precisely how to determine; beyond that limit, certain products become too expensive for the utility which they have to indemnify their consumers for what is required to obtain them."[132]

In short, utility was the basis of both a measure of value and a theory of value — and in both macroeconomic and microeconomic senses. Utility was linked to the schedule concept of demand. However, as in other areas of economics, advances in value theory which burst through the confines of the Ricardian system were opposed and obliterated by the appearance of Mill's *Principles* in 1848 and its dominance for the next several decades. The pattern was the familiar one of interpreting others' ideas in Ricardian senses — supply and demand being *quantities* supplied and demanded — and showing their inconsistencies in such terms.[133] What Jevons called the "noxious influence of authority" was sufficient to bury ideas not understood by the Ricardian school.[134] Mill's closed mind on the subject of value was evident from his youthful disparagement of "Malthus' insignificant disputes about 'value'"[135] to his more celebrated statement of his later years: "Happily, there is nothing in the laws of Value which remains for the present or any future writer to clear up; the theory of the subject is complete."[136]

SUMMARY AND IMPLICATIONS

The major substantive features of classical microeconomics revolved around the law of diminishing returns. Ricardian rent theory was obviously dependent upon it, for diminishing returns produced rent even without recourse to inferior land, and such recourse was itself evidence of already diminished returns on the superior land. Malthusian population growth presented a problem of maintaining living standards only if the additional labor input represented by the additional population did not lead to correspondingly increased increments of output. The general profit rate was likewise determined by rising marginal costs in agriculture, which raised the principle cost (food) of the principle input (labor) in manufacturing. The static law of diminishing returns was the foundation of a whole system of analysis that depended upon *historically* diminishing returns, driving up the cost of labor, increasing the landlord's rent, driving down the rate of profit, and moving the economy toward the "stationary state." In this sense, the law of diminishing returns was part of the general classical preoccupation with the problem of long-run growth.

Classical value theory was, in itself, a straightforward cost-of-production theory. The value of competitively produced commodities equaled "the" (constant) cost of production in manufacturing and a rising cost of production in agriculture. Since rent was not part of the cost of production, the latter reduced to the cost of capital and labor. Capital was considered to come "originally" in some historical sense or "ultimately" in some analytical sense from labor, so that cost and value would essentially be reducible to labor.

For all the controversy generated by the "labor theory of value" it was tangential to classical value theory, and seldom was it even alleged that any substantive conclusion would be different without it. Ricardo's elaborate catalog of modifications of the labor theory make it quite clear that he understood the role of capital, of time, etc., in the price-determination process.[137] Such disciples as McCulloch and James Mill might, in the heat of polemics, become more Ricardian than Ricardo in insisting on the ultimate role of labor, but Ricardo himself chided them for going as far as they sometimes did.[138] Marx devoted a whole volume (Vol. II) of *Capital* to the extensive modifications of the labor theory of value necessitated by varying capital turnover, before finally going full circle to the classical cost of production theory of price determination (Vol. III).

In addition to a substantive *theory* of value, classical economics spawned a number of "measures" of value, adapted to divergent purposes, from dealing with changing costs over time (Ricardo) to analyzing cyclical unemployment (Malthus). While the validity of the whole concept of a "measure" of value, and particularly an invariable measure of value, could be challenged — as it was by Samuel Bailey — once a concept was accepted, the particular measure chosen could not be challenged on the grounds of validity but only on grounds of convenience.

Supply and demand were conceived of in quantity rather than schedule terms, and "utility" meant average rather than marginal utility, so the potentialities of these concepts were lost on the central classical tradition. They had later to be rediscovered and developed as if their early exponents had never existed.

Classical Methodology

Classical economics in itself contained relatively little in the way of separate, explicit, methodological discussion, and most of that appeared late, in the writings of John Stuart Mill. However, methodological pronouncements were scattered through earlier classical writings, especially Ricardo's controversies with Malthus and his *Reply to Bosanquet* on monetary policy. Moreover, the implicit methodology of classical economics — and especially of the Ricardian school — gave rise to a voluminous critical literature. Even Adam Smith, whose *Wealth of Nations* said nothing about methodology, became in retrospect an important methodological figure repeatedly invoked by later critics of the Ricardians.

The methodological questions at issue during the classical period were very similar to those that were later to agitate neoclassical and modern economists. The controversies in classical methodology included (1) abstractions versus "reality," (2) varying concepts of causation, (3) the role of mathematics, (4) the "scientific" claims of economics, and (5) the practical relevance of classical economics. But before proceeding to analyze these topics, it may be worthwhile to briefly consider the historical development of classical methodology.

Adam Smith's methodology was eclectic. The empirical, the theoretical, the institutional, the philosophical, the static, and the dynamic were all intermingled. His definitions shifted, sometimes on the same page,[1] and, in the course of developing his classic work, he drifted back and forth between different conceptions of "value,"[2] "rent,"[3] and "real."[4] But, despite the numerous ambiguities in *The Wealth of Nations* commented on by Smith's classical successors,[5] as well as by the later scholars,[6] he moved easily around the pitfalls without disaster, being sufficiently consistent during any given chain of reasoning to avoid errors in logic.

With Ricardo economics took a major step toward abstract models, rigid and artificial definitions, syllogistic reasoning — and the direct application of the results to policy. The historical, the institutional, and the empirical faded into the background, and explicit social philosophy shrank to a few passing remarks. Comparative statics became the dominant — though usually implicit — approach. Ricardo declared: "I put these immediate and temporary effects quite aside, and fix my whole attention on the permanent state of things which will result from them."[7] Not only Ricardo, but also his disciples and popularizers, reasoned in comparative static terms — and they automatically interpreted the theories of *others* in comparative static terms as well.

The Ricardian approach did not remain unchallenged. A host of critics attacked from many directions, raising in the process fundamental and enduring questions of economic methodology.

SCIENCE

The attempt of the Ricardians to make economics more "scientific" met with both opposition and derision. Richard Jones objected that economics was a field in which "premeditated experiments" could seldom be made,[8] and denounced "the too hasty creation of whole systems" based on "a frail thirst for a premature exposition of commanding generalities."[9] Those who "snatched at general principles" ended up with principles which "will often be found to have no generality"[10] in the sense of having no historical setting in which they are literally true. Jones was concerned with "things as they exist in the world,"[11] with "institutions,"[12] with "history and statistics,"[13] and had no use for "closet philosophers"[14] or their "puerile effort to make reasoning supply the place of knowledge."[15] Jones was seconded by his literary executor, William Whewell, who contrasted Jones' historical and institutional analysis of rent with that of Ricardo:

But yet, as opinions are brought out most distinctly by their opposition, I may notice some of the remarks made at the time, by Mr. Ricardo's admirers, upon Mr. Jones's conclusions, and upon his reasonings. "Mr. Ricardo (they replied) does not pretend to give an exposition of the laws by which the rise and progress of rent, *in the ordinary and vulgar sense of the word*, is regulated. He was as well aware as Mr. Jones, or any one else that the rent, the origin and progress of which he had undertaken to investigate, was not that which is commonly called *rent*. He did not profess to examine the circumstances which practically determined the actual amount of rent in any country."

To this it was a sufficient reply to say, that the object of Mr. Jones *was* to give an account of the laws by which rent, "in the ordinary and vulgar sense of the word," is regulated. He tried to ascertain the progress and consequences of "what is commonly called rent." And the reader might be left to decide for himself which subject of inquiry may be the better worth his notice, — the rents that are actually paid in *every* country, or the Ricardian rents, which are *not* those actually paid in *any* country.

. . . Were not these *landholders* intended by Mr. Ricardo, and understood by all his readers, to be identified with the receivers of actual rent? or were they different from landholders "in the ordinary and vulgar sense of the word?" And when these disciples of his took credit to themselves, as they did, for avoiding his errors, and enforcing the identity of interest of the landlord with that of the public, who were *their* landlord, and what his interest? Was he the receiver of "what is commonly called rent," or was he an imaginary personage whose interest depends on the increase of rents "which are not paid in any country?" Was he, in short, the squire of the parish, or the creature of a definition?[16]

While most critics did not go as far as Jones and Whewell, many took similar positions on particular points. Malthus attacked the "tendency to premature generalization,"[17] and declared that before "the shrine of truth, as discovered by facts and experience, the fairest theories and the most beautiful classifications must fall."[18] Sismondi accused Ricardo of inhabiting "a hypothetical world altogether different from the real world,"[19] assuming that "a perfect equilibrium is always maintained,"[20] and "making abstraction of time and space like the German metaphysicians."[21] J.B. Say ultimately turned against the Ricardians' "method of investigation," their "vain subtleties,"[22] and "abstract principles,"[23] saying, "It is better to stick to facts and their consequences than to syllogisms."[24]

The validity of the claim of economics to be a science depended upon what was conceived to be the distinguishing feature of a science. To some a science was characterized by the precision and rigor of its *methods of analysis*; to others a science was distinguished by the *certainty of its results*. Even when critics were prepared to use the word "science" in a loose sense to describe economics, they emphasized that "the science of political economy bears a nearer resemblance to the science of morals and politics than to that of mathematics."[25] Mathematics and the natural sciences were repeatedly contrasted with economics.[26] The widespread aversion to the use of mathematics in economics during the classical period was based on a belief that "arithmetical computations" could not be made with any certainty.[27]

There was no apparent consideration that mathematics might be used to contribute to *conceptual clarity* rather than to derive numerical predictions. Cournot pointed out that mathematical analysis was used "not simply to calculate numbers" but to find "relations."[28] But, like the rest of his pathbreaking work, this made no impact whatever on classical economics. Ricardo, however, saw Malthus' argument as to the empirical uncertainty of economics as an excuse for analytical sloppiness: "Political Economy, he says, is not a strict science like the mathematics, and therefore he thinks he may use words in a vague way, sometimes attaching one meaning to them sometimes another and quite different. No proposition can surely be more absurd."[29]

Sometimes the idea that "scientific" economics meant a set of empirical propositions with a high degree of certainty might have been inferred from some of the more exuberant statements of the Ricardians that some conclusions in economics were "as certain as the principle of gravitation,"[30] "established beyond all question,"[31] "perfectly conclusive,"[32] and "unanswerable,"[33] that they possessed "all the certainty of a mathematical demonstration."[34] The theme of certainty was sometimes reinforced by tautologies used in defense of empirical propositions — notably Say's Law. One of the more remarkable predictions of this period was that of Robert Torrens: "With respect to Political Economy the period of controversy is passing away, and that of unanimity rapidly approaching. Twenty years hence there will scarcely exist a doubt respecting any of its fundamental principles."[35]

It is understandable how the emerging scientific emphasis of economics as a method of analysis could be mistaken for a belief that its empirical results would approach the degree of certainty found in the natural sciences. Both critics and defenders of the Ricardian tradition confused the two ideas from time to time. However, the Ricardians, in their more sober moments, clearly understood the difference between (1) systematically developing general principles, subject to exceptions and modifying circumstances, and (2) making concrete predictions from a priori assumptions. Ricardo wrote to Malthus: "Our differences may in some respects, I think, be ascribed to your considering my book as more practical than I intended it to be. My object was to elucidate principles and to do this I imagined strong cases that I might shew the operation of those principles."[36]

Later he wrote of Malthus: " . . . it is one of my complaints against him that he does not answer your principles but wishes to shew that you have taken your case so wide, that it could under no circumstances exist; but however limited might be your case, the same principle is involved, and it is that which should be answered."[37]

Whatever the difficulties of proceeding by general principles or "theory," Ricardo saw this as unavoidable, even by so-called practical men who imagined themselves to be sticking to "facts" and "experience." He charged that such men who are "all for facts and nothing for theory . . . can hardly ever sift their facts," and remain "credulous" unconscious theorists.[38] John Stuart Mill likewise saw that "those who disavow theories cannot make one step without theorizing."[39] The only real question was whether theorizing should be done explicitly and systematically or implicitly and with no check. Whately also argued that the avowed empirical or "practical" man was "likely to form, unconsciously, an erroneous theory."[40] He said:

> Man is so formed as to theorize unconsciously; facts *will* arrange themselves in his mind under certain classes, without his having any such design; and thus the materials he has been heaping together, will have been, as it were, building themselves up, into some, probably faulty system, while he was not aware of the process going on in his own mind.[41]

One could not "trust to accumulation of facts as a *substitute* for accuracy in the logical processes."[42] Few of the critics of classical economics — in its contemporary Ricardian form — had claimed that facts could replace theory. Many had invoked Adam Smith as an example of a *combination* of theoretical principles and empirical research.[43] Certainly Smith's systematic testing of the subsistence wage hypothesis[44] contrasts both with Ricardo's definitional approach to the subject[45] and with Malthus' aimless factual discussions used to *illustrate* — but not to test — the Malthusian population theory.[46] Sismondi was perhaps representative of contemporary critics of the Ricardian approach when he said:

> It is a natural habit of the human mind to seek to reduce
> all its operations to the simplest formula, to generalize
> all its rules, and to do everything that it can by one
> uniform procedure to avoid more complicated
> procedures.   That habit which tends to simplify
> everything, to classify everything, to generalize
> everything, is no doubt the most essential cause of the
> progress of various sciences. It is not necessary,
> however, to abandon oneself to it in an unreflecting
> manner.[47]

It was not simply that Ricardo and the Ricardians
constructed abstract models,[48] but that they applied the
conclusions from the highly restrictive models directly to the
complexities of the real world. J.B. Say considered it "a well
founded objection to Mr. Ricardo, that he sometimes reasoned
upon abstract principles to which he gives too great a
generality."[49]

Richard Jones' criticism that the Ricardians had derived
"general principles" which "have no generality"[50] went to the
heart of the issue of what was meant by, and expected of,
general or abstract reasoning. Certainly empirical universality
was *not* expected.[51]   What was sought were analytical
principles, common to a wide range of similar cases — even if
such principles were not decisive in any particular case.[52] The
institutional complement necessary for the practical application
of abstract principles was often neglected by the early
Ricardians. However, the generality of the Ricardian *principles*
was not thereby impaired. Diminishing returns, Ricardian rent,
and related principles of resource allocation apply in economies
vastly different, institutionally, from the England of Ricardo's
time. Moreover, Ricardo's systematic, deductive method of
analysis applies still more widely in time and space. Therefore,
despite the institutional omissions or parochialism of Ricardian
economics, which gave substance to the charge that it attempted
"to construct a permanent fabric out of transitory materials,"[53]

John Stuart Mill could say, "Though many of its conclusions are only locally true, its method of investigation is applicable universally."[54]

The issue of analytical generality versus empirical generality was part of an even more basic issue — whether economic principles should be founded on abstract assumptions or factual premises. Those who rejected the abstract deductive approach often pointed to the complexities of the real world as a reason for preferring empiricism. John Stuart Mill saw this as a false dichotomy. Both the "theorists" and the empirical or "practical" men used systematic reasoning, starting from given assumptions, and both derived those assumptions from something in the real world. The only meaningful question, then, was the particular manner in which the initial premises were derived from reality:

> . . . although both classes of inquirers do nothing but theorize, and both of them consult no other guide than experience, there is this difference between them, and a most important difference it is: that those who are called practical men require *specific* experience, and argue wholly *upward* from particular facts to a general conclusion; while those who are called theorists aim at embracing a wider field of experience, and, having argued upward from particular facts to a general principle including a much wider range than that of the question under discussion, then argued downward from that general principle to a variety of specific conclusions.[55]

The simple dichotomy between inductive and deductive reasoning was therefore invalid. The real difference was between direct induction from particular cases to a general conclusion — risking the *post hoc ergo propter hoc* fallacy and a threefold process of (1) induction from wider and more general experience, (2) deduction of conclusions applicable to a specific case, and (3) empirical verification of these conclusions "without which all the results . . . have little other value than that of conjecture."[56]

Precisely because of the multiplicity of causes and the inability to perform controlled experiments — features usually cited by critics of the abstract deductive approach — Mill saw little hope of finding the cause of any social phenomenon by direct induction of the facts of the particular case.[57] Only a wider survey of similar elements in a variety of circumstances was likely to suggest good working hypotheses, from which the process of deduction and verification could proceed. But finding the common element in a wide range of specific cases — i.e., abstraction — was the basis of science. The complexity of the world and the deviation of most concrete phenomena from their abstract principles was precisely what made systematic analytical procedure — science — necessary. As Karl Marx expressed it in Hegelian terms: "All science would be superfluous, if the appearance, the form, and the nature of things were wholly identical."[58] According to Marx:

> . . . the vulgar economist thinks he has made a great discovery when, as against the disclosures of the inner connection, he proudly claims that in appearance things look different. In fact, he is boasting that he holds fast to the appearance and takes it for the last word. Why, then, any science at all?[59]

Like Mill, Marx argued that the direct reasoning from "the real and concrete aspects of conditions as they are" is a method which "proves to be wrong."[60] Nothing can be done directly with "a chaotic conception of the whole," though one can proceed from reality to "gradually arrive at simpler ideas" until ultimately "we get at the simplest conception" and then "start on our return journey" to deduce conclusions, "not as a chaotic notion of an integral whole, but as a rich aggregate of conceptions and relations."[61]

Marx was one of the few economists who rejected the claim that Ricardo was "too abstract" and claimed that "the opposite accusation would be justified" — that he did not consistently restrict himself to the abstractions appropriate to the level of analysis at which he was working — a charge which Marx also made against Adam Smith.[62] No small part of the difficulties in the interpretive literature on Marxian economics derives from his use of successive approximations in *Capital* — beginning with the abstract "essence" in Volume I, introducing complications of capital turnover in Volume II, and finally in Volume III approaching "step by step" the empirical manifestations or "forms of appearance" seen by the ordinary observer,[63] and which "serve as the starting point in the vulgar conception" of economics.[64]

Given that there were to be abstractions and deductions, how should the abstract assumptions be formulated? Mill argued that it would be "mere trifling" if the assumptions bore no relation to reality. The assumption should differ from reality "only as a part differs from the whole."[65] To the degree that "the actual facts recede from the hypothesis" there must be "a corresponding deviation" of the results from those predicted.[66] Mill apparently did not recognize that this proposition was itself an empirically verifiable hypothesis, rather than an axiomatic truth. A "slightly" unreal assumption might prove to be fatal in some cases, while a "very" unreal assumption might prove to be quite serviceable in others.

CAUSATION

Methods of analysis depend upon some assumptions — implicit or explicit — about causation, and some preconception as to what kinds of phenomena should be explained. Causation can be thought of as sequential (*A* causes *B* causes *C*), as simultaneous mutual determination (as in Walrasian general equilibrium), or as a confluence of "tendencies" whose net result may bear little resemblance to any of the individual elements. What one wishes to explain may also vary, from how an existing situation came about, to what elements best explain *changes* in situations, and the degree of explanation expected may range from general guiding principles to specific predictions.

During the classical period, both orthodox and dissenting economists tended to conceive of causation in a sequential sense — as distinguished from simultaneous equilibrium — though only Sismondi formalized this in period analysis,[67] and though the Ricardians were usually content to view the process "before" and "after" in comparative static terms. Ricardo's "invariable measure of value" would have determined where a change in exchange-ratios had *originated*.[68] Malthus could deny a causal role to money in cases where it was acknowledged to be an integral part of the phenomena under discussion, if it could be shown that monetary changes were not the "original cause" or the "mainspring" of changes in real variables,[69] that "the variation had originated in the supply of commodities and not in the supply of currency."[70]

The Marxian "dialectical" approach emphasized reciprocal interaction — a sort of halfway house between sequential causation and simultaneous determination. Engels referred to the "universal action and reaction in which causes and effects are eternally changing places, so that what is effect here and now will be cause there and then and vice versa."[71] Cause and effect was, from the Marxian point of view, "a hollow abstraction" indulged by those who lack "dialectics" or an understanding of "interaction," and who reason as if "Hegel never existed."[72] In the Marxian theory of history, for example, there was no one-way causation originating in economic conditions, but rather a mutual interaction of economic and other forces, with the former being considered more powerful than the latter — in explaining *changes*, whatever its importance or unimportance in explaining *states of being*.[73]

Changes versus States of Being

The distinction between explaining changes and explaining states of being is crucial for understanding the methodology of classical economics, though it was a distinction not made explicit by the classical economists themselves (including, here, Marx).   Given multiple causation, the variable which best explains why an existing situation, relationship, or magnitude is what it is need not be the same element that best explains changes in the same situation, relationship, or magnitude. Ricardian rent theory might explain very little of existing disparities in rental payments and yet explain very much about the rise and fall of these payments over time. In terms of the Marxian theory of history, economics might explain very little of why families exist — instead of there being a wholly atomistic society or one in which people clustered in ways unrelated to biological kinship — and yet explain very much of why families have changed in the way they have from one century to another.

Ricardo's arguments about the effect of labor input on value are in reality arguments about the *changes* in labor input on *changes* in value.   Such modifying circumstances as the capital-labor ratio and the occupational wage structure might be important in explaining why values are what they are; however, they were swept aside by Ricardo on grounds that for "variations"[74] in value the occupational wage structure means little, on his assumption that "it continues nearly the same from one generation to another"[75] and while "the degree of durability of fixed capital"[76] has some effect on "variations" in prices,[77] "this cause of variation of commodities is comparatively slight in its effect."[78] He was estimating "the cause of the variations in the value of commodities"[79] — a phrase occurring 200 times in the first chapter of his *Principles*, according to one scholar's count.[80] During the classical period itself, Ricardo's great critic, Samuel Bailey, repeatedly noted that what Ricardo was really doing, especially in discussions of an "invariable measure of value" was to explain *changes* in values[81] in terms of changes in labor input. This was in keeping with the general classical concern for secular growth under conditions of historically diminishing returns, in which labor input per unit of food must rise.

Similarly, Marx's *Capital* attempts to trace *changes* in the relative shares of output going to capitalists and workers over time,[82] and the social and economic implications of such changes — the "law of motion" of capitalism[83] — not its static price determination. After completing his analytical system in the third volume of *Capital*, Marx could say that it was only in a "vague and meaningless" sense that it could still be said that the "value of commodities is determined by the labor contained in them."[84] This was *not* a change of mind between volumes, as sometimes suggested. Marx had worked out the "transformation" of values into prices in a letter to Engels written five years before publication of the first volume of *Capital*.[85] He had denied that they were identical in the first volume itself,[86] and had treated their coincidence as a rare occurrence 20 years earlier[87] — as he was to do again in the final volume of *Capital*.[88]

Much of the "institutionalist" criticism of classical economics argued that theory must explain "things as they are" — a recurring phrase in Malthus and Richard Jones, as well as later in Veblen and modern institutionalists.[89] Modern theorists have argued that the practical use of theory is to explain *changes*[90] — not states of being — and that its validity or lack of validity must be judged by how well it does that. In this, they are at one with the Marxian theory of history.[91] John Stuart Mill, however, failed to distinguish explanations of states of being from explanations of changes and in fact treated them as being the same in his *A System of Logic*:

> Before our theory of the influence of a particular cause, in a given state of circumstances, can be entirely trusted, we must be able to explain and account for the existing state of all that portion of the social phenomenon which that cause has a tendency to

influence.[92]

One way to distinguish explanations of states of being from
explanations of changes might be to see the existing state of
being as the integral of all that has gone before and changes as
the derivative at the present moment, with "human nature" a
large but constant factor in the equation.

Tendencies

One of the more elusive concepts used in classical
treatments of causation was that of "tendency." John Stuart
Mill perhaps best expressed what they meant when he
characterized a tendency as "a power acting with a certain
intensity" in a certain "direction."[93] There are no "exceptions"
to a scientifically established tendency;[94] there are only *other*
tendencies operating in other directions, leading to an
observable course of events which is the resultant of them all.[95]
But while "tendency" sometimes had this meaning, it
sometimes also meant an empirical generalization about the
observable course of events. Whately pointed out the
"undetected ambiguity" of this word which had plagued
classical economics:

> By a "tendency" towards a certain result is sometimes
> meant, "the existence of a cause which, if *operating
> unimpeded*, would produce that result." In this sense it
> may be said, with truth, that the earth or any other body
> moving round a centre, has a tendency to fly off at a
> tangent; i.e., the centrifugal force operates in that
> direction, though it is controlled by the centripetal; or,
> again, that a man has a *greater* tendency to fall prostrate
> than to stand erect; i.e., the attraction of gravitation and
> the position of the centre of gravity, are such that the
> least breath of air would overset him, but for the
> voluntary exertion of muscular force; and, again, that
> population has a *tendency* to increase beyond

subsistence; i.e., there are in man propensities which, if unrestrained, lead to that result.

But sometimes, again, "a tendency towards a certain result" is understood to mean "the existence of such a state of things that that result may be *expected to take place*." ... But in this latter sense, the earth has a greater tendency to remain in its orbit than to fly off from it; man has a greater tendency to stand erect than to fall prostrate; and (as may be proved by comparing a more barbarous with a more civilized period in the history of any country) in the progress of society, subsistence has a tendency to increase at a greater rate than population.[96]

The tragicomic ambiguity in the concept of tendency was brought out in an exchange of letters between Nassau Senior and T.R. Malthus on the Malthusian population theory. With elaborate politeness and indirection, Senior maintained that he and Malthus were "agreed" on "the facts of the case" and that their differences were "almost entirely verbal."[97] Senior confessed himself guilty of "error" in initially understanding Malthus to mean that a growing population pressing on the means of subsistence was "a more probable event" than the opposite,[98] but that would be "inconsistent" with facts which Malthus himself had stated, showing rising standards of living over time.[99] Malthus' replies did nothing to separate the two meanings of the word "tendency." Even John Stuart Mill, who had produced the most searching discussion of this word, and of classical methodology generally, lapsed back into ambiguity when defending the Malthusian population theory in his *Principles*, claiming that critics' corrections of "mere language" did not affect the substance of the problem, which was that population was in "too" large a ratio to the means of subsistence[100] — a meaningless statement, empirically and analytically.

Two of Marx's main arguments involved tendencies. Indeed, the whole dialectical approach emphasized internal conflicts which forced the entity that produced them to undergo a basic transformation.   Analogies with metamorphoses in nature abound in Marx and Engels.[101] The increasing misery of the proletariat was seen as a tendency, in both the analytical and the historical sense, for the workers' share of gross output to decline.   However, scholars who interpret this to mean an absolute reduction in real income have cited passages in which tendency is clearly used only in the analytical sense and followed by a statement of *counter*-tendencies toward rising wages.[102] The Marxian tendency of the falling rate of profit is clearly an analytical tendency, for the discussion of it is followed immediately by a whole chapter on counter-tendencies. [103]   Marx's point here is apparently to show pressures producing class conflict — spilling over into the political sphere — rather than to be concerned with the economic resultant as such.

Ricardo and the Ricardians often reasoned as if the long-run tendencies in the Ricardian system — subsistence wages, minimal profits, stationary capital and population — were in fact generally existing conditions.   Malthus fought a running battle with Ricardo on this, protesting that actual events showed these tendencies "counterbalanced by other causes," [104] "suspended . . . for a hundred years together,"[105] and generally constituting empirical exceptions in "unusual" conditions.[106] William Whewell likewise deprecated the Ricardian tendencies as guides to existing conditions, arguing how strange it would be,

> . . . if a mathematical speculator concerning the physical world should teach, as an important proposition, that all things *tend* to assume a form determined by the force of gravity; that thus the hills tend to become plains, the waterfalls to eat away their beds and disappear, the rivers to form lakes in the valleys, the glaciers to pour down in cataracts. To which the reply would be, that these tendencies are counteracted by opposite tendencies of the same order, and thus have only a small

share in shaping the earth's surface. The cohesion of
rocks, the tenacity of ice, the original structure of
mountains, are facts as real as the action of gravity; and
the doctrine that the earth's surface *tends* to a level, is of
small value and limited use in physical geography.[107]

Again, the objection to the Ricardian methodology was tied
to the uses made of the results, and depended also on whether
the Ricardian system was conceived to explain states of being
or the dynamics of change. The arbitrary designation of one
element as a tendency and other elements as "disturbing causes"
would have had little substantial significance if the Ricardians
had not slipped into the habit of regarding the former as more
common than the latter. Whewell's analogy with topography
would have been meaningless if the Ricardians had been
explicit that they were explaining *changes* rather than the state
of being — why mountains and waterfalls erode, rather than
why they exist.

Interactions

Implicit in the classical use of tendencies, counterten-
dencies and resultants is the notion that causation in the social
sciences follows the pattern of physics rather than of chemistry.
John Stuart Mill alone made this assumption explicit. Social
science was to be constructed "after the model . . . of the more
complex physical sciences."[108] In physics, the effects of "joint
forces" is "the same when they act simultaneously, as if they
had acted one after another."[109] A parallelogram of forces
shows that a body would end up at the same point whether
propelled first by one force and then the other, or whether it
followed a resultant produced by the simultaneous action of the
same two forces. In chemistry, by contrast, there is a mutually
transforming interaction, whose result is not merely the sum of
its elements. Water has "different properties" from its
constituents, hydrogen and oxygen, as Mill pointed out.[110] Nor
is the taste of a compound "the sum of the tastes of its

component elements."[111] This is why physics is a deductive science while chemistry is experimental. "Human beings in society have no properties but those which are derived from, and may be resolved into, the laws of the nature of individual man," according to Mill.[112] The peculiarities of group behavior — from committees to lynch mobs — were ignored.

Given the assumption that social causation follows the model of physics rather than of chemistry, it becomes possible to analyze by successive approximation. The simplest assumption may be used as a starting point and successive complications added as needed, one step at a time, reaching an end result which will be the same as if their complex simultaneous action had been analyzed in a "realistic" model of unmanageable complexity.[113] One may "put all these effects together, and, from what they are separately . . . collect what would be the effect of all these causes acting at once," Mill concluded.[114]

Because the nature of individual man is the analyst's starting point, Mill considered that he might derive much insight from *mental experiments* within himself.[115] Nassau Senior, however, pointed out that these mental experiments were unlikely to accurately reflect how other people from different backgrounds would behave.[116] According to Senior, "this accounts for the constant mismanagement of the lower orders and of children, madmen, and savages, by their intellectual and moral superiors."[117] Richard Jones rejected mental experiments for very similar reasons.[118]

Although the Ricardians were often accused of "geometrical" reasoning because of their syllogisms, John Stuart Mill explicitly rejected geometry as a model for reasoning in the social sciences. This was because (1) geometry was considered inconsistent with sequential causation, being "a science of co-existent facts, altogether independent of the laws of the succession of phenomena,"[119] and (2) "geometry affords no room for what so constantly occurs in mechanics and its applications, the case of conflicting forces; of causes which counteract or modify one another." [120]   One geometrical principle does not affect another; the properties of a circle are wholly unaffected by whether there is a square inscribed within it or a variety of tangents touching it or numerous other circles overlapping it. Mechanics was deductive like geometry, but permitted consideration of sequences and mutual modifications of forces or tendencies.

DEFINITIONS

Although Malthus' *Definitions in Political Economy* (1827) was the only work devoted exclusively to that topic during the classical period, a number of his contemporaries dealt with the same subject. Whately even declared "a clear definition of technical terms" to be "the most important" as well as "the most difficult" point in economics. He found "ambiguity of language" or a "fault of reasoning" to be "a more common source of error" than lack of facts or misstatements of facts.[121] Samuel Bailey likewise declared that "the strongest powers of reasoning are an insufficient security against gross error" unless accompanied by an "incessant analysis of terms and propositions" and an "intense consciousness of intellectual operations."[122] The "chameleon-like properties of language,"[123] "inaccuracy and inattention in the use of words,"[124] the ready resort to a "learned slang"[125] — general verbal carelessness — caused "more than half the difficulties in political economy."[126] While Malthus thought the problem centered on the use of the same term in different senses by different writers,[127] Bailey thought it was due to the use of the same term in different senses by the *same* writer at different times.[128]

Precisely because words are intrinsically unimportant, they require a great deal of attention to prevent their affecting substantive propositions about real things. People "are fond of supposing that they are engaged in a difficult investigation into the nature of things when they are only disagreeing about the meaning of words."[129] Bailey's *Observations on Certain*

Verbal Disputes in Political Economy (1821) said on its last page: "The foregoing Tract will, perhaps, be rejected with contempt, as a mere discussion about words. It is so; it professes to be so. It has for its object to *prevent* some discussions about words, which *do not* profess to be so, but pass themselves off for discussions about *things*, instead of what they really are."[130] While those who appreciated the need for clear definitions and careful attention to words put very great stress on the point, there were others who not only did not attach such importance to verbal precision, but who positively opposed strict definitions, on principle. The foremost of these was Richard Jones: "I have been reproached with giving no regular definition of rent. The omission was not accidental. To begin, or indeed to end, an enquiry into the nature of any subject, a circumstance existing before us, by a definition, is to show how little we knew how to set about our task — how little of the inductive spirit is within us."[131]

Sismondi likewise deliberately refused to give precise definitions in his later writings.[132] In his earlier *Richesse commerciale* (1803) he not only defined his terms mathematically[133] but also defined some of the same terms verbally in a glossary[134] — a special care for definitions which was highly unusual among economists at that time. His complete reversal in his later writings was almost certainly a reaction against the Ricardians with whom he had bitterly contended over Say's Law. James Mill, Robert Torrens, and John Stuart Mill had simply defined terms in such a way as to make Say's Law an *ex post* identity.[135] Say himself had done something similar,[136] so much so that Bailey had declared: "These affected *ways of talking* constitute, in great part, what M. Say calls his *doctrine*."[137]

While there was general dissatisfaction among economists of the classical period with each other's use of terms, and complaints of shifting or tautological definitions, there was no general agreement on what should be done about it. Malthus preferred that when common, everyday terms were used in economics, they be used in their common, everyday sense.[138]

Whately, however, argued that it was precisely "terms to which we are familiarly accustomed"[139] which produced the greatest confusion and error. This was because (1) the need for definition was not seen, due to familiarity,[140] even though the word had *several* different meanings, and (2) even if the term is specifically defined for use in a particular discipline, there will be a constant danger of "sliding insensibly into ambiguity" by using the word in one of its common popular senses."[141]

Despite Bailey's great concern for verbal precision, he opposed the widespread use of technical terms. If a technical term was borrowed from popular usage, the old connotations would continue to surround it and invite confusion.[142] New terms were also not the answer. The "*only* use of them" is where expressing the same idea without them would involve such a long string of words that the analytical connection was likely to be lost in the process.[143] Bailey did not think that this was usually the case. The initial brevity of technical terms was regarded as a short-run advantage, followed by needless, lengthy controversies due to misunderstandings. He suggested that in place of a technical term, the definition of that term could be substituted, "putting down four or five plain words here and there, instead of one that is not plain."[144] He said: "We have time enough to attend to the additional words. We have not time enough to attend to the disputes and puzzles which arise from this zeal for 'shortness.'"[145] Bailey considered much of the technical vocabulary of economics to be a result of vain imitation of more prestigious disciplines:

> To set out with a number of terms and formal definitions, gives, it is thought, an air of resemblance to mathematical accuracy. But the accuracy of mathematics does not consist in having many technical terms, which require definitions, but in having no term that *has not*, where it *is* necessary, a clear definition, and that definition constantly borne in mind.[146]

SUMMARY AND IMPLICATIONS

Economics was generally conceived of in the classical period as having a scientific core — that is, a systematic analytical method — and such additional features of science as internally consistent hypothetical truths (essential elements of Say's Law) and a stock of empirically tested principles (classical monetary theory). It was universally understood that most individual economic principles had not been, and could not be, subjected to controlled experiments and so lacked the degree of certainty of conclusions in the natural sciences. Sharp differences existed as to the implications of this fact. One school of thought regarded the impossibility of achieving scientific certainty as a reason for abandoning scientific conceptual precision and scientific methods of analysis, relying more on "experience" or common sense observation. Yet for the Ricardians the complexities and uncertainties of the real world were precisely the reason for *not* relying on direct "experience"[147] *as a source of explanatory hypotheses.* Wider experience, embracing the given phenomenon as a special case, could be used as a basis for the abstraction of principles and the deduction of conclusions — which could *then* be verified empirically from the facts of the particular phenomenon.[148] John Stuart Mill, who exemplified and elaborated classical methodology more explicitly and thoroughly than anyone else, was by no means opposed to empiricism at the stage of verification. He was indeed the first economist to systematically analyze the application of statistical theory.[149]

J.S. Mill, who best articulated Ricardian methodology, also articulated its fatal weakness — as well as exemplifying that weakness in his defenses of Say's Law, Malthusian population theory, and classical value theory. He said:

But it is, when not duly regarded against, an almost

irresistible tendency of the human mind to become the slave of its own hypotheses; and when it has once habituated itself to reason, feel, and conceive, under certain arbitrary conditions, at length to mistake these conditions for laws of nature. Let us be accustomed whenever we think of certain things, to figure them to ourselves as existing in one particular way, never in any other way, and we at last learn to think, or to feel as if we thought, that way the natural and the only possible way: and we feel the same sort of incapability of adapting our associations to any change in the hypothesis, which a rustic feels in conceiving that it is the earth which moves and the sun which stands still . . . the greatest powers of reasoning, when connected with a sluggish imagination, are no safeguard against the poorest intellectual slavery — that of subjection to mere accidental habits of thought.[150]

Ricardian economics was narrow not only in terms of its institutional base — the contemporary British economy and society — but also in terms of its theoretical aims. Although the Ricardian system was constructed to generate abstract, general principles which were hypothetically true under specified conditions, the conditions actually specified produced tendentious results geared to contemporary controversies over the Corn Laws, Poor Laws, etc. It was this practice which Schumpeter labeled the "Ricardian Vice," though one in which "many less brilliant economists sinned and still sin fully as much as that eminent man did."[151] Schumpeter observed:

. . . Ricardo's was not the mind that is primarily interested in either fundamentals or wide generalizations . . . . His interest was in the clear-cut result of direct, practical significance. In order to get this he cut that general system to pieces, bundled up as large parts of it as possible, and put them in cold storage —so that as many things as possible should be frozen and "given."

He then piled one simplifying assumption upon another until, having really settled everything by these assumptions, he was left with only a few aggregative variables between which, given these assumptions, he set up simple one-way relations so that, in the end, the desired results emerged almost as tautologies. For example, a famous Ricardian theory is that profits "depend upon" the price of wheat. And under his implicit assumption and in the particular sense in which the terms of the proposition are to be understood, this is not only true, but undeniably, in fact trivially so. Profits could not possibly depend upon anything else, since everything else is "given," that is frozen. It is an excellent theory that can never be refuted and lacks nothing save sense.[152]

The Ricardians staunchly defended not only their abstract principles, but also key empirical assumptions — *historical* diminishing returns, flexible wage rates — and a particular way of viewing the economic process — comparative statics. The methodological advance of classical economics from the loose eclecticism of Adam Smith to the systematic precision of Ricardo and the Ricardians was not without cost. These costs included (1) tendentious models based on "special cases which in the author's mind and in his exposition are invested with a treacherous generality,"[153] (2) an overlooking of questions — such as dynamics — requiring different methods, and (3) perhaps most serious of all, the tautological development of substantively meaningful propositions, such as Say's Law or the wages fund doctrine.

Many of the basic methodological issues of modern economics were raised and explored during the classical period, though not ultimately settled then any more than today. The critics of classical economics launched many of the same arguments heard later from historical, "institutionalist," and other root-and-branch opponents of modern economic theory. The later criticisms, however, more often included the charge that economics was socially conservative and apologetic, and that its abstract methodology was a means of avoiding or disguising the "real" issues. Sometimes this has been linked to a more general theory that analytical (including methodological) propositions are functions of social or political philosophy. "Experience" may seem to bear this out, since most of the strongest "institutionalist" critics of economics — from Hobson and Veblen through Galbraith and contemporary "radical political economists" — have been significantly to the left of most orthodox defenders of traditional economic methodology. However, this is itself an example of the difference between reasoning inductively from specific experience and reasoning deductively by abstracting from a wider experience. If the wider experience encompasses the critics of classical abstract deductive reasoning, it is clear that such critics were far more *conservative* than their methodological opponents, and no one more strongly defended abstract deductive reasoning than Karl Marx. On the whole, the critics and supporters of classical methodology covered a wide range of the political spectrum, suggesting that the generalization from later experience is incorrect. Even in the modern period, many exceptions are found to that generalization, the most striking being the methodological similarity of the Marxist Oskar Lange and the "conservative" Milton Friedman.[154] Judging from wider historical experience, there is no necessary and little factual relationship between political philosophy and economic methodology.

Sismondi: A Neglected Pioneer

J.C.L. Simonde de Sismondi (1773–1842) originated more fundamental economic concepts and theories than many economists of wider and more enduring fame. Yet when he is remembered at all, it is usually as one among many opponents of Say's Law, or for his questionable theories of technological unemployment, or as the reputed "father of interventionism."[1] But it was Sismondi who first developed a theory of equilibrium aggregate income, who first produced an algebraic growth model, and who anticipated more celebrated economists on a number of other points. Although Keynes lauded Malthus' *Principles of Political Economy* as a forerunner of his own *General Theory*, Marx was perhaps a little closer to the truth when he cynically characterized Malthus' *Principles* of 1820 as merely the English "translation"[2] of Sismondi's *Nouveaux Principes d'économie politique* of 1819, though in fact Malthus had already developed his ideas independently in correspondence with Ricardo before Sismondi's *Nouveaux Principes* was published.[3] But Malthus added little to what Sismondi had already said on equilibrium aggregate income.

What makes Sismondi's contribution all the more remarkable is that (1) he achieved fame primarily as an historian, (2) he had no university training,[4] and (3) his work was marred by a lack of intellectual rigor which was noted by his contemporaries as well as by later commentators.[5] The looseness of his presentation must be counted as a major — though not the sole — cause of his neglect.

LIFE AND TIMES

The man now known as Sismondi was born in Geneva in 1773 as Jean Charles Leonard Simonde. He made his surname

"Simonde de Sismondi" upon returning to Geneva in 1800 from exile in Italy, where he had discovered records of a noble Italian family named Sismondi, from whom he claimed to be descended.[6] He was sufficiently tentative or embarrassed about the change to use his original name on his first book on economics, *De la Richesse commerciale*, in 1803. However, by the time he came to write the work for which he is best known in economics, *Nouveaux Principes d'économie politique*, in 1819 he was and remained Simonde de Sismondi. The stormy and unsuccessful struggle of Sismondi with the classical school of economics was paralleled by a stormy personal life, involving three exiles, three imprisonments, a change of citizenship, a love affair frustrated by family objections to marriage plans, periods of financial strain, and a final row with political foes in Geneva just before he died of cancer in 1842.

Sismondi was a man of moderate and fluctuating fortune, as his family was forced to flee the storms generated by the French Revolution and the later reactions. Sismondi was too aristocratic for the revolutionaries, too liberal for the restorationists, and too individualistic to belong to any intellectual cult or school. As a person, he was by all accounts a man of high principles and great generosity, amiable but lacking in social graces, increasingly bitter against the neglect and misunderstanding of his economic theories, but honoring his adversaries in general and reserving special affection for Ricardo in particular.

Sismondi was a gentleman farmer, but changing political and economic fortunes led him into a variety of occupations, from clerk to professor of philosophy, the latter being one which displeased him because of "the petty intrigues" of academic life.[7] In early adulthood, he was a protégé of Madame de Staël and remained part of her intellectual circle for some years. His international travels and associations (including an English wife in 1819) made him cosmopolitan in outlook, though he returned to his native Geneva and a small circle of friends to spend his declining years.

In politics, Sismondi was a practitioner as well as a theorist. Himself a victim of the passions unleashed by the French

Revolution, he opposed all forms of dogmatism and appeals to mass actions, but in philosophy and policy he exemplified many of the values of the eighteenth-century intellectual godfathers of the Revolution. He believed in equal protection and equal opportunity, but not equal conditions.[8] "I am," he said, "a liberal, better yet, a republican, but never a democrat."[9] He repeatedly attacked slavery,[10] opposed imperialism,[11] and denounced governments for their "gigantic projects" and "pointless wars."[12] Characteristically, Sismondi refused to support Napoleon or to accept honors from him at the height of Napoleonic glory, but rallied to his support when he returned from Elba to lead a lost cause against the restorationists.[13] Sismondi was active in the political life of Geneva up to the eve of his death.[14]

In economics, Sismondi began as a disciple of Adam Smith, intending his *Richesse commerciale* as simply a systematic presentation and elaboration of the principles scattered through the rambling *Wealth of Nations*. It was, however, "not quite the Smithian brew it has been made out to be,"[15] both by later commentators and by Sismondi himself when emphasizing the new departure represented by his later works. However, in *Richesse commerciale* itself, Sismondi advanced the claim of "presenting the national balance" in an "absolutely new" manner.[16] In the text he used arithmetic examples in which (1) the output of a given year was 2.5 times the wages fund of the preceding year,[17] (2) the successive hypothetical quantities of "revenue," "expenditure," and "savings" were traced from the year 1799 to 1800 to 1801,[18] and (3) in three countries which have, respectively, no foreign trade, an export surplus, and an import surplus.[19]

The parallel algebraic reasoning underlying the arithmetic examples was elaborated in a lengthy footnote spreading over five pages.[20] This systematic model building was not only original and suggestive of modern growth models, it was in sharp contrast to Sismondi's loose reasoning in his later and better known *Nouveaux Principes*. The earlier work was not only more systematic and abstract in its aggregative model, it was more precise in its definitions, including a carefully worded glossary of terms, in sharp contrast to Sismondi's later shifting uses of such terms as "revenue" and his explicit disavowal of any attempt at precise definitions.[21] This puzzling methodological retrogression may reflect a reaction to the Ricardian method of reasoning, which was the *bête noire* of Sismondi's later economic writings — a similar change from an early "theoretical" position to a later "institutional" position occurred in Malthus — or it may reflect the Germanic influence of Madame de Staël's circle during Sismondi's early intellectual career, as against the looser French style of his later years. It might also be some combination: In criticizing the abstractions and technicalities of the Ricardian school, Sismondi likened them to the German metaphysicians.[22]

Although the early growth model of his *Richesse commerciale* marked a new departure with important potential, it made no impact, since the book itself was little noticed. Moreover, it was not used to attack or question the classical propositions now known as Say's Law — and the book closed with a strong support of this pillar of classical orthodoxy.[23] Sismondi never resumed interest in his growth models, though his *Nouveaux Principes* contained arithmetic examples whose underlying algebraic argument was essentially the same as that of his earlier work.[24]

Sismondi's break with the classical tradition came in 1815, when he wrote an article titled "Political Economy," for the *Edinburgh Encyclopedia*, in which he presented the skeleton of the argument that was later fleshed out in *Nouveaux Principes* (1819) and repeated still later (1837–38) in his *Études sur l'économie politique*. In the midst of a general survey of economics, which was quite orthodox in most respects, appeared a theory of equilibrium aggregate income. It was not, as such, an attack on Say's Law, and in fact polemics were initiated by the other side in their reviews of the same ideas when they appeared in *Nouveaux Principes*. The basic point of Say's Law — the secularly unlimited growth potential of the economy — was never challenged by Sismondi, or for that matter, by Malthus, Lauderdale, or most other supporters of "general glut" theories. But at this period in its history, Say's Law was also used to imply that equilibrium was possible at any given level of aggregate output, that *internal proportions* — not aggregate quantity — made the difference between equilibrium and disequilibrium.

Such obvious dislocations as unsold goods and unemployment were never denied by the supporters of the orthodox position, but their explanation was disproportionality rather than insufficient aggregate demand. Logically, following their premise, they concluded that equilibrium could be restored at a *higher* level of aggregate production[25] by increasing the output of goods which were in less than equilibrium proportions to other goods, rather than by reducing the latter in order to reach the same necessary proportions. Say's Law was invoked to show that there was no such thing as an equilibrium aggregate income. This set off one of the longest, most wide-ranging, and most heated controversies in the history of economics — the "general glut" controversy which reached its peak in the 1820s, involving almost every major economist of the period, as well as many minor figures and popular journals, and which continued on into the 1830s and 1840s, even after the death of most of the key participants.

A highly critical review of *Nouveaux Principes* appeared in the *Edinburgh Review* in October 1819 and drew an immediate reply from Sismondi in the *Annales de Legislation et de Jurisprudence* in 1820, as well as a passing reply on one point in Malthus' *Principles* in 1820.[26] This was met by an attack on both Sismondi and Malthus in the *Edinburgh Review* of March 1821, as well as by a lengthy rejoinder to Malthus' criticism in Torrens' *Essay on the Production of Wealth* in 1821.[27] From this point on, the articles, letters, pamphlets, books, and verbal confrontations became too numerous and involved to trace.[28] Sismondi was in the thick of the early polemics. He exchanged polemical articles with J.B. Say in the *Revue Encyclopedique* in 1824 — both articles bearing the same title, "Sur la balance des consommations avec les productions" — and placed a rejoinder to Say in the appendix to the second edition of his *Nouveaux Principes* in 1827. He encountered Ricardo while visiting England in 1819 and again in Geneva during the latter's tour of the continent in 1822 — exchanging a few words on the first occasion and having an extended argument on the second.[29] He clashed with McCulloch during a visit to Britain in 1826, in a manner which led him afterwards to fear that he (Sismondi) had been "rude" and that McCulloch would "retain some resentment against me."[30]

In general, Sismondi treated his adversaries with respect,[31] and received their good will,[32] though not always their intellectual respect[33] in return. His ideas made scarcely a dent on the Ricardians and were largely ignored in his native Geneva and in France,[34] but he apparently had an important influence on the later writings of J.B. Say. Sismondi noted on September 26, 1826: "I had this morning a visit from Say, who said to me that his friendship for M. Ricardo and his school has very often cramped him, but that in truth he finds that they have injured the science by the abstractions into which they have thrown it, and that he shall be obliged, in the new edition he is preparing, absolutely to oppose them."[35]

The fifth edition of Say's *Traité*, which appeared at the end of 1826, did in fact contain, in the chapter on the law of markets (1) an acceptance and elaboration of the Sismondian theory of equilibrium income in Sismondian language,[36] though without any reference to Sismondi by name, and (2) an observation that "it is only in abstract quantities that there are infinite progressions" while "we are studying practical political economy here,"[37] but without any specific reference to the Ricardians at this point. In a later letter to Malthus, Say frankly stated, "I will confess that my doctrine on *markets* is in fact subject to some restrictions," so much so that the recently revised *Traité* "revealed that restriction, even though Messrs. *Ricardo, Mill*, and *MacCollouch* had adopted my doctrine in that regard," because he felt it was "better to stick to facts and their consequences than to syllogisms."[38] Sismondi also reported receiving a letter from Say "with some concessions to my principles on the limits of production."[39] Unfortunately, English translations of Say's *Traité* are all from the *fourth* edition of 1821, thereby missing the important additions which appeared in Say's final edition. In a textbook, *Cours complet d'économie politique pratique*, first published in 1828–29, Say followed the chapter on the law of markets by one called "Limits to Production" — repeating part of the title of one of Sismondi's chapters[40] — in which he again set forth a theory of equilibrium income along Sismondian lines. Yet there were no repercussions of this in British economics, which was the dominant economics of the period, and it has been largely lost sight of in the history of economic thought.[41]

Sismondi's failure to affect the theoretical development of

economics and, even more important, the direction of economic policies, was a disappointment which continued bitter to the end of his days. He had no fear of secular stagnation, or even of serious depressions, growing out of the normal operation of a free market, but he feared government-sponsored programs to artificially promote economic development by growing industries "in hothouses,"[42] without regard to the state of the market. He saw in the depressions that followed the Napoleonic wars evidence of overproduction. Increasingly, his appeals were to "facts" rather than theories or reasons.

THE SISMONDIAN GROWTH MODEL

Sismondi's first economic writing, *Richesse commerciale*, had a concept of circular flows of goods and money, opposite in direction and equal in value.[43] But although the two flows "must necessarily be equal"[44] to each other, this was not an identity, but was a consequence of equilibrating tendencies: "Imagine a nation which generally has no foreign commerce at all. The product of its labor will consequently be equal to its consumption since, if it were to produce more than it could consume, making no exports, a part of the fruits of its labor would be useless, would fall in price and would arrest production for the following year."[45]

"Consumption," during this period in the development of economics, referred to aggregate demand — both investment ("productive" consumption) and consumption ("unproductive" consumption).[46] In this sense, Sismondi could say that if a nation's output in a given year "were to surpass its consumption of the same year, there would be an excess to consume in the following year, which would discourage further production, by rendering it useless."[47] Although there was nothing new here theoretically, beyond what had already appeared in the physiocrats,[48] Sismondi was launched on a course of reasoning very different from that of the contemporary defenders of Say's Law, particularly the Ricardians. The latter were concerned to show (1) the necessary equality of output and purchasing power,[49] (2) a kind of behavioral rationality which precluded attempts to hoard,[50] and (3) the ability of a free market to be cleared at any given level of output[51] — all points to which Sismondi made no objections. In addition, Ricardo argued that there could be no such thing as a theory of aggregate output,[52] and took a comparative statics approach, which contrasted with Sismondi's concern for the lagged effect of current "consumption" on future production.

Sismondi defined several key variables for use in a model of a closed economy. His variables, his definitions, and their modern equivalents are shown on the table below:

SISMONDIAN SYMBOLS	DEFINITION	MODERN SYMBOLS
P	*Production*: the total annual output of the current period.[a] In an all-agricultural economy, the most recent harvest	Y_t
N	*Salaire nécessaire*: the necessary supply price of labor in the *previous* period	W_{t-1}
X	ΔN: "the difference between the previous necessary wage and that advanced during the current year, a difference which can be either zero or positive or negative."[b]	$W_t - W_{t-1}$
D	*Dépense*: aggregate expenditure of the non-laboring classes during the current period	$(C_t + I_t) - W_t$

SOURCE: [a] *Richesse commerciale*, Vol. I, p. 105n.
          [b] Ibid., p. 107n.

Sismondi's arithmetic examples used such additional terms as "revenue" and "savings," the implied relationship in the numerical results being that revenue minus expenditure equaled savings.[53] Following the pattern above, two new "Sismondian" symbols may be added — R and E (*Revenue* and *Epargnes*) — and their corresponding modern versions, R_t and S_t.

According to Sismondi, "$P - N$ is revenue";[54] to render this first in Sismondian terms, and then in modern terms:

$$R = P - N \tag{1}$$
$$R_t = Y_t - W_{t-1} \tag{1a}$$

Current consumption "is $D + (N + X)$";[55] Sismondi's own equations can be used here:

$$D + (N + X) = P, \text{ or} \tag{2}$$
$$D = P - (N + X)$$

The modern counterpart would be:

$$(C_t + I_t) - W_t + (W_{t-1} + W_t - W_{t-1}) = Y_t \tag{2a}$$
$$C_t + I_t = Y_t$$

According to Sismondi, whether national output grows, remains stationary, or declines depends upon the difference between "revenue" and "expenditure"[56] or on X, the incremental wages fund. He did not explain why these two statements were equivalent, but it can be readily derived from equations (1) and (2) above.

$$D = P - (N + X) = (P - N) - X = R - X \tag{3}$$
$$R - D = X$$

In modern terms:

$$R_t - D_t = (Y_t - W_{t-1}) - (Y_t - W_t) = W_t - W_{t-1} \tag{3a}$$

Since R − D was definitionally "savings," then

$$S_t = W_t - W_{t-1} \tag{4a}$$

With wage payments being the only form of investment in this simplified model, incremental wage payments $(W_t - W_{t-1})$ were equal to net investment during a given period. It followed that

$$S_t = I_t \tag{5a}$$

Moving from definitions to theories, Sismondi assumed that the output of a given period was a constant (2.5) times the wages fund of the previous period.[57] This was incorporated into his numerical examples but not his explicit equations:

$$Y_t = k\,(W_{t-1}) \tag{6a}$$

Incremental output was, therefore, the same multiple of net investment:

$$Y_{t+1} - Y_t = k\,(W_t) - k\,(W_{t-1}) = k\,(W_t - W_{t-1}) = kI_t \tag{7a}$$

$$Y_{t+1} = Y_t + kI_t = C_t + I_t + kI_t = C_t + (1+k)\,I_t \tag{8a}$$

Although equation (8a) was never derived by Sismondi, even in his own terms, it fits the numerical examples in *Richesse commerciale*, as well as in *Nouveaux Principes*,[58] the only difference between the two books in this regard being that k is 2.5 in the former and 5 in the latter.[59] Modified equations were developed for an economy with international trade,[60] but the principles remained the same.

EQUILIBRIUM INCOME
AND "GENERAL GLUTS"

A "glut" in classical economics was a situation in which goods were sold at less than their cost of production (or were unsold at cost-covering prices). Everyone agreed that this could happen in particular sectors of the economy — that there could be "partial gluts." The controversy arose whether aggregate output might prove to be salable only at less than cost-covering prices — a *general* glut. A fatal ambiguity in the concept of "cost" prevented the opposing sides in the general glut controversy from coming to grips with each other's basic arguments. The classical supporters of Say's Law treated "cost" as the factor cost actually paid *ex post* while Sismondi — and, after him, Malthus and others — treated "cost" as the *ex ante* supply price. With no leakages from the circular flow, output would necessarily be sold at cost-covering prices in the sense used by Say and the Ricardians, but need not be in Sismondi's sense of receiving prices sufficient to cause their reproduction in subsequent time periods.

Sismondi's *Richesse commerciale* defined the "necessary price" as that required so that the producers do not "become disgusted and quit their work," the "relative price" as representing the "sacrifices which the buyer is willing to make," and the "extent of the market" as the quantity of goods for which consumers "offer a relative price equal to the intrinsic price." These terms appeared again in *Nouveaux Principes*,[61] but without definitions. In his later *Études*, costs were defined as "not what it has cost now, but what it would cost hereafter."[62]

Differences between expectations *ex ante* and results *ex post* permitted aggregate supply to differ from aggregate demand. Sismondi's emphasis on costs as supply prices rather than as actual factor payments reflected the fact that he was not concerned with *clearing the market* but with the *sustainability* of a given volume of aggregate output. Moreover, Sismondi's costs reflected the underlying disutility of production, and demand its underlying utility. His analysis, in fact, began with a man stranded alone on a desert island, to show how the two were balanced by him,[63] and then, by extension, by society at large.[64] In society, the complexity of the market made miscalculations *possible*,[65] but the price mechanism tended to maintain equilibrium[66] — except where governmental policies interfered: "The development of nations proceeds naturally in all directions; it is scarcely ever prudent to obstruct it, but it is no less dangerous to hasten it . . . ."[67]

Contrary to interpretations in the literature, it was not inherent defects of the capitalist economy[68] but the deliberate policies of contemporary governments which Sismondi regarded as the primary cause of glutted markets. Government growth schemes were "indiscriminately pushing production"[69] and trying to grow industries in "hothouses."[70] Although the private capitalist's interest would lead him "to do what suits the country best," Sismondi feared that the "ardor" of "all governments" who had artificially "excited every species of production," brought about "a disproportion between labor and demand,"[71] with disastrous consequences.

Reasoning still in the lagged terms of his earlier work, Sismondi argued that an artificial increase in investment in one period would raise wages temporarily, causing a growth of population which would turn out to be unemployable in later periods, as reduced returns on capital led to disinvestment.[72] In such circumstances, when governments find themselves "charged with a population which they have created, by demanding superfluous labor," Sismondi urged intervention on grounds that governments have an "obligation to provide for their needs,"[73] to "intervene at least to destroy the evil which they have created."[74] While Sismondi recommended, in general, only "indirect means" of dealing with economic problems through government policy, in emergency conditions "legislation must come to the rescue in a more direct manner,"[75] but he was by no means a *dirigiste*: "By allowing the greatest freedom to capital, it will go where profits call, and these profits are the indication of national needs."[76]

While Sismondi accepted laissez-faire as a principle, he opposed it as a dogma. He was not prepared to "reduce political economy to the simplest maxim . . . to *laisser faire* and *laisser passer*."[77] He urged the principle of guaranteed wages to be pressed upon industries in order to prevent short-run increases of demand for labor from creating an excess dependent population.[78] He suggested that the government use its "indirect influence" by promoting transportation and communication, good tax laws, a good system of justice, etc., and perhaps in that way compensate for its harmful mercantilistic measures.[79]

The concept of an equilibrium income is implicit in the idea of a general glut, but with Sismondi (in contrast to Malthus, Lauderdale, and others) the term "equilibrium" is explicit and occurs repeatedly throughout his writings.[80] He saw clearly the distinction between his theory of an equilibrium income and the Say-Ricardo theory that there could be no aggregate overproduction but only internal disproportionality:

> You have produced too much, say some. You have not produced enough, say the others. Equilibrium will be re-established, peace and prosperity will be created again, only when you have consumed all this surplus of merchandise which remains unsold on the market, and when you have regulated your production thereafter by the demand of the buyers. Equilibrium will be re-created, say the others, provided that you redouble the efforts to accumulate as well as to produce. You are mistaken when you believe that our markets are glutted. Our stores are only half filled; let us similarly fill the other half, and these new riches, exchanged against the others, will revive commerce.[81]

The question of "the balance of consumption and production" was for Sismondi "the fundamental question in political economy."[82] He was concerned to explain "violent crises,"[83] not secular stagnation:

> I have sought to show that the natural course of nations was the progressive increase of their prosperity, the consequent increase of their demand for new products, and of their means of paying for them. [84]

Although Sismondi had no theory of secular stagnation, as sometimes suggested,[85] he did not believe that equilibrium was immediately re-established after every disturbance. There were difficulties of exit for capital, businessmen, and specialized labor.[86] There were, in some cases, backward bending supply curves.[87] Moreover, fixed capital would continue to operate at a loss whenever closing down would involve a bigger loss.[88] Education was also "a sort of fixed capital"[89] and, like other fixed capital, it continued to produce for less than its long-run supply price during periods of depression."[90] Additionally, speculative inventory accumulation by merchants and consumers alike retards still further "the period when the balance can be re-established between consumption and production."[91] These frictions and destabilizing responses did not make a depression permanent, but exacted a toll before recovery: "a certain equilibrium is re-established, it is true, in the long run, but it is by a frightful suffering."[92]

Money played no essential role in Sismondi's theory of overproduction. Indeed, the theory was first developed in a Robinson Crusoe model and then in a barter economy "deliberately," according to Sismondi, in order to show that money was not necessary to explain it.[93] Like his classical contemporaries, Sismondi treated money as a "veil." It "simplified all mercantile operations and complicated all philosophic observations, of which the same operations are the object."[94] But also like his classical contemporaries, he recognized that monetary phenomena were involved in cyclical downturns, though he did not regard such phenomena as playing an initiating role or as affecting the end result. Although he referred, in general terms, to the stability of monetary velocity,[95] this did not imply — for him or for his contemporaries — that velocity remained constant during all phases of the business cycle.   Indeed, he referred to monetary contractions during downturns[96] and considered controlled reflation as a policy at such times.[97] None of this was original with Sismondi, and in fact he acknowledged his debt to the writings of Henry Thornton on these points.[98]

One of the key concepts used in Sismondi's discussions of equilibrium income and general gluts was "revenue" — literally a *return*. While "revenue" is translatable as "income,"[99] such a translation misses what Sismondi himself called the "mysterious and incomprehensible" nature of the concept,[100] which he referred to by the same word in English as in French,[101] although he knew the English word "income,"[102] and in fact wrote in English as well as in French. Revenue was not synonymous with income or output.   In *Richesse commerciale*, Sismondi had defined revenue as current output minus previous labor costs $(P - N$ or $Y_t - W_{t-1})$,[103] literally a return on previous investments — wage payments, as noted earlier, being the only form of investment in this simplified model. In *Nouveaux Principes* this definition reappeared as one among several which were used interchangeably without warning. Sometimes "revenue" meant a "value by which the finished product surpasses the advances made to produce it"[104] — as originally — but "revenue" was also used as the sum of property incomes plus the workers' "ability to work,"[105] though Sismondi recognized that the latter was "incommensurable" with material wealth.[106] In his *Études*, revenue was also used "in the largest sense" to include all incomes — wages, profits, and rents[107] — without abandoning his earlier definitions or the conclusions based on them.

The basic idea running through Sismondi's arguments and definitions was that "revenue" was a supply price which determined *re*production in the next time period.   The profitability of past production as discovered in the current period $(P - N)$ fitted this general pattern of thought, as did the attempt to add together property incomes from past investments and current labor income — the "ability to work" counted as "revenue" only when actually employed[108] — in order to be able to compare aggregate demand with aggregate output. According to Sismondi, "the national revenue is composed of two quantities, of which one is past and the other present — or, if you will, one present and the other future."[109] This revenue was considered in terms of the units of labor which it could purchase, like Malthus' "labor command" or Keynes' "labor units":

> Wages do not represent an absolute quantity of labor, but only a quantity of subsistence which sufficed to support the workers in the previous year. The same quantity of subsistence will put in motion, the following year, a greater or lesser quantity of labor, and from that fluctuation in the proportion between these two values results the increase or decrease of the national wealth, the comfort or poverty of the productive class, the multiplication or the destruction of population.[110]

In making the equality of revenue and output an equilibrium condition rather than an identity,[111] Sismondi was not guilty of the crude underconsumptionism of believing that output somehow exceeded income, nor was he anticipating later Keynesian or Marxian arguments[112] involving monetary phenomena: "It is not money which the consumer is in want of, but revenue."[113] Even in a barter economy, expectations could cause over-investment, rising wages (reducing the labor command per unit of output), and then declining rates of return on capital. Aggregate revenue, measured by its labor command, would be insufficient to reproduce the same quantity of output subsequently. In this sense, it is possible to understand how Sismondi could refer to output and revenue as being sometimes equal,[114] sometimes unequal,[115] sometimes rising at different rates or even moving in opposite directions.[116]

POPULATION

Sismondi attacked the dominant Malthusian population theory of his time, questioning the famous "ratios" of food and population growth, not simply on empirical grounds but because he had detected the fatal ambiguity in Malthus' shifting use of the word "tendencies." Sismondi saw that Malthus' "tendencies" sometimes referred to abstract potentialities (population had the *capability* of growing faster than the food supply) and sometimes to empirical facts (population *historically* grew as much as the food supply permitted it to grow). Nassau Senior and Richard Whately were later to attack Malthus on the same ground [117] — and while Senior's criticism was said to be "the first break with Malthus' doctrine by a leading economist,"[118] Sismondi preceded him by a decade. Moreover, Sismondi pointed out that Malthus considered the abstract potentiality of population growth in comparison to an historical generalization about the growth of the food supply. It was "completely sophistical" to compare "the possible growth of the human population" with "the positive growth of animals and vegetables," he said.[119]

Sismondi compared them on the same bases: the abstract growth potential of people and food, and then the historical growth of people and food. In consistent senses, it was by no means apparent, or even plausible, that population tended to increase faster than the food supply. First he considered the situation with regard to potentialities: "Abstractly speaking, the multiplication of vegetables follows a geometric progression infinitely more rapid than that of animals, and the latter is in its turn infinitely more rapid than that of men . . . ."[120] Here the "power of multiplication is virtual in vegetables, animals, and men,"[121] and there was no tendency for man to increase faster than his food supply. In an empirical sense also, according to Sismondi, "human generations do not grow as fast as subsistence."[122]

The proposition that population is *limited* by the food supply — often confused with a more dubious proposition that population *varies* with the food supply — was accepted by Sismondi as "true only abstractly but in a manner inapplicable to political economy," because population "has never reached those limits and probably never will."[123] Differential class fertility, with the greatest fertility being in the poorest class, showed that "what Malthus regards as a law of human nature" was in fact a social phenomenon, since "nourishment is not lacking" among the wealthy and the aristocratic.[124] Actual population growth was "regulated solely by revenue" — that is, "revenue limited and distributed as it is,"[125] and with people's ideas of an adequate standard of living varying from class to class. The rapid population growth among the poor was a social phenomenon, rather than a general characteristic of human nature, and was due to the hopelessness of the position of "proletarians"[126] and the impossibility of their foreseeing and planning for their economic future.[127] Sismondi argued that "the natural limits of population are always respected by men who have something, and always exceeded by those who have nothing."[128]

Sismondi believed that wages above subsistence caused population to grow, and therefore the adult labor force to grow with a lag.[129] Because of this lagged response of the labor force to higher wages, he was greatly concerned that the demand for labor be stable rather than have painful downward adjustments of population size recurring because of wage and employment fluctuations.[130] His scheme of guaranteed wages and employment was intended to deal with this problem by (1) reducing a firm's incentive to increase hiring to meet a temporary demand, and by (2) supporting the workers during periods of slack demand for labor at the expense of the industry in which they were employed, instead of allowing unstable industries to externalize part of their labor costs to public charity.

Unlike his classical contemporaries, Sismondi supported poor-law relief, and did not believe that it increased improvident marriages.[131] He welcomed the empirical work of John Barton, which indicated to him that (1) periods of population growth often varied inversely with wage movements, [132] that (2) the marriage rate was continually declining despite the popular arguments that poor-laws were increasing it, [133] and that (3) the great population growth which others attributed to economic causes was in fact due to improvements in public health and the advances of medicine, which reduced mortality. [134] Sismondi was not optimistic about the condition of the poor, however. He regarded the problem of caring for the unemployed poor as "the most difficult problem to resolve in political economy," [135] and recognized the danger that poor-laws could add to population problems. [136] He regarded technological unemployment as a great menace, [137] along with cyclical fluctuations and the growth of an urban proletariat without sufficient hope to restrain themselves in producing children.

METHODOLOGY

Sismondi continued to regard himself as a disciple of Adam Smith, [138] even after developing his heretical views — which he treated as "modifications" or "complements" to Smith's system [139] — and this was nowhere more apparent than in his discussions of methodology in economics. What Sismondi admired most about Smith was his *combination* of facts and theory. According to Sismondi, Smith had recognized that "it was only from a judicious observation of facts that one could deduce principles." [140] Before Smith there had been theories which were "ingenious but not well founded." [141] Smith's system was "no less ingenious, but better nourished with facts and observations." [142] He contrasted this with "the abstractions" of Smith's "new disciples" in England. [143] But despite Sismondi's many attacks on the abstractions of the Ricardians, [144] which have caused him to be regarded as an early "institutionalist" or "historical" economist, [145] his objection was not to abstraction as such, but to its abuse:

> It is a natural habit of the human mind to seek to reduce all its operations to the simplest formulas, to generalize all its rules, and to accomplish this uniform procedure whenever it can to avoid more complicated procedures. That habit, which tends to simplify everything, to classify everything, to generalize everything, is no doubt the most essential cause of the progress of various sciences. It is not necessary, however, to abandon oneself to it in an unreflecting manner . . . .[146]

Sismondi himself was not at all averse to abstracting from money,[147] international trade,[148] or all agricultural goods besides wheat,[149] or to developing theories from Robinson Crusoe models,[150] or using many mathematical examples throughout his economic writings.[151]

Abstraction was treated as unavoidable. Precisely because of the intertwining and transformation of capital and revenue into one another in the real world, the analytical distinction between them was important.[152] Because income flows were so difficult to grasp in a complex economy, the principle had to be illustrated by referring to "a single family."[153] Sismondi did not consider it "necessary to renounce the defense of what appeared to me to be the truth because that truth was abstract, difficult to grasp," and likely to be misinterpreted.[154] He noted that even those "practical" men who reject "theory" were implicitly following defunct theories which persisted as popular prejudices.[155] At other times, however, Sismondi invoked "practical" men against the supporters of Say's Law.[156] His objection to Ricardo's abstractions was that they abstracted from precisely what was crucial to the issue at hand — by assuming constant equilibrium in capital and labor markets[157] — and that Ricardo's reasonings were all based on "a hypothetical world completely different from the real world,"[158] a world of abstractions which he never left.[159]

Sismondi, like Smith, regarded economics as a direct

instrument of policy,[160] rather than as a system of principles as Ricardo did.[161] Economics was with Sismondi a branch of political science.[162] As a direct instrument of policy, it needed institutional information[163] rather than "intellectual systems."[164] Instead of "isolating principles or examining them in an imaginary world," it was necessary to follow their action "in the midst of society and in the cross currents of all the complications of current interests."[165] Nor was Sismondi prepared simply to accept generalizations from facts. Economics (and other social sciences) were *experimental*, even though the experiments were not controlled.[166] History was not simply a record of facts but a test of theories.[167] The economic crises of the 1820s were cited as showing events which were "completely unexpected" by followers of the dominant economic theories while they "conformed perfectly" to "explanations which I had given in advance."[168]

The key point made against the Ricardians, by their contemporaries as well as by later commentators on "the Ricardian Vice," was that they ended up with real-world policies directly on the basis of their abstract model. A similar idea was suggested by Sismondi, who said that they were often guilty of "jumping over the intermediate links in a chain of reasoning."[169]

Sismondi opposed "systems" in political as well as economic theory. He said that "dogmatic writers, all those who wished to raise a system, need to attach it to some striking idea understood by all,"[170] as something "at the disposal of the most limited mind, and as deriving rigorously from a small number of indisputable principles,"[171] the kind of "general rules" by which "young people, barely out of the university, can believe themselves ready to present constitutions to their country and all countries."[172] Economics could not be based "on a mathematical succession of theorems, deduced from obscure maxims, given as indisputable truths,"[173] at least not in the policy sense conceived by Sismondi.

SUMMARY AND IMPLICATIONS

Sismondi originated a number of significant advances in economics which would have been important "contributions" if they had been accepted into the ongoing stream of classical economics. As it was, many were rejected or ignored and had to be rediscovered and redeveloped by later economists as if Sismondi had never lived. Among his more fundamental advances were these:

1. *The theory of equilibrium income.* Sismondi explicitly applied the concept of "equilibrium" to aggregate output and produced a theory of its determinants — namely, the balance of the disutility of production and the utility of output, as reflected in factor-supply conditions and product-demand conditions.[174]

2. *The development of growth model equations.* Sismondi advanced beyond the mere *conception* of an economy as a whole and the role of its aggregates — which the physiocrats had before him — to a set of crude equations yielding results similar to modern post-Keynesian models.

3. *The distinction between increased demand and increased quantity demanded.* The Ricardians, including John Stuart Mill as well as Ricardo's contemporary disciples, meant by demand *the quantity demanded ex post* — or rather, their long-run equilibrium model made no distinction between *ex ante* and *ex post*. In this sense, supply and demand were always equal. Sismondi, however, distinguished an increased quantity of sales during overproduction from an increased

quantity of sales resulting from an increased desire or ability to pay. Only the latter — more sales "at the same price"[175] was an increased demand. The purely quantitative concept of demand characteristic of the Ricardians[176] was necessarily equal to supply — an identity used in defense of Say's Law[177] — but Sismondian demand equaled supply only when it covered costs.[178] Sismondi's sketchy but repeated discussions of this point were more systematically developed in Malthus.[179]

4. *A theory of destabilizing responses to disequilibrium.* While both Sismondi and the supporters of Say's Law recognized the possibility of disequilibrium (overproduction and disproportionality, respectively) and the tendency of the economy to automatically correct it, Sismondi alone developed a theory of behavior (backward bending supply curves and inventory speculation) which would take the economy further away from equilibrium, though he implicitly assumed that these would ultimately be overcome by other tendencies bringing it back.

5. *The concept of a shutdown point for the firm.* It had long been recognized that individual firms would sometimes be forced to *sell* at less than cost-covering prices, but Sismondi argued that they would *continue to produce* at less than cost-covering prices, where the alternative was to lose still more money by shutting down. He did not specify the shutdown conditions, but only indicated that firms were more prone to produce below cost when there was much fixed capital.

In addition, Sismondi advanced methodologically beyond his contemporaries in clarifying the meaning of the Malthusian theory of population and in bringing to the surface the difference between dynamic analysis and the comparative statics of the Ricardians. Shrewd intuitive and analytical insights were Sismondi's forte; consistency, rigor, and system building were not. The best that can be said for his theory of technological unemployment is that he abandoned it under fire.[180] All in all, Sismondi was a pioneer, with all that this implies, not only of primacy but of crudity.

The almost total neglect of Sismondi's ideas remains a mystery. In Sismondi's own view, it was due to his attacking a dominant *system*[181] which had an attractive symmetry, determinacy, and comprehensiveness. To some extent, he was undoubtedly right: it takes a system to beat a system, and his rambling examples and shifting terms make it difficult to see the system underlying it all. Another major factor was Sismondi's intellectual isolation. He belonged to no school in economics and his policy positions put him at the opposite end of the political spectrum from "general glut" economists such as Malthus, Lauderdale, and Chalmers, whose proposals involved favoring landlords, government sinecurists, and fundholders in the national debt rather than Sismondi's "proletarians."

Although the basic Sismondian analysis and that of Malthus are practically identical as theory, Malthus was never as much a promoter of Sismondi as Sismondi was of him, possibly because Sismondi preceded him into print with ideas which Malthus already held, as revealed in his correspondence with Ricardo.[182] Sismondi received equally shabby treatment from Karl Marx and his followers, who owed several ideas to Sismondi.[183] Marx's voluminous *Theories of Surplus Value*, the first great history of economic thought, deliberately omitted Sismondi,[184] although covering other economists who were even less well known, and he was dismissed with patronizing references elsewhere in Marx and received little better treatment from Marx's disciples.[185]

Sismondi's independence and distrust of rigid systems —

perhaps born of his experiences with the French Revolution and the later reactions — made him unwilling to raise a banner or to fall in behind anyone else's banner. He was simply a man who sought truth and tried to deal with the sufferings he saw around him. This made his name and his doctrines of little use to leaders of contemporary crusades or founders of dogmatic movements. Perhaps the traits which best characterized Sismondi are those which he admired in Ricardo — "urbanity, good faith, and love of truth."[186]

The Enigma of John Stuart Mill

Few thinkers have ever so dominated the whole intellectual landscape of their age as John Stuart Mill did. He not only wrote the leading economic treatise of the mid-nineteenth century, he also wrote the leading treatise of his day on logic, as well as other writings in philosophy, and his writings on political science at both popular and scholarly levels were the leading contemporary works in that field. Mill's *A System of Logic* in 1843 first established him as a landmark figure, after many years as simply one of the leading lights of the time. His *Principles of Political Economy* in 1848 remained the foremost book on economics until replaced by Alfred Marshall's *Principles of Economics* in 1890 — and, even so, Mill's *Principles* continued to be used as a text in some colleges and universities on into the early twentieth century. Yet, despite Mill's unchallenged pre-eminence in a number of fields simultaneously in his own time, his reputation in later generations was not as great as that of some others who had never achieved such intellectual dominance in their own lifetimes.[1]

This is one of many enigmas surrounding Mill's work. The enigmas of the man are no less intriguing. His stances on political issues are not easy to pigeon-hole and portions of his views on the role of government can be quoted by believers in laissez-faire or in social activism extending all the way to socialism.

Mill's precepts on the role of ideas were sometimes in sharp contrast with his own practices. A man of enormous integrity and great sympathies for the less fortunate, he was in his own personal life woefully lacking in understanding or empathy with those around him, including members of his own family.[2] The influence of Mill's ideas is still with us today, even among people who have never read his writings, but who have absorbed some of those ideas from the general atmosphere of our times, which already incorporate many of the beliefs and opinions of John Stuart Mill.

MILL AND HIS TIMES

The earliest letter of John Stuart Mill that has survived was written to his father's friend Jeremy Bentham who, like Mill, was a much more prominent figure in his own lifetime than he would be in retrospect. Mill wrote:

> MY DEAR SIR,
>   Mr. Walker is a very intimate friend of mine, who lives at No. 31 in Berkeley Square. I have engaged him, as he is soon coming here, first to go to your house, and get for me the 3.^{d} and 4.th volumes of Hooke's Roman history. But I am recapitulating the 1.st and 2.^{d} volumes, having finished them all except a few pages of the 2.^{d}. I will be glad if you will let him have the 3.^{d} and 4.th volumes.
>   I am yours sincerely,
>   JOHN STUART MILL

This letter was written on July 28, 1812 — which means that John Stuart Mill was six years old.[3]

The hothouse development of Mill's intellect from his earliest years under the stern tutelage of his father, James Mill, left their mark not only in an enormously learned and highly structured and disciplined mind, but also in an under-developed, if not emotionally starved, personal life.

Young John Stuart Mill grew up in a social circle that included some of the intellectual giants of his time. Among these were his father, who had risen from obscurity in Scotland to national prominence with his writings on politics and economics, and especially his monumental *History of British India*. As a result, James Mill's friends included not only Jeremy Bentham and his disciples in the Utilitarian philosophy and its associated political movements, but also the great classical economist David Ricardo. Moreover, the young John Stuart Mill was not simply an observer and listener but, at an early age, also a participant in the controversies that surrounded their work. His first published writings appeared in newspapers, beginning when he was fourteen. At sixteen, he began publishing in the leading intellectual journals of his time. By the time he was twenty, he was a veteran of the wars of the mind in economics, philosophy, history, political science and the various issues of the day.

David Ricardo took a personal interest in the young Mill. Writing to James Mill in 1821, when John Stuart Mill was 15 years old, Ricardo regretted that the elder Mill was unsure whether he would be able to pay a planned visit but said:

> I wish too you would bring John with you, I desire much to see him after his long visit to foreign parts, and to hear the history of his adventures from his own mouth. It would give me pleasure to see him although it should happen that you cannot find time to come: he will have his time for reading and study nearly as much undisturbed here as at home and will benefit a little by mixing with strangers — it may tend to remove the shyness which you say still adheres to him.[4]

Two years later, this leading economist of his era critiqued a paper on economics by the young Mill.[5] In his *Autobiography*, John Stuart Mill wrote of this period:

> My being a habitual inmate of my father's study made me acquainted with the dearest of his friends, David Ricardo, who by his benevolent countenance and kindliness of manner, was very attractive to young

persons, and who after I became a student of political
economy, invited me to his house and to walk with him
in order to converse on the subject.[6]

It is hardly surprising that Ricardo inspired the kind of
personal loyalty later exhibited by the mature John Stuart Mill in
defense of Ricardian economics, even in areas where Mill was
moving beyond some of its tenets, as he more forthrightly moved
beyond the philosophy of Bentham and his Utilitarian followers.

The first great influence on Mill outside the circle of his
father's intellectual allies and personal friends was Harriet
Taylor. The relationship between Mrs. Taylor and Mill was a
subject of some speculation during their lifetimes and has been
ever since. Though there may have been no physical intimacy
between them while her husband was alive, Harriet Taylor was
nevertheless the first great emotional attachment of Mill's life.
His autobiography, centered on his childhood, does not mention
his mother even a single time. Of his father, he says that the
younger children "loved him tenderly," adding "and if I cannot
say so much for myself, I was always loyally devoted to him."[7]

Prior to meeting Harriet Taylor, Mill went through what he
called "a crisis in my mental history." During a lull in his hectic
writing pace, he asked himself whether, if all the goals he was
pursuing were achieved, that would make him happy. When he
realized that the answer was *No!* "my heart sank within me; the
whole foundation on which my life had been constructed fell
down."[8]

His worries now included the doctrine of predestination,
which "weighed on my existence like an incubus."[9] He fretted
over the fact that there were just eight notes in the musical scale,
which meant that only a finite amount of music was possible.[10]
Mill himself later wrote of this period of nameless malaise: "If I
had loved any one sufficiently to make confiding my griefs a
necessity, I should not have been in the condition I was."[11] These
melancholy preoccupations receded, however, when he met
Harriet Taylor, whom he later called "the chief blessing of my

existence."[12]

When they met, Mill was twenty-five, she was twenty- three — and already married and a mother. Throughout their lives, he showered the most extravagant praise on her, both publicly and privately. In his autobiography, for example, he said, "I have learned more from her teaching, than from all other sources taken together."[13] His extraordinary assessment of her intellect was unmatched by that of anyone else who knew her[14] — except Harriet Taylor herself. She was a beautiful, headstrong woman, confident to the point of dogmatism and energetic to the point of stridency. Her letters to him are imperious, his to her submissive.[15] She took Mill's writings in a more radical direction on social issues and, in later years, he credited her with the ideas behind his *On Liberty*.[16] But nothing that Harriet Taylor published in her lifetime, or that has been published since then,[17] has attracted any great notice or praise even faintly resembling that from John Stuart Mill.

The frequency with which Mill and Harriet Taylor began to see each other did not go unnoticed in Victorian England, least of all by her husband. Failing to get her to stop seeing Mill, John Taylor accommodated himself to the situation, accepting her assurances that there was nothing improper between them and absenting himself on evenings when Mill came over to dine. The tensions of this period led Mill to break even old friendships with those who said or did anything that would reflect on his relationship with Harriet Taylor. Even members of his own family, with whom he continued to live, were in fear of what they might inadvertently say or do — or not do — as regards Harriet Taylor that might provoke his wrath. Meanwhile the tensions in the Taylor household led Harriet's husband to provide her with a small place in the country, where Mill would visit her and spend weekends.

Mill's *Logic* in 1843 was the last of his publications to go into print without Harriet Taylor's input during her lifetime. She critiqued and influenced the writing of Mill's *Principles of Political Economy* and even involved herself in shaping the terms of his contract with the publisher.[18] In appreciation, Mill proposed a fulsome dedication to her. But when she passed on this idea to her husband, he called it something showing "a want of taste and tact which I would not have believed possible."[19] The dedication was never published but was included in gift copies to their friends.

John Taylor died in 1849, and Harriet Taylor and John Stuart Mill were married in 1851. Mill's family was not invited to the wedding, as they had failed to make a customary call on Harriet after being informed of marriage plans, and this omission marked a lasting break between Mill and his siblings. Decades later, when Mill exchanged letters with one of his sisters, he noted in passing that he did not know how many children she had.[20]

From the age of fifteen, John Stuart Mill worked at India House in London, where his father had become a high official, as a result of the elder Mill's magnum opus, *History of British India*. The post at India House was a lifetime job and one whose demands were sufficiently light that John Stuart Mill could write numerous articles and all his books while working there. Indeed, he wrote his massive *Principles of Political Economy* in just 18 months while working at India House.[21] At the age of 49, Mill was able to retire on a generous pension. A year later, Harriet died and a year after that their joint work, *On Liberty*, was published. After her death, Mill said: "It is doubtful if I shall ever be fit for anything public or private again."[22] *On Liberty* was in fact to be his last major work.

MILL'S ROLE IN ECONOMICS

The three great controversies in economics during John Stuart Mill's lifetime were disputes over Say's Law, the Malthusian overpopulation theory, and the theory of value. Whatever advances were made in all these areas during the early nineteenth century were set back by the appearance of Mill's *Principles of Political Economy* in 1848. Its role in snuffing out the early beginnings of a utility theory of value and a schedule concept of demand has already been noted in the earlier essay,

"Classical Microeconomics." Much the same pattern can be seen in Mill's discussions of Say's Law and of Malthusian overpopulation theory.

Say's Law

As we have already seen,[23] those who challenged Say's Law challenged it in that particular form in which it had been used to deny the possibility of a theory of equilibrium aggregate income. When Sismondi and Malthus argued that there could be a "general glut," that was a logical corollary to the theory of equilibrium aggregate income, which implied that there can be aggregate incomes above or below the equilibrium level. This Ricardo, and John Stuart Mill after him, denied categorically. In discussing the phenomena of depressions, Ricardo said, "it is at all times the bad adaptation of the commodities to the wants of mankind which is the specific evil, and not the abundance of commodities."[24] John Stuart Mill likewise declared, "production is not excessive, but merely ill-assorted."[25]

Although Jean-Baptiste Say himself eventually acknowledged the possibility of disequilibrium in aggregate income in the fifth edition of his *Traité d'économie politique* and in his subsequent textbook, *Cours complet d'économie politique pratique*,[26] Mill's *Principles* did not even acknowledge that this was the issue. Instead, Mill ascribed to Sismondi and Malthus a belief in a "permanent" glut,[27] despite all their statements to the contrary.[28] This was not a deliberate distortion. There is simply no evidence that Mill went back and read what Sismondi and Malthus had written on this subject, decades earlier, when he wrote his *Principles* at breakneck speed while working at India House.

There was not a single quotation or page reference in Mill's published writings or correspondence to any discussion of general gluts in Sismondi or Malthus, even though his *Principles* abounded in quotations and page citations from almost every leading economist of the era — including Sismondi and Malthus on other issues.[29] Mill simply did not spend time on old ideas which he regarded as having been refuted by his father, Say, and

Ricardo years earlier. This was part of a larger pattern in Mill's approach to issues and ideas, pointed out by J.A. Schumpeter:

> . . . Mill, however modest on his own behalf, was not at all modest on behalf of his time. "This enlightened age" had solved all problems. And if you knew what its "best thinkers" thought, you were in a position to answer all questions. ... [T]his attitude, besides being ridiculous, made for sterility and — yes — superficiality. There is too little attention to groundwork. There is too little thinking-things-through and much too much confidence that most of the necessary thinking had been done already.[30]

Mill's treatment of Sismondi and Malthus represented a fundamental contradiction between his precepts and his practices. In his *Essays on Some Unsettled Questions of Political Economy*, written more than a decade earlier, Mill wrote of a need for "seeing that no scattered particles of important truth are buried and lost in the ruins of exploded error."[31] But this precept was violated both in this book and in his later *Principles* because he did not bother to examine the doctrines which he regarded as discredited because others whom he respected had treated them as discredited.

Although he declared that his *Principles* was intended to incorporate "new ideas and new applications of ideas,"[32] from the recent literature of economics, it was clear from Mill's correspondence that the new applications were his primary concern. The point was to show how various new practical schemes which Mill favored — such as Wakefield's colonization plan — "do not contradict but *fit into*" the classical theory.[33] On the theoretical level, Mill considered himself to be "sticking pretty close to Ricardo" and added: "I doubt if there will be a single opinion (on pure political economy) in the book, which may not be exhibited as a corollary from his doctrines."[34] There was no apparent intention here of rethinking the basic principles of economics, much less of re-exploring old heresies, such as those of Sismondi and Malthus. This was a book with more of a social than an intellectual agenda. In the language of a later era, Mill wished to be "relevant." In this, he wanted to rescue economics from other contemporary economists:

> My object in writing a treatise on Pol. Economy was to rescue from the hands of such people the truths they misapply, & by combining these with other truths to which they are strangers, to deduce conclusions capable of being of some use to the progress of mankind.[35]

Given Mill's policy focus and limited theoretical objectives, and his emphasis on the *applications* of existing economic theory, it is possible to understand how and why he could have completed a book of more than a thousand pages in less than two years of writing, while holding down an ostensibly full-time job.

Mill's willingness to rely on what others had said, or on the general impressions of his times, led to another remarkable situation. Although he wrote extensively on socialism, Mill began to study this subject by setting out to familiarize himself with what were "the best socialistic writers" on the European continent[36] — which is to say, he did not canvas the vast socialist literature and then decide for himself what was the best. As a consequence, he lived in London for two decades as a contemporary of the leading socialist writer of all time — Karl Marx — without the slightest indication in any of Mill's published writings or voluminous correspondence that he had any awareness of the existence of such a person. Marx was by no means famous at the time but neither was he wholly unknown, and he was a force to be reckoned with in the radical movements of his day. John Stuart Mill's ignorance both of Marx and of the substantive arguments of the equilibrium income theorists before him reveal a major blind spot in Mill's approach to the study of ideas.

Mill did not exclude competing viewpoints. On the contrary, he sought them out. His extensive correspondence with Thomas Carlyle and August Comte, and his writings on the works of Coleridge, show a man consciously seeking different ways of looking at the world. Nor did he overlook Marx because of any aversion to socialist ideas, which he in fact wrote about sympathetically. Mill simply allowed reputation to pre-select what he would study and take seriously. His own massive reputation then played a major role in banishing from economics promising beginnings toward theories of equilibrium aggregate income and modern supply-demand analysis based on marginal utility — ideas which had to be rediscovered later, as if their early pioneers had never existed.

Another complicating factor in Mill's work was his loyalty in defense of the intellectual legacy of Ricardo and James Mill, especially as regards Say's Law. Mill's correspondence gives some clues to his treatment of the issues raised in the controversies over general gluts. Although he wrote to a friend in 1834 that there was "much new speculation" on the subject which would be "added to" his then unpublished essay on gluts,[37] when that essay actually appeared in print, it claimed that *nothing* had been "added to" or "subtracted from" Say's Law as it had been previously presented in the classical tradition.[38] Either Mill had ignored the new speculations after all, or he was not being completely candid. There certainly was no such sophisticated analysis of the role of money in economic downturns as that of John Stuart Mill's *Essays on Some Unsettled Questions of Political Economy* in the writings of either James Mill or David Ricardo, or in the earlier writings of Say that introduced Say's Law.

In another letter, Mill expressed a fear of "giving a handle to the enemies of the science; which such men as Torrens and Malthus and even Senior are constantly doing, and which I systematically avoid." He urged this course on others: "I am anxious that in your article on the theory of a 'glut of capital,' you should avoid the phrase 'glut' or any other word which will bring you into seeming collision (though not real) with my father's and

Say's doctrine respecting a general glut."[39] Yet, as we have seen, Say himself had been willing to accommodate Sismondi's theory of equilibrium aggregate income in his later writings. By nailing his flag to the mast of a sinking ship, Mill allowed himself to be among those sweepingly dismissed by John Maynard Keynes in a later era.[40]

One of the earliest challengers of Say's Law was James Maitland, 8th Earl of Lauderdale. It was, in fact, in the course of criticizing Lauderdale that James Mill first developed his own version of Say's Law, to which his son would remain so loyal. Like Sismondi and Malthus, Lauderdale reasoned in terms of period analysis and disequilibrium conditions, rather than in the comparative statics of Ricardo and the Ricardians. However, John Stuart Mill, as the last of the Ricardians, not only reasoned in comparative statics terms, he translated the views of Lauderdale and other dissenting economists into comparative statics terms and then refuted them in such terms.

Lauderdale, as noted in an earlier essay,[41] wrote in criticism of a proposal to have the government invest budget surpluses, in order to build up a "sinking fund" to pay off the national debt. Because this investment was presumed to be made without regard to its effect on the rate of return on capital, Lauderdale challenged the notion that there was no equilibrium level of investment — his interpretation of Adam Smith's claim that more savings and investments were beneficial to the economy and promoted economic growth. In an era when static and dynamic analyses had not yet become sharply distinguished, Lauderdale may well have misunderstood Smith but he was quite clear as to his own views on capital accumulation.

To Lauderdale, the government's taxing away money that would otherwise have gone into consumption, in order to build up a "sinking fund," meant that it was converting consumption expenditures into capital investments, without regard to inherent limits on how much capital could be profitably invested at a given time, under given technology, without driving down the rate of return to a level that would subsequently cause private investors to disinvest. In other words, there was an equilibrium level of investment — and investments beyond that level were unsustainable in subsequent time periods. Lauderdale was concerned with "future reproduction," [42] with what is "subsequently produced,"[43] with whether there would be an "encouragement"[44] or a "discouragement to future production."[45]

Similar reasoning appeared in Sismondi and in Thomas Chalmers, the latter saying that "capital is hemmed on all sides by a slowly receding boundary." [46] The equilibrium limit to sustainable capital investment would recede because the short-run limit to the amount of capital that could be invested at a self-sustaining rate of return would, in the longer run, increase as advances in technology raised the productivity of capital. Put differently, in the absence of technological advance, capital investment opportunities at a sustainable rate of return were not unlimited. As Sismondi put it more loosely, "a country which cannot make progress should not make savings."[47]

Here again, John Stuart Mill was able to refute the heretics only by interpreting their words in Ricardian comparative statics terms — and then presenting the same analysis and conclusions in different words. For Mill, there was indeed an equilibrium level of sustainable capital investment. He said, "the rate of profit is habitually within, as it were, a hand's breadth of the minimum, and the country therefore on the verge of the stationary state." Mill added:

> By this I do not mean that this state is likely in any of the great countries of Europe, to be soon actually reached, or that capital does not still yield a profit considerably greater than what is barely sufficient to induce the people of these countries to save and accumulate. My meaning is, that it would require but a short time to reduce profits to the minimum, if capital continued to increase at its present rate, and no circumstances having a tendency to raise the rate of profit occurred in the meantime. The expansion of capital would soon reach its ultimate boundary, if the boundary itself did not continually open and leave more space.[48]

Mill was then at pains to point out that this did not conflict with the idea that supply creates its own demand:

> The difficulty would not consist in any want of a market. If the new capital were duly shared among many varieties of employment, it would raise up a demand for its own produce, and there would be no cause why any part of that produce should remain longer on hand than formerly. What would really be, not merely difficult, but impossible, would be to employ this capital without submitting to a rapid reduction of the rate of profit.[49]

More than a quarter of a century before Mill wrote this, an anonymous monograph of 1821, probably written by Samuel Bailey,[50] pointed out the irrelevance of such statements as answers to those with general glut or equilibrium aggregate income theories:

> Nobody denied, that a new product will always, or almost always, find a *market*: The question is, at what price? Whether a profitable market? Whether its production and sale will bring in what were before the usual average profits of stock or less?[51]

By the same token, the same monograph said, no one ever denied that capital "might be '*employed*' if you did not care what profits it brought."[52] Yet, decades later, Mill wrote about the static declining marginal productivity of capital as if it were completely compatible with his earlier dismissal of people who believed in "the fallacy of the universal glut," which he regarded as among the "refuted, and now almost forgotten errors."[53] In his *Principles of Political Economy*, Mill said:

...unless a considerable portion of the annual increase of capital were either periodically destroyed, or exported for foreign investment, the country would speedily attain to the point at which further accumulation would cease, or at least spontaneously slacken, so as no longer to overpass the march of invention in the arts which produce the necessaries of life. In such a state of things, a sudden addition to the capital of the country, unaccompanied by any increase of productive power, would be of but transitory duration; since, by depressing profits and interest, it would either diminish by a corresponding amount the savings which would be made from income in the year or two following, or it would cause an equivalent amount to be sent abroad, or to be wasted in rash speculations.[54]

Even though this analysis required Mill to leave the world of Ricardian comparative statics, he gave no consideration to the possibility that an earlier generation of economists whose analysis was outside that framework might have had a point — if read within their own framework. Their work still represented to Mill simply "refuted, and all but forgotten errors" — because he did not bother to go back to read them.

Ironically, Mill in a different context warned of the "almost irresistible tendency of the human mind to become the slave of its own hypotheses," to "reason, feel, and conceive under certain arbitrary conditions, at length to mistake these conditions for laws of nature." He added, "the greatest powers of reasoning, when connected with a sluggish imagination, are no safeguard against the poorest intellectual slavery — that of subjection to mere accidental habits of thought."[55]

ON LIBERTY

Among the many writings of John Stuart Mill, the one most likely to have been read by people living today is *On Liberty*, and the ideas expressed in it taken as most characteristic of Mill's philosophy. Yet this small and plainly written work is often profoundly misunderstood.

Although *On Liberty* has become a symbol invoked against the intrusions of government into people's personal lives or its stifling of ideas, Mill was unmistakably clear that intrusive government was *not* the object of his concern in this particular essay. He asserted, "the era of pains and penalties for political discussion has, in our own country, passed away."[56] Even a government press prosecution the year before *On Liberty* was published "has not" in Mill's words, "induced me to alter a single word of the text."[57] Various other government restrictions Mill dismissed as "but rags and remnants of persecution."[58] The government was not what Mill feared nor what *On Liberty* was meant to warn against. It was the social "tyranny of the majority"[59] and "the despotism of Custom"[60] that he opposed in *On Liberty*. He said:

> In England, from the peculiar circumstances of our political history, though the yoke of opinion is perhaps heavier, that of law is lighter, than in most other countries of Europe; and there is considerable jealousy of direct interference, by the legislative or the executive power, with private conduct; not so much from any just regard for the independence of the individual as from the still subsisting habit of looking on the government as representing an opposite interest to the public.[61]

What then is the subject of *On Liberty*? Mill says in the first paragraph of that essay that its subject is "the nature and limits of the power which can be legitimately exercised by society over the individual"[62] — society, not government. Mill declared:

> Like other tyrannies, the tyranny of the majority was at first, and is still vulgarly, held in dread, chiefly as operating through the acts of the public authorities. But reflecting persons perceived that when society itself is the tyrant — society collectively, over the separate individuals who compose it — its means of tyrannizing are not restricted to acts which it may do by the hands of its political functionaries. Society can and does execute its own mandate: and if it issues wrong mandates instead of right, it practices a social tyranny more formidable than many kinds of political oppression.[63]

While society's disapproval is "not usually upheld by such extreme penalties" as government may have at its disposal, there are "fewer means of escape," with social disapproval "penetrating more deeply into the details of life, and enslaving the soul itself."[64] Mill says in *On Liberty*: "Our merely social intolerance kills no one, roots out no opinions, but induces men to disguise them, or to abstain from any active effort for their diffusion."[65] Admitting that some rules of conduct must be imposed, both by law and by pubic opinion, Mill nevertheless thought that "the sole end for which mankind is warranted, individually or collectively, in interfering with the liberty of any of their number, is self-protection."[66] *On Liberty* argued that individuals should be free to do as they like "without detriment to their estimation" in the eyes of others.[67] This was, however, an asymmetrical principle, as Mill applied it. To say that people should be free to do as they like "without detriment to their estimation" in the eyes of others is to say that others have no right to express their own opinions or even to quietly shun those whose conduct they disapprove.

This central principle elaborated in *On Liberty* is asymmetrical in yet another way. It becomes clear, especially in the later parts of *On Liberty*, that Mill's special concern is with the effects of public opinion and customs on the intellectual elite. "Customs are made for customary circumstances and customary characters,"[68] he says. Exceptional people should be exempt from the influence of mass public opinion — but mass public opinion should not be exempt from the influence of the intellectual elite. On the contrary, one of the arguments for the exemption of the elite from the social influence of the masses is that this will enable the elite to develop in ways that can then enable them to exert social influence over the masses:

> There is always need of persons not only to discover new truths, and point out when what were once truths are true no longer, but to commence new practices, and set the examples of more enlightened conduct, and better taste and sense in human life. It is true that this benefit is not capable of being rendered by everybody alike: there are but few persons, in comparison with the whole of mankind, whose experiments, if adopted by others, would be likely to be any improvement on established practice. But these few are the salt of the earth; without them, human life would become a stagnant pool.[69]

Thus *On Liberty*, which seems at first to be an argument for being non-judgmental towards individuals in general, turns out to be an argument for a *one-way* non-judgmental attitude toward special individuals who are to apply social influence on others that others are to refrain from applying to them.

Throughout Mill's writings over his lifetime, special intellectual elites were depicted as the salvation of society in general and of the masses in particular. Great things could be achieved, Mill said in one of his early writings, "if the superior spirits would but join with each other" for social betterment.[70] He called upon the universities to "send forth into society a succession of minds, not the creatures of their age, but capable of being its improvers and regenerators."[71]

According to *On Liberty*, democracy can rise above mediocrity, only where "the sovereign Many have let themselves be guided (which in their best times they always have done) by the counsels and influence of a more highly gifted and instructed One or Few."[72] *On Liberty* is an argument for the differential treatment of an intellectual elite, cast in the language of greater freedom for all. In this and in Mill's other writings, it is these elites — "the best and wisest,"[73] the "thinking minds,"[74] "the most cultivated intellects in the country,"[75] "those who have been in advance of society in thought and feeling"[76] — that he looked to for the progress of society. What Mill called "the general progress of the human mind" was in reality the special progress of special minds who were to lead others. Even when they lacked the power or influence to carry out this role, the intellectual elite had the duty of "keeping alive the sacred fire in a few minds when we are unable to do more," as Mill wrote to a friend.[77]

In short, the excogitated conclusions of the intellectual elite were more or less automatically assumed to be superior to the life experiences of millions, as distilled into social values and customs. The role of the masses was to be taught by their betters and the role of their betters was to be taught by the best. Mill wrote to Harriet Taylor that they must write in order to provide material from which "thinkers, when there are any after us, may nourish themselves & then dilute for other people."[78] As for the masses, Harriet Taylor wrote to Mill that "for the great mass of peoples I think wisdom would be to make the utmost of sensation while they are young enough & then die."[79]

SUMMARY AND IMPLICATIONS

The contrast between Mill's dominating reputation in his own time and his subsequent downgrading, or being ignored, may reflect a number of factors. One that does Mill credit is that he did not announce his own innovations to the blare of trumpets — certainly not in economics, where he portrayed himself as "sticking pretty close to Ricardo,"[80] when in fact his own explorations of the role of monetary contractions during economic downturns was more sophisticated than anything in

Ricardo's *Principles* or the rest of the classical literature. Mill's systematic explorations of methodological issues in his youthful but insightful *Essays on Some Unsettled Questions of Political Economy* and in his later *A System of Logic* were a major advance over both his classical predecessors and their more "institutionalist" critics, though Samuel Bailey's earlier critique of the Ricardian school and especially his analysis of the "general glut" controversy was a very worthy predecessor and was in some ways superior.[81]

A less admirable aspect was Mill's unwillingness to concede anything explicitly to heretical critics of the Ricardians, while in fact expounding much the same doctrines as the heretics in different words. Mill's condemnation of the Earl of Lauderdale's oversaving doctrine while saying virtually the same thing himself was all too typical. He was open to Marx's indictment of the whole classical school on Say's Law, that it "admits the same phenomenon as present and necessary when it is called A but denies it when it is called B."[82]

John Stuart Mill's dual goals of defending the classical tradition against heretics and using his own *Principles of Political Economy* as a vehicle for policy applications not only led to his giving short shrift to distracting theoretical heresies, such as those of Sismondi and Malthus, it also led to one of Mill's characteristic patterns that extended beyond economics — attempts to combine for practical purposes theories that were not merely divergent but mutually contradictory. Perhaps the most notable of his attempts to square the circle was his distinction between "laws of production" and "laws of distribution."

Laws of Production and Distribution

Mill attempted to show how laws of production, such as the law of diminishing returns, were "strongly distinguished" from laws of income distribution. The laws of production "partake of the character of physical truths," according to Mill. "There is nothing optional or arbitrary in them."[83] They are determined "by the constitution of external things," and by "the inherent properties" of human beings. By contrast, the distribution of output "is a matter of human institution solely."[84] Once things have been produced, "mankind, individually or collectively, can do with them what they like"[85] — placing them "at the disposal of whomsoever they please, and on whatever terms."[86] It is all a matter of "the laws and customs of society," "the feelings and opinions" of its ruling elements, and is "very different in different ages and countries" and can vary still further "if mankind so chooses."[87]

Taken very literally, Mill's words might suggest that production is a matter of economics while distribution is a matter of social philosophy. Obviously production and distribution cannot be so completely independent of each other when the manner in which a given period's output is distributed affects the use of inputs — and therefore output — in subsequent periods. Mill was well aware of this:

> We have here to consider, not the causes, but the consequences, of the rules according to which wealth may be distributed. Those, at least, are as little arbitrary, and have as much the character of physical laws, as the laws of production. Human beings can control their own acts, but not the consequences of their acts to themselves or to others. Society can subject the distribution of wealth to whatever rules it thinks best: but what practical results will flow from the operation of those rules, must be discovered, like any other physical or mental truths, by observation and reasoning.[88]

The original distinction between laws of production and laws of distribution thus collapses. In the same sense in which society may distribute as it pleases and take the consequences, it may also produce as it pleases and take the consequences. In substance, Mill does not postulate any greater freedom in one area than in the other. Mill had created a distinction without a difference.

This pattern of bold assertion and devastating proviso likewise marked Mill's position on the question whether, in the legal system, laws were better to be made — excogitated — or to grow or evolve out of existing traditions. Mill said:

> The laws of Moses, those of Mahomet, were made, and did not grow; they had, it is true, the direct sanction of religious faith; but the laws of Lycurgus, the laws of Solon, were *made*, and were as durable as any laws which *grew* have hitherto been found.[89]

But here, as with laws of production and distribution, Mill's assertions were devastated by his provisos. Those who "make" law, according to Mill, must take into account "what the people will bear" and that is a function of their "ancient habits" or of their "durable and strenuous convictions, without which the whole system of laws would become inoperative." The "acquiescence of mankind" thus "depends upon the preservation of something like continuity of existence in institutions" representing "those innumerable compromises between adverse interests and expectations, without which no government could be carried on a year, and with difficulty even for a week."[90] Mill's desire to be useful in some practical way sometimes too readily led to a relaxation of intellectual rigor, to the point of amalgamating things that were incompatible — blurring distinctions of principle, while creating other meretricious verbal distinctions, in order to avoid explicitly conceding points made by writers from rival schools of thought.

Originality
Ironically, Mill's emphasis on practical applications in his *Principles of Political Economy* went counter to his own assessments of his strengths and weaknesses in his *Autobiography*, where he said that he "always had a humble opinion of my own powers as an original thinker, except in

abstract science (logic, metaphysics, and the theoretic principles of political economy and politics)." His venture into applications of economics he attributed to Harriet Taylor, with his intellectual role in relation to her being the role that he had fulfilled with regard to others, "that of an interpreter of original thinkers, and a mediator between them and the public."[91]

An attempt to depict John Stuart Mill as "one of the most original economists in the history of the science" by one of the leading scholars on the history of economics[92] seems to contradict Mill's modest estimate of his own originality. Among the things with which Professor George J. Stigler credited Mill was having "introduced the concept of demand as a schedule or function" because Mill had noted that a greater "quantity demanded" than "quantity supplied" would lead to a rise in price and the opposite would lead to a fall, so that "the value which a commodity will bring in any market is no other than the value which, in that market, gives a demand just sufficient to carry off the existing or expected supply."[93] Yet Mill's use of the term "demand" to mean quantity demanded would seem like the antithesis of a schedule concept of demand, even in the absence of his dismissal of Malthus' schedule concept of demand as "insignificant disputes about 'value'"[94] and his assertion that neither he (Mill) nor anyone else needed to add to the existing theory of value.[95]

The idea that prices rise when the quantity demanded exceeds the quantity supplied, and fall when the reverse is true, was spelled out as explicitly in the previous century by Adam Smith as it was later by John Stuart Mill.[96] When Jean-Baptiste Say said the same thing in 1803 — before Mill was born — he characterized his own discussion as being familiar to the point of being "trivial" even then.[97] Indeed, despite Stigler's claims of originality for Mill on this point, elsewhere Stigler said that "demand functions, as a set of empirical relationships, were already an established part of economic analysis" in Adam Smith's time.[98]

Professor Stigler also credited Mill with originality in recognizing "the fact that rent is a cost of production" in those cases "when land has alternative uses."[99] But, again, Adam Smith had long before recognized that rent was a price-determining production cost when the land had alternative uses.[100] Stigler likewise credited Mill with being "penetrating as well as original" in recognizing "the limitation of the proposition that there cannot be an overproduction of all commodities" simultaneously, i.e., Say's Law. But not only had Sismondi and Malthus preceded Mill in seeing this limitation of Say's Law, Say himself came to recognize that limitation in the fifth edition of his *Traité* and in his later *Cours complet*.[101] Anyone can be considered original if his predecessors are ignored. In the case of John Stuart Mill, not only did he have predecessors in general, his specific discussions of the monetary aspects of economic downturns in the economy had already been stated by Robert Torrens and G.P. Scrope before him.[102]

Nevertheless, among Professor Stigler's insights into the general role of originality in the advancement of a discipline that are worth noting is this:

> A new idea does not come forth in its mature scientific form. It contains logical ambiguities or errors; the evidence on which it rests is incomplete or indecisive; and its domain of application is exaggerated in certain directions and ignored in others. These deficiencies are gradually diminished by a peculiar scientific ageing process, which consists of having the theory "worked over" by many men.[103]

It was precisely this process of critical examination and refinement which John Stuart Mill prevented by his sweeping dismissals of "Malthus' insignificant disputes about 'value'" and by similarly dismissing equilibrium income theories challenging one aspect of Say's Law as "refuted, and now almost forgotten errors." Only someone with Mill's well-deserved reputation as a man of integrity and tolerance could have so completely slammed the door shut on such promising developments in the evolution of economic analysis through what W. Stanley Jevons was later to call "the noxious influence of authority."[104] Stigler noted in passing that, unlike other periods of intellectual ferment among economists, "economics was stuffy from 1850 to 1870."[105] But Stigler failed to note that this was essentially the period between the publication of Mill's *Principles* in 1848 and the epoch-making marginalist revolution led by Jevons and Menger in the 1870s.

Another great scholar on the history of economic thought — perhaps the greatest — J.A. Schumpeter, saw Mill very differently. Despite "J.S. Mill's own belief that he was only qualifying Ricardian doctrine," Schumpeter pointed out that Mill's "qualifications affect essentials of theory." Moreover, despite the broad sweep of Mill's work within and beyond economics, Schumpeter said:

> You can travel far and wide and yet wear blinkers wherever you go. Mill's comprehension never went below certain layers . . . and his intellect never got over certain barriers. What was below these layers and beyond those barriers he put down as nonsense . . . .[106]

Schumpeter attributed Mill's limitations to the distractions of "his unflagging interest in current issues" and his work at India House which, "though not very arduous" nevertheless created interruptions and perhaps accounted for "the incessant hurry that all his writings display."[107] Certainly Mill's magnum opus in economics, his *Principles of Political Economy*, was written in an enormous hurry — more than a thousand pages in eighteen months — that left no time for re-examining the writings of those economists whose ideas he dismissed, not only from this book but, because of Mill's enormous stature and the long-lasting influence of his *Principles*, from economics as a whole.

Mill and History

In an age of increasing specialization, it is doubtful whether there will ever again be anyone who will be pre-eminent in so many fields simultaneously as John Stuart Mill was in his time. It seems even less likely that there will be anyone whose intellectual development, virtually from infancy, will produce someone so learned and accomplished at an early age in the social sciences and humanities, where child prodigies are even rarer than in fields like mathematics, chess, or music. It may be hoped that there will be no one who is left so emotionally starved by a hothouse intellectual development.

Mill's contributions to economics considerably exceed those particular analyses in which he can be regarded as truly original. To have re-organized and presented as a structured whole the broad sweep of classical economics for the first time in his *Principles of Political Economy* was no small feat. Following in the wake of Ricardo's difficult to understand writings, Mill's making economics accessible to generations to come was a real service. His earlier *Essays on Some Unsettled Questions of Political Economy*, written in his twenties, was perhaps a greater contribution, from the standpoint of originality, to a narrower audience of those already well versed in the economics of the time. These essays clarified controversial theoretical issues without being distracted by an attempt to be "relevant" to policy issues of the day and general social uplift, as Mill's later *Principles* would be.

Both books, however, suffered from the theoretical distraction of trying to defend not only the substantive analyses of Ricardo, but also many of the conceptual peculiarities of the Ricardian system and its assumptions that have not stood the test of time — such as the Malthusian overpopulation theory that was an integral part of that system — as well as particular formulations that were needlessly constricting. The greatness of Ricardo's work could easily have survived explicit revisions, without Mill's having to obliterate contributions from other schools of thought that operated within different frameworks and with different assumptions.

John Stuart Mill's position as the unchallenged leader in economics and in other fields in his time was due not only to the quality of his own work but also to the happenstance that people of comparable stature did not come along at that time to contest his methods and conclusions. He was like a track star running against the clock instead of against another track star. He was never pushed — either by the criticism or the competing theories of comparably able contemporaries — to reach his utmost potential. In the long run, his reputation suffered accordingly, because in the long run there are always people of comparable stature.

The Mysteries of Marxian Economics

Like other systems of thought which have influenced or controlled the lives of millions of people, Marxism is an elaborate construction, whose interpretation has generated a whole priesthood of those familiar with its intricacies and ambiguities, and with the special vocabulary in which these are expressed. Many of the difficulties of unraveling the mysteries of Marxian economics derive more from the language in which Marx's ideas are expressed, and from the particular philosophic and economic frameworks from which its concepts are derived, rather than from the intrinsic difficulties of the analysis itself. Joseph Schumpeter's description of what is necessary for understanding Marxian economics can also be read as a reason why so many economists have misunderstood him:

> There is no point whatever in perusing selected bits of Marx's writing or even in perusing the first volume of *Das Kapital* alone. Any economist who wishes to study Marx at all must resign himself to reading carefully the whole of the three volumes of *Das Kapital* and of the three volumes of *Theorien über den Mehrwert* [*Theories of Surplus Value*]. Further, there is no point whatever in tackling Marx without preparation. Not only is he a difficult author but, owing to the nature of his scientific apparatus, he cannot be understood without a working knowledge of the economics of his epoch, Ricardo in particular, and of economic theory in general. This is all the more important because the necessity for it does not show on the surface.[1]

The difficulties in trying to understand Marxian economics — or other aspects of Marxism — without the necessary preparation has sometimes led to the fatalistic notion that you can "prove anything" about Marx's meaning by quoting selected passages. The clearest refutation of this notion is that some fashionable interpretations of Marxism — by its followers and opponents alike — cannot produce a single citation of anything ever written by Karl Marx or Friedrich Engels to substantiate these interpretations.[2]

Before proceeding to the substance of Marxian economics, a brief discussion of some Hegelian and Ricardian concepts may help avoid the pitfalls indicated by Schumpeter.

THE MARXIAN FRAMEWORK

First of all, it is necessary to distinguish between Marx's using certain words, phrases or concepts from Hegel or Ricardo and any claim that what Marx said substantively repeated what Hegel or Ricardo had said. This may be illustrated by parallel passages from Hegel's *Philosophy of History* and from Marx's *Capital*, both describing the emergence of the modern world. First Hegel:

> These three events — the so-called Revival of Learning, the flourishing of the fine Arts and the discovery of America and of the passage to India by the Cape — may be compared with that *blush of dawn*, which after long storms first betokens the return of a bright and glorious day.[3]

Then Marx:

> The discovery of gold and silver in America, the extirpation, enslavement and entombment in mines of

> the aboriginal population, the beginning of the conquest
> and looting of the East Indies, the turning of Africa into
> a warren for the commercial hunting of black-skins,
> signalised the rosy dawn of the era of capitalist
> production.[4]

This is just one example of how similar forms can express very different substance, not only with Hegel but with Ricardo as well.

Hegelian Concepts

It is not necessary to elaborate the whole Hegelian system of thought, or even to assess how accurately or inaccurately Marx and Engels may have interpreted it, in order to understand how its concepts were used in Marxian economics. What is necessary is to understand how the concepts that Marx and Engels took and adapted from Hegel and the neo-Hegelian tradition affected the substantive meanings of their presentations of their own ideas.

Here "Marxian" ideas will refer to the ideas developed jointly by Karl Marx and Friedrich Engels. Despite attempts by some interpreters to claim that Engels misconstrued Marx's ideas in his own writings,[5] they have failed to demonstrate substantive differences. Nor is it hard to see why they failed. Engels and Marx collaborated for nearly four decades, exchanged letters with great regularity,[6] and each wrote part (or all) of some writings that appeared under the other's name,[7] in addition to their explicit co-authorship of many writings. It is no small task to separate Marx from Engels intellectually, nor has this task been seriously undertaken by those who depict Engels — an intelligent and well-read man — as misunderstanding a friend whose ideas he was more familiar with than anyone else in the world. Moreover, Engels' most extensive discussion of Hegelian ideas occurs in his book popularly known as *Anti-Dühring,* which he read to Marx and discussed with him before it was published, in addition to Marx's having written one of the chapters himself.[8]

Both in Marx's *Capital* and in his *Critique of Political*

Economy, as well as in Engels' correspondence, the Hegelian concept of dialectics was referred to as a "method" of thinking,[9] rather than a set of substantive beliefs about the real world. More specifically, dialectics as used by Marx and Engels referred first of all to seeing the world as a set of dynamic *processes* rather than a set of static *things*. Understanding the nature of these processes was seen by Marx and Engels as the key to understanding how economic and social systems evolved, much like following the metamorphoses of living creatures. Social analogies to metamorphoses in nature abound in the writings of Marx and Engels.[10]

Marx also referred repeatedly to his presenting of the analysis in the three volumes of *Capital* in a "dialectical" way, meaning in this context by successive approximations. That is, the simplified assumptions used in the analysis of the first volume of *Capital* are made progressively more complex in the analysis in the second and third volumes. In various places in the first volume, Marx referred to particular puzzling economic phenomena which could not be dealt with there, under the many simplifying assumptions of that volume, but which would be explained later in the third volume.[11] More specifically, he said:

> We have in fact assumed that prices=values. We shall, however, see in Volume III, that even in the case of average prices the assumption cannot be made in this very simple manner.[12]

Engels warned Marx — in vain — that this method of proceeding invited gross misunderstandings of what he was saying, even by scholars, because they "were no longer at all accustomed to this kind of thinking."[13] Events proved Engels right. The most famous refutation of *Capital*, by Austrian economist Eugen von Böhm-Bawerk, proceeded on the assumption that the discussion of value in the first volume was Marx's theory of prices and therefore Böhm-Bawerk made criticisms of the labor theory of value that were essentially the same as Marx's criticisms of the labor theory of value in manuscripts not yet published until long after his death.[14]

The method of successive approximation was described by Marx in Hegelian terms as advancing from the inner "essence" to the outward "appearance." Early in the third volume of *Capital*, Marx announced that now the economic phenomena to be discussed would "approach step by step that form which they assume on the surface of society, in their mutual interactions, in competition, and in the ordinary consciousness of the human agencies in this process."[15] In this final approximation, the idea that a commodity's price is determined by the labor time that went into producing it disappears — or rather, appears "only in a vague and meaningless form," in Marx's own words.[16] Value is still defined in terms of labor time but such definitional values do not equal empirical prices because competition, as Marx said in a letter to Engels, "does *not* reduce commodities to their *value*, but to their *cost prices*, which are *above, below* or *equal* to their *value*" according to other complications now taken into consideration in the third volume of *Capital*. Some interpreters have conjectured that Marx simply changed his mind between volumes. But in fact Marx explained all of this in a letter to Engels before the first volume of *Capital* was published.[17]

Ricardian Concepts

In the writings of David Ricardo, where value was measured by labor time, the value of the worker's own wages was therefore measured by the amount of labor that went into producing what the worker consumed. Thus, if rising productivity allowed profits, rents, and wages all to increase in absolute terms simultaneously, but the relative share going to the workers declined, Ricardo would call that a fall in wages. To Ricardo, this fall in the worker's wages "will not the less be a real fall, because they might furnish him with a greater quantity of cheap commodities than his former wages."[18] As John Stuart Mill put it, Ricardo used the term value "in a sense peculiar to himself, to denote cost of production."[19]

This Ricardian conception of rises and falls in wages did not remain confined to Ricardo, however. Marx adopted it as well:

> The value of wages has to be reckoned not on the basis of the quantity of necessaries which the worker receives, but on the basis of the quantity of labour which these necessaries cost — actually the proportion of the working day which he appropriates for himself; the proportionate share of the total product, which the worker receives. It is possible that, reckoned in use values (quantities of commodities or money), his wages may rise as productivity increases, and yet reckoned in value they may fall, and *vice versa.* It is one of Ricardo's greatest merits that he made an examination of relative wages and established them as a definite category. Previously wages had always been looked upon as a simple element, and consequently the worker had been regarded as an animal. In Ricardo, however, he is considered in his social relationship. The position of the classes in relation to each other depends to a greater extent on the proportion which the wage forms than on the absolute amount of the wage.[20]

Despite Marx's reading of his own social or ideological concerns into Ricardo, in reality Ricardo made no such inference. To determine the worker's condition, Ricardo said that he would "estimate his condition by the abundance of necessaries which those money wages would procure him."[21]

While the Marxian conception of "rises" and "falls" in wages were in Ricardian relative terms, that did not preclude wages falling in absolute terms as well, since that would be just a special case of a decline in Ricardian-Marxian value terms. On this point, there really was a change of mind by Marx and Engels over the years. During the economic distress years of the 1840s — sometimes known as "the hungry forties" — Marx and Engels expected the actual real income of workers to decline under capitalism. In an 1847 article, Marx declared:

> In the course of development, there is a double fall in
> wages:
> *Firstly*: relative, in proportion to the development of
> general wealth.
> *Secondly*: absolute, since the quantity of
> commodities which the worker receives in exchange
> becomes less and less.[22]

Other Marxian writings of the 1840s — notably *The Poverty
of Philosophy* (1847) and the *Communist Manifesto* (1848) —
discuss the worker's standard of living in absolute terms, the
latter saying that the worker "sinks deeper and deeper"
economically with the progress of capitalism and the former
saying that the "natural price of labour is no other than the wage
minimum."[23] In later years, however, as the standard of living of
the working class was visibly rising, Marx's views changed,
though he was neither graceful nor prompt in announcing such
changes. Decades later, Engels said in a footnote to a new edition
of *The Poverty of Philosophy* that German socialist Ferdinand
Lasalle's "iron law of wages" was based on what he and Marx
had said in the 1840s about wages remaining at subsistence, but
which they no longer believed.[24] Marx referred publicly to
Lasalle's "outrageous retrogression" on this point in view of
recent and more "scientific" understanding of the subject — but
without mentioning that he, Marx, was the source of both the
ideas to which Lasalle was retrogressing and of the new view of
the matter.[25]

The more fundamental Marxian objection to the fate of the
worker under capitalism was not only that Marx and Engels did
not expect the proletariat to share equally in the growing output
of the system but also that work would no longer be fulfilling.
The notion of metamorphosis again surfaced in Marxian writings
on the role of work. A caterpillar *grows* into a bigger caterpillar;
it *develops* into a butterfly. Not so the worker under capitalism:
"If the silk worm were to spin in order to continue its existence as
a caterpillar, it would be a complete wage-worker."[26] Yet work
can be an end in itself, and its performance a satisfaction:

"Milton produced *Paradise Lost* for the same reason that a silk worm produces silk. It was an activity of his nature."[27]

Under capitalism, Marx argues, work no longer fulfills this vital role in the lives of the people. The division of labor under capitalism "attacks the individual at the very roots of his life."[28] It converts the worker into a "crippled monstrosity" by developing his manual dexterity in a narrow detail "at the expense of a world of productive capabilities and instincts; just as in the States of la Plata they butcher a whole beast for the sake of his hide or his tallow."[29] What is more relevant to the present question, Marx declares that this process must grow worse over time under capitalism. The same methods which increase productivity are methods which "mutilate the labourer into a fragment of a man" and "estrange him from the intellectual potentialities of the labour-process in the same proportion as science is incorporated in it as an independent power."[30] This is a vital part of the picture which leads Marx directly to the conclusion that "in proportion as capital accumulates, the lot of the labourer, be his payment high or low, must grow worse."[31]

Although this aspect of well-being (or lack of well-being) is often overlooked by his interpreters, it was supremely important to Marx himself. He described it as "a question of life and death" that the worker under capitalism, "crippled by life-long repetition of one and the same trivial operation, and thus reduced, to the mere fragment of a man" be replaced by "the fully developed individual . . . to whom the different social functions he performs are but so many modes of giving free scope to his own natural and acquired powers."[32]

Marx's doctrine of the increasing misery of the proletariat under capitalism was never a purely economic concept. But, for the sort of increasing misery that he envisioned to lead the workers to a revolution overthrowing the capitalist system, it would be necessary for the workers themselves to see the situation the same way Marx did and history has now made plain that this is not what has happened.

THE MARXIAN "LAW OF VALUE"

While Marx followed Ricardo in seeing the value of a commodity as the labor time that went into its production, this was for Marx simply a *definition*, rather than a theory of prices. Although this was spelled out only in the final approximation in the third volume of *Capital*, Marx was quite clear in his correspondence, even before the first volume of *Capital* was published in 1867, that values so defined did not and could not equal prices in the real world. In a letter to Engels in 1862, Marx spelled out with numerical examples why prices necessarily deviated from values, because of different capital/labor ratios among producers and the effect of competition in equalizing profit rates.[33] The same explanation, with the same kinds of numerical examples, would reappear in the third volume of *Capital*, when it was published, decades later, after Marx's death.[34]

When Marx began writing *Capital*, it was the prevailing view of the classical economists that the values of commodities reflected the respective amounts of labor that went into their production. Marx took this prevailing theory as his starting point, with some caveats — such as that the amount of labor must be "socially necessary," given the state of technology and the demand for the output — but turned this *theory* of value into a *definition* of value. Marx referred specifically to his "definition" of value and his "concept" of value in letters to Engels and to "value as defined" in the first volume of *Capital*.[35] The Marxian definition was the starting point for discussing the principles governing the allocation of resources — what Marx called the "law of value." In the third volume of *Capital*, he said:

> Only as an internal law, and from the point of view of the individual agents as a blind law, does the law of value exert its influence here and maintain the social equilibrium of production in the turmoil of its accidental fluctuations.[36]

In short, the Marxian "law of value" was about resource allocation, using the existing classical concept of labor time as value to symbolize how resources were directed and redirected under capitalism. Marx was flabbergasted that critics wanted him to prove a definition, when the whole point was to analyze resource allocation:

> The nonsense about the necessity of proving the concept of value arises from complete ignorance both of the subject dealt with and of the method of science. Every child knows that a country which ceased to work, I will not say for a year, but for a few weeks, would die. Every child knows too that the mass of products corresponding to the different needs require different and quantitatively determined masses of the total labour of society.[37]

The "law of value" — that is, resource allocation theory — was important in both Marxian microeconomics and macroeconomics. In a microeconomic sense, resource allocation was intimately affected by price fluctuations and prices were influenced by, though not identical with, values defined as labor costs. In a macroeconomic sense, gross misallocations of resources among sectors of the economy — disproportionality as distinguished from underconsumption — brought on economic downturns called recessions or depressions today but called economic "crises" by Marx.

Some have thought that Marxian values were expected to come into their own under communism, with the government prescribing prices based on the amount of labor that went into the production of goods and services. This was an idea common among various non-Marxian socialists, but it was rejected with contempt by Marx and Engels. Marx said of one such socialist:

Let M. Proudhon take it upon himself to formulate and lay down such a law, and we shall relieve him of the necessity of giving proofs. If, on the other hand, he insists on justifying his theory, not as a legislator, but as an economist, he will have to prove that the *time* needed to create a commodity indicates exactly the degree of its *utility* and marks its proportional relation to the demand, and in consequence, to the total amount of wealth.[38]

People like Proudhon "reduce socialism to an elementary misconception" of economics, according to Marx.[39] They wish to eliminate the very process of market competition which tends to produce the equality of price and product cost that they desire. This would destroy the whole allocation process, as Engels explained: "Only through the undervaluation or overvaluation of products is it forcibly brought home to the individual commodity producers what things and what quantity of them society requires or does not require." Without this mechanism, Engels wondered "what guarantee we have that necessary quantity and not more of each product will be produced, that we shall not go hungry in regard to corn and meat while we are choked in beet sugar and drowned in potato spirit, that we shall not lack trousers to cover our nakedness while trouser buttons flood us in millions... . "[40] Ironically, the situation described by Engels became a chronic problem in the Soviet Union, where unsold goods accumulated in warehouses while people suffered shortages of other things that could have been produced by the resources that had been wasted producing a surplus of other things.

MARXIAN ECONOMIC "CRISES"

Resource allocation theory — the Marxian "law of value" — was applied by Marx and Engels to the macroeconomic problem of explaining economic downturns or "crises." Contending explanations of such downturns before Marx's time might be divided into (1) underconsumption and (2) disproportionality. Underconsumptionists such as Sismondi and Malthus saw the problem as inadequate aggregate demand to sustain the existing level of aggregate output and employment.   But those like Ricardo and John Stuart Mill saw the fundamental imbalance as being between the different sectors of the economy — too many resources being devoted to producing furniture, perhaps, and not enough to producing wheat.   Ricardo said: "Men err in their productions, there is no deficiency of demand."[41]   Marx's writings show him repeatedly on the side of those who saw crises precipitated by disproportionalities, though in the course of adjustments to these disproportionalities, aggregate demand could also be reduced.

Microeconomic and macroeconomic applications of the Marxian "law of value" were linked because price determination and resource allocation were seen as inseparable parts of the same process. In keeping with their dialectical approach, Marx and Engels did not look at prices as *things* determined in static equilibrium, but focussed instead on the *process* by which prices were determined and saw economic crises as a by-product of that process. While writing *Capital,* Marx wrote to Engels that his analysis of crises in that work would show that "things remain as you have already quite aptly described them" in an obscure essay of the 1840s — an essay that had led Marx to seek out Engels and begin their lifelong collaboration. Here is what the young Engels had written in 1844:

> The law of competition is that demand and supply always strive to complement each other, and therefore never do so. The two sides are torn apart again and transformed into flat opposition. Supply always follows close on demand without ever quite covering it. It is either too big or too small, never corresponding to demand; because in this unconscious condition of mankind no one knows how big supply or demand is. If demand is greater than supply, the price rises and, as a result, supply is to a certain degree stimulated. As soon

as it comes on to the market, prices fall; and if it
becomes greater than demand, then the fall in prices is
so significant that demand is once again stimulated. So
it goes on unendingly — a permanently unhealthy state
of affairs — a constant alternation of overstimulation
and collapse which precludes all advance — a state of
perpetual fluctuation perpetually unresolved. This law
with its constant balancing, in which whatever is lost
here is gained there, seems to the economist marvelous.
It is his chief glory — he cannot see enough of it, and
considers it in all its possible and impossible
applications. Yet it is obvious that this law is a purely
natural law, and not a law of the mind. It is a law which
produces revolution.[42]

Revolution eventually results from these price fluctuations
because of workers' bitter reactions to economic depressions, or
"trade crises" in Engels' words, which "reappear as regularly as
the comets, and of which we have on the average one every five
to seven years." The economists' law of supply and demand is in
a sense vindicated by these fluctuations of price and output, but
not in the smooth and easy way suggested by the economists:

Of course, these trade crises confirm the law, confirm it
exhaustively — but in a manner different from that
which the economist would have us believe to be the
case. What are we to think of a law which can only
assert itself through periodic crises? It is just a natural
law based on the unconsciousness of the participants. If
the producers as such knew how much the consumers
required, if they were to organise production, if they
were to share it out amongst themselves, then the
fluctuations of competition and its tendency to crisis
would be impossible. Produce with consciousness as
human beings — not as dispersed atoms without
consciousness of your species — and you are beyond all
these artificial and untenable antitheses. But as long as
you continue to produce in the present unconscious,

thoughtless manner, at the mercy of chance — for just
so long trade crises will remain; and each successive
crisis is bound to become more universal and therefore
worse than the preceding one; is bound to impoverish a
larger body of small capitalists, and to augment in
increasing proportion the numbers of that class who live
by labour alone, thus visibly enlarging the mass of
labour to be employed (the major problem of our
economists) and finally causing a social revolution such
as has never been dreamt of by the school-wisdom of the
economists.[43]

The crucial elements later elaborated by Marx in *Capital*
were already present in this 1844 publication by Engels:

1. Crises are inherent in capitalist commodity
   production because producers cannot
   accurately predict the demand of the
   consumers or the supply of other producers.
2. Price fluctuations reflect — and correct —
   production imbalances or disproportionalities among the various sectors of the
   economy, but in a way that can lead to crises,
   rather than to the smooth adjustments
   suggested by economists.
3. Successive crises become progressively worse
   because they are ever widening in their scope
   ("more universal"),[44] rather than ever deepening
   in their declines, as often suggested in the
   interpretive literature.[45] The ever-widening
   crises are consistent with the Marxian view of
   the capitalist system as beginning as part of a
   given economy and then spreading out to
   become the whole national economy and
   finally becoming international in its scope.[46]
4. The growing size of an impoverished

proletariat eventually leads to social
revolution, in conjunction with the crises.

Neither underconsumption nor a permanent economic
"breakdown" plays any role in this picture — nor later in Marx,
despite an interpretive literature driven to the desperate expedient
of quoting numerous post-Marxian writers and ignoring Marx
himself.[47]
The underconsumption interpretation of Marx often
concludes that some permanent breakdown of the capitalist
economy will eventually occur, due to the economy's inability to
achieve sufficient aggregate demand to revive production after a
depression or economic crisis.[48] But no such theory exists in
Marx, who repeatedly referred to the *transitory* nature of
individual crises. They were referred to by Marx in such terms as
"general stoppages of a transient nature,"[49] a "momentary
suspension" of economic activity,[50] or in Engels' words
"temporary overproduction."[51] According to Marx: "The crises
are always but momentary and forcible solutions of the existing
contradictions, violent eruptions which restore the disturbed
equilibrium for a while."[52] More fundamentally: "There are no
permanent crises."[53] It is hard to imagine a more unequivocal
rejection of the economic breakdown theory which has been
attributed to Marx by his interpreters.
Attempts to salvage the underconsumptionist breakdown
interpretation of Marx have sometimes fastened on his use of
words like "contradiction" or "negation" to suggest that Marx
meant that capitalism reaches an insoluble impasse or somehow
annihilates itself as an economy. Perhaps no Hegelian term has
created more misconceptions of Marxian economics than the
word "contradiction." Joseph Schumpeter was one of the few
economists to be aware that this word had a special Hegelian
meaning:

The untutored reader of Marx's writings may wonder
why Marx speaks so often of 'contradictions' of

capitalism when he means nothing but mutually counteracting facts or tendencies: these *are* contradictions from the standpoint of Hegelian logic.[54]

Marxian metaphors about metamorphoses are again relevant here, as are the concepts of "essence" and "appearance." The end of capitalism was foreseen by Marx as being analogous to that of a germinating seed:

> Centralisation of the means of production and socialisation of labour at last reach a point where they become incompatible with their capitalist integument. This integument is burst asunder. The knell of capitalist private property sounds. The expropriators are expropriated.
>
> The capitalist mode of appropriation, the result of the capitalist mode of production, produces capitalist private property. This is the first negation of individual private property, as founded on the labour of the proprietor. But capitalist production begets, with the inevitability of a law of Nature, its own negation. It is the negation of the negation.[55]

Words like "contradiction" and "negation" used by Marx in a Hegelian sense might suggest a nullification of capitalism, in the sense of an economy experiencing a catastrophic breakdown, when those words are interpreted in their ordinary sense, and some interpreters have in fact reached such conclusions.[56] But contradiction in the sense of contending forces, such as those within a germinating seed which breaks through its integument, is very different. Hegel said: "Contradiction is the very moving principle of the world: and it is ridiculous to say that contradiction is unthinkable."[57] As for "negation," that too had a special Hegelian meaning as transformation or metamorphosis, not self-annihilation. According to Hegel, negation "resolves itself not into nullity, into abstract Nothingness, but essentially only into the negation of its *particular* content."[58] A capitalist economy thus "begets . . . its own negation," in Marx's words,[59] when it changes its content to become a socialist economy.

The Hegelian language of "essence" and "appearance" is part of this vision of metamorphosis. The essence is what explains the processes that a given natural or social organism goes through. The appearance is not simply a delusion; on the contrary, it represents empirical reality, though only on a superficial level at a given moment. The proverbial blind men who felt different parts of an elephant were literally in touch with empirical reality, even though that led them to differing and erroneous conceptions of an elephant. Similarly, the empirical reality of a given stage of metamorphosis is quite real but may be a completely inadequate and misleading representation of what an acorn, a caterpillar, a tadpole, or an apple blossom will lead to. All these things develop into something quite different from their existing appearance at a given point in time.

More important, from the standpoint of Marxian analysis, all these things are transformed *from within* by forces inherent in them, struggling against one another — that is, by their "internal contradictions." That is how Marx and Engels expected capitalism to be transformed, not by some economic impasse like the classical stationary state but by active forces inherent in capitalism and contending with one another, leading ultimately to its transformation into socialism.

Those who interpret Marx to be predicting a catastrophic breakdown of capitalist economies have been forced into strained explanations as to why they cannot find anything in his voluminous writings to support that interpretation. Paul Sweezy, for example, postulates that Marx *would have* developed an underconsumptionist theory of economic breakdown had he lived to complete the writing of *Capital*, so that "Marx's silence" as to whether economic crises "must occur first in the consumption-goods department" only shows "that he never worked the 'underconsumptionist' theory out in any detail."[60] But Marx was not "silent" on this at all. He said the direct opposite, that "crises do not show themselves, nor break forth, first in the retail business, which deals with direct consumption, but in the spheres of wholesale business and banking."[61]

More fundamentally, it is completely misleading to depict *Capital* as an *analytically* unfinished work, even though it was, in a literary sense, far from a finished piece of writing when Marx died in 1883. However, Marx wrote to Engels in 1866 that the entire manuscript of *Capital* was "finished," though far from a publishable condition, and that even the first volume still needed "*polishing of style*"(Marx's emphasis).[62] Indeed, Marx insisted on seeing *Capital* "as a *whole*" before sending the first volume off to the printer.[63]

After Marx's death, Engels wrote to one of Marx's daughters that the third volume (in which "crisis" theory was developed) had been "complete since 1869–1870 and has never been touched since."[64] It took Engels more than a decade to decipher Marx's handwriting and pull together overlapping and repetitious manuscripts into reasonably organized books for Volumes II and III of *Capital*, but the "essential parts" of Volume III had been completed before Marx published Volume I in 1867, as Engels explained in a preface to the second volume.[65] In short, the evidence shows that *Capital* was completed by Marx as a piece of analysis, though not as a piece of writing, in his own lifetime, so the speculation as to what his analysis would have contained had he lived is gratuitous.

An earlier voluminous draft of the book that was eventually to become *Capital* has since been published as Marx's *Grundrisse* — and it too contains no underconsumptionist breakdown theory. It too emphasized disproportionality among the various sectors of the economy, rather than aggregate underconsumption. The *Grundrisse* stated that "if the supplied product is unsaleable, it proves that too much has been produced of a supplied commodity and too little of what the supplier demands."[66] This was a classic disproportionality explanation, repeating what had been said by members of the Ricardian school for decades.

In short, for Marx, overproduction in one sector of the economy was balanced by underproduction in other sectors. Therefore capital "withdraws" from one sector and "throws itself" into another sector in response to competitive pricing. But Marx pointed out here, as elsewhere, that "this necessity of evening up already *presupposes* the unevenness" which is inherent in capitalism and the precursor of crises.[67] A similar point was made in the 1840s in Marx's pamphlet *Wage Labour and Capital*, where he said: "If the price of a commodity rises considerably because of inadequate supply or disproportionate increase of the demand, the price of some other commodity must necessarily have fallen proportionately," leading to capital migrations toward the more profitable sectors of the economy.[68]

Disproportionality was present — and underconsumption absent — from Marx's economic writings over a period of more than three decades.

Precipitating Factors

Marx depicted the disproportionality theorists as having understood the fundamental nature of capitalism better than those theorists who emphasized a deficiency of aggregate demand.[69] This was somewhat ironic because the disproportionality school of economists were supporters of Say's Law, and proponents of that doctrine often used it to dismiss fears of depressions, which were seen as short-lived happenstances. Marx, however, was a bitter critic of Say's Law, which he called "preposterous,"[70] "a paltry evasion,"[71] "childish babble,"[72] and "pitiful claptrap."[73] J.B. Say himself he denounced as "inane,"[74] "miserable,"[75] "thoughtless,"[76] "dull,"[77] and a "humbug."[78] For Marx, disproportionality did not end with a smooth restoration of equilibrium but precipitated further complications that ended in aggregate overproduction relative to a shrinking monetary demand.

Marx recognized that the classical supporters of Say's Law had admitted "the glut of the market for particular commodities," and had denied only "the *simultaneity* of this phenomenon for all spheres of production, and hence general overproduction."[79] According to classical economics, too much production of *A* implied too little production of *B* but not too much output in the aggregate.[80] This was because total supply equals total demand

(Say's Law) and therefore each excess of either supply or demand in the case of a given commodity was necessarily offset by a corresponding deficiency or excess in the case of some other commodity. This equality of supply and demand existed from the outset in the mind of each producer, who supplied commodities only because of — and only to the extent of — his demand for other commodities.[81]

Marx, however, spotted the fatal flaw in this reasoning — that the supplier could only *attempt* to equate his own supply with his own demand by imagining what price he would receive for his own output. If he guessed wrong, his individual supply might not equal his own individual demand — and since all producers were in the same position, aggregate supply as *conceived* need not equal aggregate demand as *realized*. While Marx recognized that "commodities are equated beforehand in imagination, by their prices, to definite quantities of money,"[82] he did not assume that they were necessarily correctly equated. He said:

> My supply and demand are thus as different as something conceptual is from something real. Further, the quantity I supply and its value stand in no proportion to each other. The demand for the quantity of use-value I supply is however measured not by the value I wish to realise, but by the quantity which the buyer requires at a definite price.[83]

Here Marx was developing an idea originated decades earlier by Sismondi, who had likewise sought to explain "violent crises,"[84] and who considered "the balance of consumption and production" to be "the fundamental question in political economy."[85] Sismondi said that producers' attempts to balance their own supply with their own demand — quantities "independent of one another" — could only proceed by "divination" because "even the most knowledgeable have only conjectural knowledge."[86] Marx was familiar with the work of

Sismondi, who anticipated him in other areas as well,[87] but deliberately neglected to cover Sismondi's economic theories in his massive *Theories of Surplus Value*, the first great history of economic thought.

While Sismondi had indicated much earlier that the attempt to equate supply and demand was likely to fail in a complex capitalist economy, Marx elaborated more rigorously and mathematically (in the second volume of *Capital*) just how complex the relationships were among the various sectors of the capitalist economy and among various flows of purchasing power. These interrelationships became quite complex, even under the assumption of "simple reproduction"[88] — that is, unchanging total output from year to year — and still more so under the more realistic assumption of "accumulation and reproduction on an enlarged scale,"[89] or a growing capitalist economy. Dynamically growing capitalism — the only kind of capitalism Marx thought possible[90] — was one in which there was no "predestined circle of supply and demand"[91] known to the producers beforehand. Moreover, growing output might be absorbed for some time by wholesalers before reaching the stage where the ultimate consumer demand for it was put to the test:

> . . . the entire process of reproduction may be in a flourishing condition, and yet a large part of the commodities may have entered into consumption only apparently, while in reality they may still remain unsold in the hands of dealers, in other words, they may still be actually in the market. Now one stream of commodities follows another, and finally it becomes obvious that the previous stream had been only apparently absorbed by consumption. The commodity-capitals compete with one another for a place on the market. The succeeding ones, in order to be able to sell, do so below price. The former streams have not been utilized, when the payment for them is due. Their owners must declare their insolvency, or they sell at any price in order to fulfill their obligations. This sale has nothing whatever

to do with the actual condition of the demand. It is merely a question of a demand for payment, of the pressing necessity of transforming commodities into money. Then a crisis comes. It becomes noticeable, not in the direct decrease of consumptive demand, not in the demand for individual consumption, but in the decrease of exchanges of capital for capital, of the reproductive process of capital.[92]

There were other complicating factors in crises. A growing capitalist economy implied, for Marx, the sporadic formation and liquidation of hoards of money at various places and unpredictable times. These added to the conditions of capitalism which "become so many causes of abnormal movements, implying the possibility of crises, since a balance is an accident under the crude conditions of this production."[93]

The crucial question for Marx, as for Sismondi before him, was not how particular imbalances — overproduction in a particular sector, for example — might arise, but how that led to *general* overproduction, to economic crises. Both Sismondi and Marx recognized that the pricing mechanism tended automatically to restore imbalances through declining prices for overproduced goods, rising prices for underproduced goods, and rising or falling interest rates according to supply and demand in the capital markets. But both also argued that beyond some magnitude of imbalance, this no longer worked — that there were destabilizing responses to extreme conditions, responses that took the economy further away from equilibrium rather than back toward it. Sismondi's destabilizing responses[94] were somewhat different from Marx's, but like Marx's they served to delay rather than to prevent eventual equilibrium. According to Sismondi, "a certain equilibrium is re-established, it is true, in the long run, but it is by a frightful suffering."[95] To Marx, these frightful sufferings provoke a political revolt against the whole capitalist system. It was this political revolt — not an economic "breakdown" — that ends capitalism, in the Marxian vision.

Destabilizing Responses

The destabilizing force in Marxian economics was the monetary and credit system. Money and credit turned partial overproduction into general overproduction. Marx did not consider money and credit as initiating causes of crises — "both make their appearance long *before* capitalist production, without crises occurring"[96] — but they were mechanisms which could make sectoral disproportionalities become general overproduction, relative to a declining demand, provided that the initial imbalances were large enough. According to Marx: "For a crisis (and therefore also overproduction) to be general, it is sufficient for it to grip the principal articles of trade."[97] When particular producers or middlemen — like the wholesalers already mentioned — suddenly find themselves financially over-extended through excessive output or inventory, and unable to pay previously contracted debt obligations, their immediate demand for money may be more than the system can supply while maintaining existing output and employment. Although monetary crises could occur as independent entities, according to Marx,[98] they were, more generally, seen as phases of larger crises growing out of overproduction in particular sectors — disproportionality.

Overproduction in particular sectors thus generates financial panic in those sectors, when money receipts are insufficient to meet existing fixed contractual obligations when they are due. Rather than face bankruptcy, producers sell whatever output is on hand, at whatever price they can get, and use the proceeds to meet financial obligations, rather than to spend for consumer goods or to re-order new supplies. Marx said:

> A man who produced has not the choice whether he will sell or not. He must sell. And in crises appears precisely the circumstance that he cannot sell, or only below the price of production, or even that he must sell at a positive loss. What does it avail him or us, therefore, that he has produced in order to sell? What

concerns us is precisely to discover what has cut across
this good intention of his.[99]

In response to Ricardo's argument that producers sell in order
to spend on consumption or on new production — all of which
would make their demand equal their supply — Marx replied:
"Ricardo even forgets that a man may sell in order to pay, and that
these compulsory sales play a very significant role in crises."
Marx added: "During the crisis the man may be very pleased
when he has made a sale, without any immediate thought of a
purchase."[100] His demand need not equal his supply at that point
in the process.

In short, there is an increasing demand to hold money during
unsettled economic conditions — a point made by many other
economists before and since. But Marx did not "seek to explain
crises by these simple *possibilities* of crises"[101] — an approach
he criticized in John Stuart Mill.[102] Rather, he sought to show
how the disproportionality inherent in capitalist production
would episodically reach levels that would precipitate financial
panics and contractions of aggregate monetary demand. This was
not only because of a failure to re-spend on the part of some
capitalist producers, but also because others could not re-spend or
even went into credit default.

When there are "debts due to A from B, to B from C, to C
from A, and so on,"[103] — in short, "an ever-lengthening chain of
payment"[104] or "mutual claims and obligations"[105] — then a
monetary crisis develops "from the non-fulfillment of a whole
series of payments which depend on the sale of these particular
commodities within this particular period of time."[106] A general
financial panic ensues. According to Marx, "in periods of crisis
when credit collapses completely . . . nothing goes any more but
cash money."[107]

With the shrinkage of credit, aggregate money demand
becomes insufficient: "At a given moment the supply of all
commodities may be greater than the demand for all
commodities, because the demand for the general commodity,

money, exchange value, is greater than the demand for all particular commodities."[108] Marx was aware that the insufficiency of demand was an insufficiency only at given prices:

> The excess of commodities is always relative, that is, it is an excess at certain prices. The prices at which the commodities are then absorbed are ruinous for the producer or merchant.[109]

The lower prices are ruinous because the whole price structure cannot deflate smoothly: "The fixed charges . . . remain the same, and in part cannot be paid."[110] Even commodities which were not among those which had been overproduced "are now suddenly in *relative* overproduction, because the means to buy them, and therewith the demand for them, have contracted."[111] Thus, "in times of general overproduction, the overproduction in some spheres is always the *result*, the *consequence*, of overproduction in the leading articles of commerce."[112]

What Marx did not explain was why the monetary contraction originating in sectors that were overproducing and incurring losses was not offset by monetary expansion originating in other sectors that were underproducing and making unusually high profits due to the rising prices of their unusually scarce goods. An earlier exponent of a similar theory, Robert Torrens, was more explicit. Torrens' theory that "a glut of a particular commodity may occasion a general stagnation"[113] was based on his assumption that "multiplied failures in agriculture, manufacturers, and trade, would strike a panic into the holders of floating capital, and they would refuse to grant accommodation upon securities, which in more prosperous times they would be disposed to consider unobjectionable."[114] In short, it was not only the producers who happened to be in distressed conditions, but the economy as a whole, that would have a rising demand for money — a desire to be more liquid than usual — and these desires could not be realized simultaneously without causing a declining aggregate money demand for output. This seems consonant with Marx's theory, though the Marxian theory was less explicitly stated. Marx did say, however:

> During crises — *after* the moment of panic — during the standstill of industry, money is immobilized in the hands of bankers, billbrokers, etc.; and, just as the stag cries out for fresh water, money cries out for a field of employment where it may be realized as capital.[115]

This not only indicates why there were crises, but also suggested why crises were transient. The purchasing power needed to restore prosperity was never annihilated, but only temporarily withdrawn from circulation pending restoration of sufficient confidence for the normal incentives of profit-seeking to draw it back into circulation again.

Periodicity

In Marx, crises were not merely episodic — as might be expected from a purely random process, in which sectoral disproportionalities exceed certain critical limits at unpredictable intervals, by chance. Rather, crises occur in a "periodic cycle,"[116] at relatively regular intervals. Marx and Engels saw these periodical recurrences of crises as having begun in 1825.[117] Over the years they revised their estimates of the length of the period between crises. In *Capital* Marx referred to the "decennial cycle,"[118] but after his death Engels said that "the ten-year cycle seems to have broken down."[119] Earlier, Engels had estimated the cycle as from five to seven years.[120] Marx seemed not to attach any great significance to the exact period of business cycles, as compared to their inevitable recurrence. He seemed to suggest that the economic life of fixed capital was related to the business cycle, presumably because so much capital was invested simultaneously during the recovery phase after a crisis:

> To the same extent that the volume of the value and the
> duration of the fixed capital develop with the evolution
> of the capitalist mode of production, does the life of
> industry and of industrial capital develop in each
> particular investment into one of many years, say of ten
> years on an average . . . However, it is not a question of
> any one definite number here. So much at least is
> evident that this cycle comprising a number of years,
> through which capital is compelled to pass by its fixed
> part, furnishes a material basis for the periodical
> commercial crises in which business goes through
> successive periods of lassitude, average activity,
> overspending, and crisis. It is true that the periods in
> which capital is invested are different in time and place.
> But a crisis is always the starting point of a large amount
> of new investments. Therefore it also constitutes, from
> the point of view of society, more or less of a new
> material basis for the next cycle of turn-over.[121]

This aspect of Marx's theory was left in a very sketchy state,
perhaps because periodicity was not in itself crucial to his picture
of the end of capitalism. After Marx's death, Engels began to
suggest that the periodic cycle had been superseded by chronic
economic stagnation.[122] But no coherent theory was presented to
account for this, any more than there had been a coherent theory
for the earlier Marxian assertions of regular periodicity.

SUMMARY AND IMPLICATIONS

In Marxian economics, a relatively straightforward set of
theories have been obscured in mists of interpretive controversy
because Marx chose to express those theories in the language of
two writers notoriously difficult to understand — Hegel and
Ricardo. Marx compounded these difficulties by presenting the
three volumes of *Capital* as successive approximations,

operating under different sets of assumptions in each volume. Thus, the first volume defined value as labor time, and treated these definitional values as empirical prices, while mentioning in passing in footnotes that in reality that this was not so, and that the assumed correspondence between value and price would be changed in the third volume.[123] To Engels' concern that the way *Capital* was being constructed invited misunderstandings and objections, Marx replied that a fuller explanation "can be set forth only in the third book." He added:

> If I were to *silence* all such objections *in advance*, I should ruin the whole dialectical method of development. On the contrary, this method has the advantage of continually *setting traps* for these fellows which provoke them to untimely demonstrations of their asininity.[124]

Marx expected publication of the succeeding volumes of *Capital* to follow fast upon publication of the first volume,[125] so that his idea of embarrassing the critics of his first approximation may have been understandable. In reality, however, for various reasons — notably failing health — Marx never had the later volumes published, despite living sixteen years after publication of the first volume. Following his death, it took Engels many years to decipher and laboriously piece together the handwritten manuscripts left by Marx, so that more than a quarter of a century elapsed between publication of Volume I and Volume III of *Capital*.

By that time, critics and disciples alike had hardened their positions, taken on the basis of a first approximation. Moreover, this was a quarter of a century of decisive change in economics. The classical framework, which Marx was able to take for granted as a familiar intellectual setting for explaining his own analysis, was devastated by the rise of revolutionary new "marginalist" concepts of utility and value — concepts which were dominant in economics by the time the third volume of *Capital* finally appeared. What Marx wrote in the 1860s was interpreted in the context of a new framework of economics in the 1890s. The classic "refutation" of *Capital* was made by a leading figure in the new economics, Eugen von Böhm-Bawerk. His refutation repeatedly misunderstood what it was refuting, and unknowingly repeated criticisms that Marx had already made of Ricardo's labor theory of value in manuscripts still unpublished at that time.

The very assumption that Marx was trying to prove a particular price theory would be inconsistent with his attempt to overthrow the economic system in which prices were determined by market competition. Why would anyone devote so many years of work to an incidental aspect of a transient economic system, whose transience he was trying to ensure? However, Marx's linking of price determination and resource allocation went to the heart of his picture of capitalism's instability, as expressed in recurrent economic crises that in Marx's view ultimately threatened the existence of capitalism when the working class would finally revolt at the sufferings entailed by these depressions.

Periods of depression, unemployment, or economic "crises" in Marx's terminology were seen by some schools of economists as resulting from a lack of proportion between the output of some sectors — not by an excess of total output. Marx and Engels repeatedly took this position in writings that spanned the decades from Engels' first economic essay of the early 1840s to the elaborate vision of Marx's *Capital* fully unfolded half a century later. The competing school, which saw crises originating in excessive total output — notably Sismondi and Malthus — was explicitly repudiated by Marx, and the ever-popular underconsumption versions ridiculed unmercifully.

Marxian economics did, however, move beyond the classical disproportionality theory by arguing that monetary reactions to severe disproportionality could in fact temporarily reduce aggregate demand below aggregate supply, in defiance of Say's Law.

Attempts to interpret Marx as an underconsumptionist who foresaw a permanent breakdown of the capitalist economy have had to rely on speculation rather than concrete statements by Marx or Engels. Yet these speculations fly in the teeth of massive evidence of disproportionality theory pervading the Marxian vision of capitalism.

The Marx-Engels vision of economic crises encompassed not only individual depressions but also the pattern of their recurrence over the years. Crises were expected to widen in their scope as capitalism itself spread — not deepen in their severity otherwise, as too often assumed by interpreters. A regularity in the period between crises was claimed by Marx and Engels but neither a fixed period nor a developed theory of periodicity was ever determined. Nor was either essential to their over-all economic or social vision.

As an intellectual construct, *Capital* was a masterpiece. But, like some other intellectual masterpieces, it was an elaborately sophisticated structure erected on the foundation of a primitive misconception. That misconception was that there was something special about labor as a source of output. It was a misconception that lasted nearly a century, from Adam Smith's *The Wealth of Nations* in 1776 until Marx's *Capital* in 1867, the latter being the last major treatise within the classical framework. Yet the marginalist revolution of the 1870s showed that neither labor nor any other input determined price because it was not cost of production that was crucial, but the utility of the output to the consumer, which determined whether or to what extent the consumer would be willing to pay to cover those costs.

Even among inputs to the production process, labor had no special causal significance, as compared to managerial or entrepreneurial skills. Countries with much labor and little capital or entrepreneurship typically do not have more output, more valuable output, or a higher standard of living. On the contrary, usually such countries are poor. Nor can a mere transfer of capital make them prosperous, as the failure of massive foreign aid programs in Third World countries has demonstrated repeatedly. The first nation to put into practice the Marxian notion that capitalists were useless parasites — the Soviet Union — immediately paid a tragic price in a collapsing economy. In Lenin's own words, there was a "fuel crisis" which "threatens to disrupt all Soviet work," and in general "ruin, famine and dislocation," in the country. Contrary to his writings before the Bolshevik revolution, Lenin now saw a need for people "who are versed in the art of administration" and admitted that "there is nowhere we can turn to for such people except the old class" — that is, the capitalist businessmen.[126] Lenin's New Economic Policy restored much of the functioning of the capitalist economy, which in turn brought a desperately needed economic upturn. Later, when Stalin launched his five-year plans to "build socialism," he did so by importing both technology and managerial talent from capitalist countries. Moreover the managerial class that ran the Soviet economy was disproportionately descended from capitalists of the past.

However factually or logically discredited the Marxian idea of labor as the real source of wealth, from which parasitic capitalists profited, ideologically it remained a powerful and compelling vision. As Edmund Wilson put it, "once we have read *Das Kapital*, the conventional works on economics never seem the same to us again; we can always see through their arguments and figures the realities of the crude human relations which it is their purpose or effect to mask."[127] It is a powerful vision and one which Marx and Engels themselves saw as their major intellectual contribution — "laying bare" the extraction of "surplus value" from the proletariat as the essence of capitalism.[128]

It would be hard to conceive of any other vision, outside the realm of religion, which has seized the imaginations of more millions of people around the world and caused so many of them to dedicate their lives — and even risk or forfeit their lives — in its service. In the realm of ideas in general, the Marxian vision — including his theory of history — has not only dominated various fields at various times, it has survived both the continuing prosperity of capitalism and the economic debacles of socialism. It has become axiomatic among sections of the intelligentsia, impervious to the corrosive effects of evidence or logic.

But what did Marx contribute to economics? Contributions depend not only on what was offered but also on what was accepted, and there is no major premise, doctrine, or tool of analysis in economics today that derived from the writings of Karl Marx. There is no need to deny that Marx was in many ways a major historic figure of the nineteenth century, whose long shadow still falls across the world of the twenty-first century. Yet, jarring as the phrase may be, from the standpoint of the economics profession Marx was, as Professor Paul Samuelson called him, "a minor post-Ricardian."[129]

Thoughts on the History of Economics

The history of economics is part of the history of ideas in general, and though there are some ways in which economics has evolved differently from other disciplines, many of the issues involved in the general history of ideas arise in the history of economic thought as well. Intellectual issues involved in the history of economics include the dynamics of controversy, the role of ideological bias, the reciprocal effect of ideas and events, and questions of individual originality and contributions to the discipline.

The focus of this book has been on the era of classical economics, broadly conceived, so as to include dissenters from the classical tradition, such as Sismondi, and to conclude with Karl Marx, the last major figure to write within the broad framework of the classical economists, though reaching very different conclusions from those of Smith, Ricardo, or John Stuart Mill. Modern reductionist attempts to show what the classical economists were "really" trying to do look small and cheap beside the monumental works of thinkers who were as guileless as any in the history of ideas — guileless not only in their work, but in their lives as well, with the notable exception of Karl Marx, who could be quite devious.[1]

Smith, Ricardo and John Stuart Mill were not men preoccupied with academic in-fighting or influence-mongering in the political arena. Though Ricardo and Mill served briefly in Parliament, they were essentially anti-politicians in a political institution, and their distaste for it was apparent. Ricardo voted consistently against his own self-interest and that of his class, and Mill a generation later refused to have anything to do with what is today called "constituent service" or with the cheap arts of campaigning. When Ricardo entered Parliament, he wrote to a friend:

I wish that I may never think the smiles of the great and
powerful a sufficient inducement to turn aside from the
straight path of honesty and the convictions of my own
mind.[2]

Perhaps the clearest indication of the integrity of the classical
economists was that Marx — who coined the term — never
accused Smith or Ricardo of class apologetics, or treated them as
anything other than thinkers whose ideas he disagreed with, even
though their policy conclusions were at the opposite pole from his
own.   Indeed, with Smith especially, even when Marx pointed
out what he regarded as errors, he also attempted to show that
those errors were "historically justified" as of the time they were
made, when Smith was pioneering in intellectually uncharted
territory.[3]   If the leading classical economists were not
paragons of virtue, they were remarkably close to it, at least for
those of us who have a constrained vision of human possibilities.
Certainly their intentions can seldom be faulted, even in the case
of Mill's *On Liberty*, a work with ugly implications, that is
revered in proportion to its being misunderstood.[4] Even Mill's
distortions of others' promising beginnings in the development of
a utility theory of value, a schedule concept of demand, and
aggregate income theory were honest misunderstandings and a
blindness deriving in part from his loyalty to Ricardo.

What does classical economics have to say to us today? Is its
analysis not already incorporated into the latest textbooks, with
the classical insights rendered into diagrams and equations, and
the classical errors and misstatements decently buried without
fanfare? Certainly one need not have read a word of Smith or
Ricardo in order to get an economics degree, tenure, or an
appointment to the Council of Economic Advisers. But if one is
still old-fashioned enough to want to be an educated individual,
then an understanding of how ideas evolve and how the dynamics
of polemics can drive both parties to untenable positions should

be part of that education. John Stuart Mill stands as a painful object lesson in how an honest, inquisitive, learned, and brilliant thinker could so grossly misunderstand the early pioneers in aggregate income theory and deliberately canvas the literature of socialism without any inkling of the writings, or even the existence, of someone whose lifespan overlapped Mill's for more than half a century, who was a fellow resident of London for decades, and who was the most famous socialist of all time — Karl Marx.

While free market economics is regarded by many today as an old conservative idea, it was in fact one of the most revolutionary concepts to emerge in the long history of ideas. For centuries, landmark intellectual figures from Plato to Machiavelli had discussed which principles wise thinkers might propose to guide personal, social, and political actions or which policies wise leaders might impose for the benefit of society in various ways. Now, for the first time, it was argued that — in the economy, at least — all of this was giving "a most unnecessary attention," in Adam Smith's words,[5] to things that could be sorted out better by vast numbers of individuals interacting with one another, and making their own mutual accommodations, than by those who presumed to guide them from above.

The idea of a spontaneously self-equilibrating system — the market economy — first developed by the physiocrats and later made part of the tradition of classical economics by Adam Smith, represented a radical departure, not only in analysis of causation but also in seeing a reduced role for political, intellectual, or other leaders as guides or controllers of the masses. Even today, many have not yet grasped the full implications of self-equilibrating interactions or have not been able to accept the humbling thought that their own presumably superior wisdom and virtue might be superfluous, if not damaging.

THE DYNAMICS OF CONTROVERSY

One of the painful lessons of the history of economic thought, and of the history of ideas in general, is that highly intelligent thinkers with good will can nevertheless talk past each other for years. This is quite aside from continuing disagreements on substantive issues, based on different readings of evidence and different assumptions about the world and about human nature. These latter conflicts of visions can last for centuries.[6] However, this does not make the history of ideas simply a spectacle of futility. It does, however, underscore the need for scrutinizing definitions and making implicit frameworks of assumptions explicit. There has clearly been progress in these matters over time. Increasingly more rigorous methods have kept economics from being just an arena for a clash of opinions. Any comparison of twentieth-century economics with eighteenth-century economics shows major progress in more precise thinking — helped by, though not identical with, a growing use of mathematics.

Has this made economics a science? That question is still as debatable today as it was in the days of classical economics. However, such things as the rise and fall of the Phillips Curve in the second half of the twentieth century suggests that progress has been real. Those attracted to the idea of a systematic trade-off between inflation and unemployment may have welcomed the initial empirical findings of the Phillips Curve as consonant with the Keynesian view of the economy, while those who were initially skeptical may have resisted because of a very different set of assumptions about how the economy works. But, whatever personal bias may have influenced these respective initial positions, what is crucial is that both sides recognized something higher than their own assumptions, biases, or ideologies as decisive. This intellectual progress was not simply a result of the happenstance that more or better data, or more sophisticated methods of analyzing data, are available now than in the days of classical economics. The data available in the nineteenth century were enough to get John Stuart Mill to admit that the food supply had increased faster than the population — and yet he continued to come up with verbal formulations to defend Malthusian overpopulation theory. For that matter, people outside the economics profession continue to defend it in the twenty-first century. But the fact that economics does not is one sign of the progress of the profession.

Mathematics has made its contribution to this process, not simply by facilitating more penetrating analyses or through the development of statistical techniques for dealing with data, but more fundamentally by constraining the amount of evasion made possible by the flexibility of words. When an assertion that $y = x^n$ is empirically refuted, there is little opportunity to evade that refutation as John Stuart Mill continued to verbally evade the empirical refutation of the Malthusian overpopulation theory. More important, the economics profession as a whole can abandon empirically discredited doctrines and move on to apply its mental resources to other things.

Not all controversies can be resolved empirically, however. When controversies envelop whole schools of thought, not only opposing theories, but whole concepts and incidental insights may be rejected along with the particular theories objected to. One of the recurring sources of confusion in economics has been a failure to distinguish concepts — the apparatus used in the expounding of theory — from the actual substance of the theories themselves. Much futile controversy surrounded such concepts as "no-rent land," which was wholly unessential to the classical theory of rent. "Measures of value" were likewise needlessly disputed as if they were theories of price, as Marxian "value" would be in a later era, despite being what Marx repeatedly called a "definition" or "concept"[7] and never a theory. The Keynesian "consumption function" was similarly a piece of apparatus through which a given set of Keynesian beliefs could be expressed, but which could also be used to express very different beliefs, as was done by Milton Friedman.[8]

If mathematics can help clarify ideas, polemics can obscure them. Virtually all Marxian writings were polemical, including the massive three volumes of *Capital*. What this has meant is that it is often nearly impossible to understand what Marx and Engels were writing without knowing what they were writing against. As the passing years and generations put more and more time between the controversies in question and the present, it becomes more and more obscure what Proudhon or Dühring or Bakunin said that caused Marx or Engels to say what they did *in reply*. The "dictatorship of the proletariat" is a classic example of a phrase whose meaning at the time was wholly different from what it has come to mean in the light of twentieth-century Communist dictatorships.

Marx and Engels were arguing against not only defenders of capitalism but also against many competing individuals and movements on the political left, including some who preferred a road to socialism that did not include class warfare and others who thought that government itself could and should be dispensed with after a revolution. The challenge to Marx and Engels was not simply to emphasize their disagreements with such political competitors but also to de-emphasize what has been aptly called an "inconveniently large expanse of common ground"[9] with their adversaries on the right, for Marx not only believed in a post-revolutionary government, he saw the desirable features of such a government as including universal suffrage and civil liberties — what people today loosely call democracy, and what at the time represented a wide area of agreement with nineteenth-century laissez-faire liberals.[10]

In Marx's time, using the phrase "the dictatorship of the proletariat" to describe the electoral dominance of the working class in a post-revolutionary society served the purpose of differentiating the Marxian product from that of both the anarchists and the classical liberals — substantively from the former and verbally from the latter. One of the painful ironies of history is that this convenient catch phrase would in the next century be seized upon by Lenin and his successors to justify a dictatorship in a tragically different sense.

The classical economists' controversies likewise led them to make statements that were both misleading and unnecessary for their own theories. Because classical economics began with

Adam Smith's attack on the concepts of wealth behind the mercantilists' desire to accumulate gold for the sake of national power, the whole classical tradition de-emphasized the role of gold or money in the economy in sweeping terms that were inconsistent with their many other statements acknowledging the substantive role that changing quantities of money can have on such real variables as output and employment. Similarly, the Ricardians' controversies with Sismondi, Malthus, and other critics of Say's Law led them to take positions that were unnecessarily rigid — and in fact more rigid than the position taken by Say himself after he began to acknowledge and incorporate into his own work the theories of aggregate income determination by Sismondi and Malthus.

The problems created by the polemics of the past illuminate not only those long-ago controversies but also the way controversies in general, including those of the present and future, carry the inherent danger of either or both sides reacting to the other by taking more rigid positions than required to defend their respective beliefs, and therefore introducing erroneous or misleading statements which make either reconciliation or — more important — the search for the truth more difficult or impossible to achieve.

IDEAS AND EVENTS

There is perhaps no more famous statement of the relationship between ideas and events by an economist than that of John Maynard Keynes that "the ideas of economists and political philosophers, both when they are right and when they are wrong, are more powerful than is commonly understood." He added:

> Practical men, who believe themselves to be quite exempt from any intellectual influences, are usually the slaves of some defunct economist. Madmen in

authority, who hear voices in the air, are distilling their frenzy from some academic scribbler of a few years back. I am sure the power of vested interests is vastly exaggerated compared with the gradual encroachment of ideas.[11]

Keynes' view of the relationship between ideas and historic events was quite different from that of Karl Marx or John Stuart Mill or many others inside and outside of economics.

Marx's views have been widely misunderstood to mean that people act on the basis of their own economic self-interest. On the contrary, the individual's subjective motivations are based on "tradition and upbringing," according to Marx,[12] and "the tradition of all the dead generations weighs like a nightmare on the brain of the living."[13] But the Marxian theory of history does not attempt to explain what happens by simply determining what particular individuals intend. In Engels' words, "what each individual wills is obstructed by everyone else and what emerges is something that no one willed." Theory attempts to predict results — what emerges — not intentions.

The Marxian theory of history sees the sources of subjectively felt values and imperatives as originating in the socioeconomic positions of the various individuals and the experiences deriving from these positions. Such experiences and ideas vary by class — and are therefore at variance with one another. In short, class struggle is inherent, not directly because of competing economic interests — which might well be reconciled in one way or another — but by irreconcilable differences in ultimate bedrock beliefs, values, and ideologies, based on the very different positions from which different classes experience and perceive the economic and social worlds. The periodic economic "crises" which Marx foresaw were then to become catalysts for a class struggle, which he assumed would end with the triumph of the proletariat.[14]

Marx's theory of history was in part a conscious reaction against the notion of social evolution being a result of "the general progress of the human mind," as so often proclaimed by John Stuart Mill. In Mill's words, "the order of human progression in all respects will mainly depend on the order of progression in the intellectual convictions of mankind, that is, on the law of the successive transformation of human opinions."[15] For Mill, the intellectual elite was the vanguard of progress, which was one reason for those elites to be released from the constraints of other people's opinions, even as the elite would then seek to guide that public opinion.

Marx's theory of history has often been misconstrued as one of economic motivations determining events, as exemplified by Charles E. Beard's theory that the Constitution of the United States was a result of the economic self-interests of those who wrote it. This was the kind of theory that Marx himself denounced in his day as "facile anecdote-mongering and the attribution of all great events to petty and mean causes."[16]

While Marx's real insight into the unfolding of history has been that external socioeconomic circumstances — and especially changes in those circumstances — explain much of what people do has been a contribution to our understanding of social phenomena, and an advance beyond "great man" theories of history or John Stuart Mill's theory, Marx's emphasis on circumstantial explanations of history can too easily become an over-emphasis. Different social groups can react very differently to the same physical, economic, or social surroundings because each group trails the long shadow of its own cultural legacy. When the children of Jewish and southern Italian immigrants to nineteenth-century America grew up in very similar economic circumstances in the same neighborhoods and sat side-by-side in the same school rooms, did their very different reactions and performances there[17] reflect their immediate circumstances or the very different cultures which had developed over the centuries before they were born into those cultures?

Another theory of the relationship between ideas and events has arisen from quarters more numerous, though perhaps not so distinguished, as Keynes, Marx, and Mill. This is the theory that ideas in general, or economic theories in particular, have been

responses to events in the real world — for example, that
Ricardian analysis was a response to issues arising in early
nineteenth-century England and that Keynesian economics was a
response to the Great Depression of the 1930s. These examples
may be striking but, aside from risking the *post hoc* fallacy, they
are remarkable for being so few in the centuries-long history of
economics.

When diametrically opposed theories arise during the same
era, are they each reflecting the same events? Conceivably they
might be different ways of trying to deal with the same reality but,
when a new idea arises alone, is there usually something in the
circumstances of the time that would have caused that idea to
arise when it did, rather than a generation or a century earlier or
later? Were falling objects more numerous or more socially
significant when Newton developed his law of gravity? The great
shift within nineteenth-century economics from a theory of price
determined by production costs to a theory of price determined by
consumer demand was not in response to changes in either
production costs or consumer demand. During the period of the
industrial revolution, the prevailing practice among the leading
economists was to hold technological change constant in their
analyses.

Even when the same idea occurs simultaneously and
independently to different people, is that evidence that there was
something about the events of the times which evoked that idea?
What in the mid-nineteenth century would have led Jevons and
Menger to independently develop a theory of marginal utility?

Simultaneous discoveries, whether in economics or in
science, may be more compatible with a very different
explanation — namely, that the progress of an intellectual
discipline is advanced more by its own internal pressures to
resolve the inevitable ambiguities and puzzles that arise in the
course of groping for truth and clarity. In other words, internal
intellectual agendas based on unfinished business in the
discipline, and their resulting controversies, concentrate efforts
that lead to discoveries.

That such internal developments are not wholly divorced

from the real world does not fit the events-cause-ideas theory, for the external connection might have originated a decade, a century, or a millennium earlier. The desire to fly, for example, goes back to ancient times, but it cannot explain why the Wright brothers succeeded in the early twentieth century, at a time when others around the world were also working on airplanes, many of which took off in the same era as the Wright brothers' flight. This would suggest that the internal development of science and technology had reached the point where the ages-old desire to fly was now within reach, and would have been soon fulfilled, even had the Wright brothers died prematurely.

In economics, the utility theory of value had a similarly long pedigree before it was gotten off the ground, as it were, by Jevons and Menger and became established parts of the framework of modern economic analysis. The utility theory of value was sufficiently widespread in earlier centuries to provoke Adam Smith to attempt to refute it. Indeed, Schumpeter traces "an unbroken line of development" of utility theory in continental Europe, even after Smith and Ricardo had substituted the labor theory of value in England.[18] That Jevons and Menger simultaneously found an acceptable way to make the utility theory of demand part of economics everywhere may have been a coincidence, but it was a well-prepared coincidence.

George J. Stigler aptly observed, "it is a sign of the maturity of a discipline that its main problems are not drawn from immediate, changing events." It is "neither popular economic problems nor heroic events" which have a great effect on the development of economic theory but rather "the set of internal values and pressures of the discipline." Because "imperfection is as inevitable in theory as it is in man," successive attempts to grapple with the imperfections of these theories move economic analysis forward, not external events, however momentous those events may be in themselves. Stigler said: "A war may ravage a continent or destroy a generation without posing new theoretical questions."[19]

THE DEVELOPMENT OF ECONOMICS

Whether the development of economics has been a result more of external influences or internal pressures, a question arises as to why some theories succeed in becoming part of the on-going body of economic analysis and others do not. This is especially puzzling when a theory that was vanquished in one era later emerges to succeed, and even become central and dominant, in another. Striking examples include the theory of equilibrium aggregate income, which failed to become part of the accepted body of economics after a long and bitter struggle in the early nineteenth century,[20] and yet became the reigning orthodoxy after Keynes' *General Theory* was published in 1936. Other examples include schedule concepts of demand and supply, and the utility theory of value.

Ignored pioneers, whose contributions later had to be made from scratch by other economists who had never heard of them, include not only rediscovered heroes like Augustin Cournot, but also people whose work remains as obscure as ever two centuries later, of whom Sismondi is perhaps the prime example.

J.A. Schumpeter's encyclopedic *History of Economic Analysis* observed: "The distinctive feature of Sismondi's analysis is that it is geared to an *explicit dynamic model in the modern sense of this phrase.*"[21] Yet, despite the algebraic growth model in Sismondi's *Richesse commerciale*, even Schumpeter did not include Sismondi among the pioneers in the application of mathematics to economics.[22] Sismondi's most striking achievement — his theory of equilibrium aggregate income at a time when Ricardo denied that there could even be such a theory,[23] — has gone almost completely unrecognized, in contrast to the fact that a similar achievement in the twentieth century made Keynes a landmark figure in the history of economics.

This is not to claim that Sismondi was another Keynes. He was not. But he was a precursor of Keynes, at least as much as Malthus, whom Keynes explicitly recognized as a predecessor. One of the many differences between Sismondi and Keynes is that Sismondi was an outsider to economics and, by the time he wrote his magnum opus in economics, *Nouveaux Principes d'économie politique*, in 1819 he was a much looser thinker than he had been when he wrote *Richesse commerciale* in 1803. That Sismondi wrote primarily in French was apparently not a major handicap in getting his work noticed by his English-speaking contemporaries, who published critiques of his work, but may have helped consign his writings to obscurity in later years, especially after John Stuart Mill essentially dismissed all equilibrium income theorists.

Even before he wrote *The General Theory*, Keynes was not someone who could be dismissed. The author of a massive treatise on monetary theory and a man with a flair for writing on many subjects, Keynes was in the center of economics and what he wrote had to be confronted. Moreover, there is simply no question that the substance of *The General Theory* was more rigorous and more compelling than that of the more loosely woven *Nouveaux Principes*, from which a theory could be extracted, but only with effort. Much the same could be said of Malthus' *Principles of Political Economy*, which was published a year after Sismondi's *Nouveaux Principes*, though its ideas had already been vetted in letters to Ricardo in earlier years,[24] so that Marx's cynical insinuation of plagiarism will not stand up under scrutiny.

Even by the standards of their times, the writings of Sismondi and Malthus did not come up to the level of systematic reasoning found in the writings of Ricardo, James Mill, or the young John Stuart Mill. In addition to the analytical or literary shortcomings in the writings of Sismondi and Malthus, as well as in the writings of some lesser known critics of Say's Law, they appeared on the stage as outsiders, seen as attacking economics itself, provoking fierce resistance publicly and disdain privately.[25] Yet the final consignment of their ideas to oblivion was essentially the work of one man, John Stuart Mill. There was no one in such a position to obliterate ideas from economics in the twentieth century.

Whatever role analytical sloppiness had in the failure of equilibrium aggregate income theory to get a foothold in economics in the nineteenth century, such sloppiness cannot provide a *general* explanation of ignored pioneers. One of the books published during the era of classical economics, Cournot's *Researches into the Mathematical Principles of the Theory of Wealth* in 1838, had a rigor and elegance far beyond anything written by the leading classical economists themselves, as well as offering substantively new analytical work that would not be performed by others for another century. The calculus and graphs in Cournot's book also make it seem like the work of a later century.

Drawing the now familiar graph of a demand curve, but with price and quantity axes the reverse of later convention, Cournot pointed out that the quantity demanded meant the quantity demanded per unit of time,[26] that the total revenue ("the total value of the quantity annually sold") is maximized at that quantity where its first derivative is zero,[27] that profit is maximized at the output where the first derivative of total revenue equals the first derivative of total cost, and said that cost curves were U-shaped.[28] Among other things, he also went into questions about what would later be called the elasticity of demand[29] — all this a decade before the first edition of John Stuart Mill's *Principles* was published. Yet Cournot was, if anything, even more completely ignored than Sismondi. Nearly forty years passed before his work was discovered by Jevons and Walras, and was then praised in the highest terms by Edgeworth and Alfred Marshall.[30] But, by then, Cournot was dead.

What Cournot and Sismondi, so different in many ways, had in common was that they both wrote within a framework unfamiliar to their contemporaries. They also both wrote in French but that would not have been a serious barrier to the predominantly English-speaking leading economists of their era.[31] Moreover, their economic writings made little impact in French-speaking countries as well, though Cournot was honored in France for his work as a mathematician.

These two extremes do not of course exhaust the possible varieties of intellectual innovation or the reasons for their acceptance or rejection. Some new analyses may simply arrive at the wrong place at the wrong time while others arrive just when everyone is most receptive to the new message. There is no way of knowing whether Keynes' *General Theory* would have been such an instant and runaway success had it arrived during the prosperity of the 1920s rather than during the Great Depression of the 1930s.

It may be tempting to say that new ideas should always be welcomed, or at least examined carefully. But resources of time and energy are not free goods available in unlimited abundance. Nor can any discipline be prepared to tear down its whole framework at a moment's notice and try reconstructing another one on a different foundation. George Stigler has suggested that there is an optimum rate of innovation, and that higher rates of innovation exceed the profession's capacity to sort out the good theories from the bad, make the improvements necessary in even the best new theories and salvage whatever insights may be found in other theories that should be discarded.[32] There may also be an optimum amount of newness, in the sense that theories which deviate too far from existing accepted doctrines in either substance or presentation raise barriers to their own acceptance.

As regards the history of ideas in general, Thomas Kuhn's work argues that there is a fundamental difference between a developed scientific field and a less developed one. In the early stages of a science "men confronting the same particular phenomena" might "describe and interpret them in different ways." But, after a science becomes mature, these divergences, according to Kuhn, "disappear to a very considerable extent and then apparently once and for all."[33] Oxidation theories and phlogiston theories might co-exist for a while in chemistry but not indefinitely, while opposing political, social, and moral theories can co-exist for centuries. The history of economics has had enough discarded theories, from those of the mercantilists to the labor theory of value to the Phillips Curve, to at least be placed closer to the scientific end of the spectrum in the history of ideas.

NOTES

Social Philosophy of Classical Economists

1. Karl Marx, *Critique of Political Economy* (Chicago: Charles H. Kerr & Co., 1904), p. 56.
2. Karl Marx, *Capital* (Chicago: Charles H. Kerr & Co., 1906), Vol. I, p. 93n.
3. Karl Marx, *Theories of Surplus Value: Selections* (New York: International Publishers, 1952), p. 202.
4. See Thomas Sowell, "Marx's *Capital* After One Hundred Years," *Canadian Journal of Economics and Political Science*, February 1967, pp. 66–67.
5. John Maynard Keynes, *The General Theory of Employment, Interest and Money* (New York: Harcourt, Brace & Co., 1936), pp. 3n, 4–22.
6. J. R. Hicks, "Mr. Keynes and the Classics," *Econometrica*, April 1937, p. 147.
7. John Maynard Keynes, *The General Theory*, pp. 29, 289, 296.
8. For example, Henry Thornton, *An Enquiry into the Nature and Effects of the Paper Credit of Great Britain*, ed. F. A. v. Hayek (New York: Augustus M. Kelley, 1965), pp. 96–97, 232–233; David Ricardo, *The Works and Correspondence of David Ricardo*, edited by Piero Sraffa, Vol. III (Cambridge: Cambridge University Press, 1951), p. 90; Alfred Marshall, *Official Papers* (London: Macmillan & Co., 1926), pp. 267–268; Irving Fisher, *The Purchasing Power of Money* (New York: Augustus M. Kelley, 1963), pp. 159–160.
9. Ricardo himself credited Malthus and West with priority. See David Ricardo, *The Works and Correspondence of David Ricardo*, Vol. I: *Principles of Political Economy and Taxation* (Cambridge: Cambridge University Press, 1951), p. 5.
10. As suggested in Robert L. Heilbroner, *The Worldly Philosophers* (New York: Simon & Schuster, 1961), p. 42.
11. Sir James Steuart, *The Works: Political, Metaphysical &*

Chronological of Sir James Steuart (London: T. Cadell and W. Davis, 1805 [originally 1767]), Vol. I, pp. 310–312.

12. Ibid., pp. 313–314.

13. Ibid., pp. 326–327.

14. Thomas Mun, *England's Treasure by Forraign Trade* (New York: Augustus M. Kelley, 1965 [originally 1664]), p. 21.

15. Sir James Steuart, *Works*, Vol. I, p. 347. See also p. 360.

16. Thomas Mun, *England's Treasure by Forraign Trade*, p. 5.

17. Ibid., p. 7.

18. Sir James Steuart, *Works*, Vol. I, p. 337.

19. Adam Smith, *An Inquiry into the Nature and Causes of the Wealth of Nations* (New York: Modern Library, 1937), p. 79.

20. John Stuart Mill, "Speech on the British Constitution," *Collected Works of John Stuart Mill,* Vol. XXVI: *Journals and Debating Speeches*, edited by John M. Robson (Toronto: University of Toronto Press, 1988), p. 373.

21. Adam Smith, *The Wealth of Nations*, pp. lx, 321, 419.

22. Ibid., p. 238.

23. Ibid., p. 415; David Ricardo, *The Works and Correspondence of David Ricardo*, Vol. I, pp. 133–134; John Stuart Mill, *Principles of Political Economy*, ed. W. J. Ashley (London: Longmans, Green and Co., 1909), pp. 580–581. This edition of Mill's *Principles* is cited hereafter as "Ashley edition." In the variorum edition published by the University of Toronto Press, cited hereafter as "Toronto edition," the *Principles* constitute volumes II and III of Mill's *Collected Works*, with pages numbered consecutively through both volumes, so that specifying the particular volume is unnecessary. The corresponding passage in this edition is therefore John Stuart Mill, *Principles of Political Economy* (Toronto: University of Toronto Press, 1965), pp. 592–593.

24. Adam Smith, *The Wealth of Nations*, p. 325.

25. Ibid., p. 559.
26. Ibid., p. 900.
27. Ibid., p. 582.
28. James Mill quoted in J.A. Hobson, *Imperialism* (Ann Arbor: University of Michigan Press, 1965), p. 51.
29. David Ricardo, *The Works and Correspondence of David Ricardo*, Vol. I, Chapter XXV.
30. Adam Smith, *The Wealth of Nations*, pp. 80–81.
31. Ibid., p. 365.
32. Ibid., p. 365.
33. David Ricardo, *The Works and Correspondence of David Ricardo*, Vol. V (Cambridge: Cambridge University Press, 1952), p. 483.
34. See Michael St. John Packe, *The Life of John Stuart Mill* (New York: Macmillan Co., 1954), pp. 423–427.
35. John Stuart Mill, *Principles of Political Economy*, Ashley edition, p. 251; Toronto edition, p. 247.
36. Ibid., Ashley edition, p. 253; Toronto edition, p. 249.
37. John E. Cairnes, *The Slave Power* (New York: Harper & Row, 1969 [originally 1862]), pp. 55–56.
38. Ibid., pp. 62, 180.
39. Ibid., pp. 81–83, 143–144, 147–148, 176–177.
40. Ironically, the *analytic* approach of the mercantilists has been revived in the theories and policies of modern groups with radically different social philosophies. See Thomas Sowell, "Economics and Black People," *Review of Black Political Economy*, Winter-Spring 1971, pp. 14–16.
41. Adam Smith, *The Wealth of Nations*, p. 128; see also pp. 249–250, 402–403, 429, 438, 579.
42. Ibid., p. 460.
43. Ibid., p. 250.
44. Ibid., p. 128.
45. "It is the business of a statesman to judge of the expediency of different schemes of economy, and by degrees to model the minds of his subjects so as to induce them, from the

allurement of private interest, to cooperate in the execution of his plan" (Sir James Steuart, *Works*, Vol. I, p. 4); ". . . nothing is impossible to an able statesman" (p. 15); the statesman is "constantly awake" on economic matters (p. 73), as the "great genius of Mr. de Colbert" and the "genius of Mr. Law" show them to be "born statesmen" (p. 88).

46. Adam Smith, *The Wealth of Nations*, p. 435; see also p. 329.
47. Loc. cit.
48. Ibid., pp. 249, 250.
49. Ibid., p. 247.
50. Ibid., p. 49.
51. John Stuart Mill, *Principles of Political Economy*, Ashley edition, p. 818; Toronto edition, pp. 819–820.
52. Ibid., Ashley edition, p. 422; Toronto edition, p. 416.
53. Ibid., Ashley edition, p. 429; Toronto edition, p. 423.
54. Ibid., Ashley edition, p. 231; Toronto edition, p. 228.
55. Ibid., Ashley edition, p. 748; Toronto edition, p. 754.
56. Adam Smith, *The Wealth of Nations*, p. 14.
57. Adam Smith, *The Theory of Moral Sentiments,* Part II, Section II, Chapter VI (Indianapolis: Liberty Classics, 1976), p. 98.
58. Ibid., pp. 97–98.
59. Adam Smith, *The Wealth of Nations*, p. 423.
60. Ibid., p. 594.
61. Ibid., p. 308.
62. Ibid., pp. 247–248; David Ricardo, *The Works and Correspondence of David Ricardo*, Vol. I, pp. 83, 125, 335–336, 337.
63. David Ricardo, *The Works and Correspondence of David Ricardo*, Vol. I, pp. 27, 35, 110, 115, 118, 132, 159, 205, 214, 215, 226, 289, 296, 323, 333, 404n, 411.
64. John Stuart Mill, *Principles of Political Economy*, Ashley edition, p. 208; Toronto edition, p. 207.
65. Jean-Baptiste Say, *A Treatise on Political Economy,*

translated by Clement C. Biddle (Philadelphia: Grigg & Elliot, 1834), p. liii.

66. John Stuart Mill, "Miss Martineau's Summary of Political Economy," *Monthly Repository*, May 1834, pp. 318–322. Reprinted in John Stuart Mill, *Collected Works of John Stuart Mill*, Vol. IV: *Essays on Economics and Society* (Toronto: University of Toronto Press, 1967), pp. 225–228.

67. Karl Marx and Frederick Engels, *Selected Correspondence* (New York: International Publishers, 1942), p. 57; Karl Marx, *Capital*, Vol. I, pp. 17–18.

68. John Stuart Mill, *Principles of Political Economy*, Ashley edition, p. 235; Toronto edition, p. 232.

69. Adam Smith, *The Wealth of Nations*, p. 61.

70. Ibid., p. 14.

71. Ibid., p. 574.

72. Ibid., p. 596.

73. Ibid., pp. 734, 737–740.

74. David Ricardo, *The Works and Correspondence of David Ricardo*, Vol. I, pp. 249–250, 385.

75. John Stuart Mill, *Principles of Political Economy*, Book II, Chapter IV, both Ashley and Toronto editions.

76. See, for example, Jacob Viner, "Adam Smith and Laissez-Faire," *Journal of Political Economy*, April 1927, pp. 198–232.

77. Adam Smith, *The Wealth of Nations*, p. 683.

78. Ibid., p. 794.

79. Ibid., p. 777.

80. John Stuart Mill, *Principles of Political Economy*, Ashley edition, pp. 381–383; Toronto edition, pp. 376–378.

81. Adam Smith, *The Wealth of Nations*, p. 438.

82. John Stuart Mill, *Principles of Political Economy*, Ashley edition, p. 795; Toronto edition, p. 799.

83. Ibid., Ashley edition, p. 950; Toronto edition, p. 945.

84. Ibid., Ashley edition, p. 947; Toronto edition, p. 941.

85. Ibid., Ashley edition, p. 945; Toronto edition, pp. 939–940.

86. Ibid., Ashley edition, p. 961; Toronto edition, p. 955.
87. Ibid., Ashley edition, p. 956; Toronto edition, p. 950.
88. Ibid., Ashley edition, p. 949; Toronto edition, p. 943.
89. David Ricardo, *The Works and Correspondence of David Ricardo*, Vol. VIII (Cambridge: Cambridge University Press, 1952), p. 133.
90. Ibid., p. 49.
91. Adam Smith, *The Wealth of Nations*, pp. 581–582.
92. James Mill, *Commerce Defended* (London: C. & R. Baldwin, 1808), p.128.
93. Ibid., p. 130.
94. John Stuart Mill, "Speech on the British Constitution," *Collected Works of John Stuart Mill*, Vol. XXVI, p. 373.
95. Jean-Baptiste Say, *Œuvres diverses de J.-B. Say* (Paris: Guillaumin et Cie, 1848), p. 397.
96. Adam Smith, *The Wealth of Nations*, p. 872.
97. Ibid., p. 878.
98. Loc. cit.
99. David Ricardo, *The Works and Correspondence of David Ricardo*, Vol. IX (Cambridge: Cambridge University Press, 1952), p. 180.
100. See Adam Smith, *The Wealth of Nations*, pp. 738–739; Alexander Bain, *James Mill* (London: Longmans, Green, and Co., 1882), p. 49; Michael St. John Packe, *The Life of John Stuart Mill*, p. 424.
101. Adam Smith, *The Wealth of Nations*, p. 728.
102. Ibid., pp. 717–720.
103. Francis W. Hirst, *Adam Smith* (New York: Macmillan Co., 1904), pp. 115–116; John Rae, *The Life of Adam Smith* (London: Macmillan & Co., 1895), pp. 167–168, 170–171.
104. "A Memoir of David Ricardo" [by one of his brothers], David Ricardo, *The Works and Correspondence of David Ricardo*, Vol. X (Cambridge: Cambridge University Press, 1955), p. 13.
105. John Rae, *The Life of Adam Smith*, p. 437.

106. David Ricardo, *The Works and Correspondence of David Ricardo*, Vol. VI, p. 122; ibid., Vol. X, pp. 113, 118, 131, 133.

107. F. A. v. Hayek, "Introduction," Henry Thornton, *Paper Credit of Great Britain*, p. 23.

108. Ibid., p. 25.

109. Richard Whately, *Introductory Lectures on Political Economy*, second edition (London: B. Fellowes, 1832), p. 2.

110. Michael St. John Packe, *The Life of John Stuart Mill*, p. 484.

111. Quoted in Jacob Viner, "The Economist in History," *American Economic Review*, May 1963, p. 13.

112. Adam Smith, *The Wealth of Nations*, pp. 66–67.

113. Graham Wallas, *The Life of Francis Place* (New York: Burt Franklin, 1951), Chapter VIII.

114. Ibid., pp. 206–207.

115. David Ricardo, *The Works and Correspondence of David Ricardo*, Vol. VIII, p. 316.

116. Graham Wallas, *The Life of Francis Place*, p. 99.

117. Michael St. John Packe, *The Life of John Stuart Mill*, pp. 57–58.

118. Mark Blaug, *Ricardian Economics* (New Haven: Yale University Press, 1958), p. 196.

119. Marian Bowley, *Nassau Senior and Classical Economics* (London: George Allen & Unwin, 1937), Part II.

120. Élie Halévy, *The Growth of Philosophic Radicalism* (New York: Kelley & Millman, no date), Part III.

121. Graham Wallas, *The Life of Francis Place*, p. 161.

122. J.A. Schumpeter, *History of Economic Analysis* (New York: Oxford University Press, 1951), p. 402.

123. David Ricardo, *The Works and Correspondence of David Ricardo*, Vol. I, p. 108.

124. Thomas Sowell, *Say's Law: An Historical Analysis* (Princeton: Princeton University Press, 1972), pp. 20,

126–127.
125. See Max Lerner, "Introduction," Adam Smith, *The Wealth of Nations*, pp. ix–x.
126. David Ricardo, *The Works and Correspondence of David Ricardo*, Vol. V, pp. 467–468.
127. Ibid., Vol. X, p. 278.
128. John Stuart Mill, *Principles of Political Economy*, Ashley edition, pp. 211–217; Toronto edition, pp. 210–214.
129. John Rae, *The Life of Adam Smith,* pp. 26–29.
130. Ibid., pp. 26, 208.

Classical Macroeconomics

1. Adam Smith, *An Inquiry into the Nature and Causes of the Wealth of Nations* (New York: Modern Library, 1937).
2. David Ricardo, *The Works and Correspondence of David Ricardo*, edited by Piero Sraffa, Vol. I: *Principles of Political Economy and Taxation* (Cambridge: Cambridge University Press, 1951), p. 5.
3. Adam Smith, *The Wealth of Nations*, p. 59.
4. Jean-Baptiste Say, *A Treatise on Political Economy*, translated by Clement C. Biddle (Philadelphia: Grigg & Elliott, 1834), p. xxxvii; James Mill, *Commerce Defended* (London: C. & R. Baldwin, 1808), p. 76n; Adam Smith, *The Wealth of Nations*, p. 643.
5. Pierre François Joachim Henri Le Mercier de la Rivière, *L'Ordre naturel et essential des sociétés politiques* (London: Jean Nourse, 1767), Vol. II, p. 249.
6. Ibid., p. 337.
7. Ibid., pp. 262–264.
8. Ibid., p. 262.
9. Ibid., p. 264.
10. Ibid., p. 258.
11. Ibid., p. 296.

12. Ibid., p. 291.
13. Ibid., p. 140.
14. Ibid., p. 272.
15. Ibid., pp. 138, 142, 250.
16. Ibid., p. 250.
17. Ibid., pp. 138, 271.
18. Ibid., pp. 138–139.
19. Jean-Baptiste Say, *A Treatise on Political Economy*, p. xxxvii.
20. Jean-Baptiste Say, *Traité d'économie politique* (Paris: Deterville, 1803), Vol. II, pp. 358–359; James Mill, *Commerce Defended*, p. 76n.
21. Joseph J. Spengler, "The Physiocrats and Say's Law of Markets," *Essays in Economic Thought*, ed. J. J. Spengler and W. R. Allen (Chicago: Rand McNally & Co., 1960), pp. 161–214; Ronald L. Meek, *The Economics of Physiocracy* (Cambridge: Harvard University Press, 1963).
22. Jean-Baptiste Say's mentor, DuPont de Nemours, reminded Say how much of the latter's own analysis derived from the physiocrats. Jean-Baptiste Say, *Œuvres diverses de J.-B. Say* (Paris: Guillaumin et Cie, 1848), p. 365.
23. Adam Smith, *The Wealth of Nations*, p. 321.
24. Ibid., p. 323.
25. Ibid., p. 407.
26. Loc. cit.
27. Loc. cit.
28. James Mill, *Commerce Defended*, p. 81.
29. Ibid., p. 83; Adam Smith, *The Wealth of Nations*, pp. 321–322.
30. Adam Smith, *The Wealth of Nations*, p. 322; Jean-Baptiste Say, *Traité d'économie politique*, 1803 edition, Vol. II, p. 177n.
31. John Stuart Mill, *Principles of Political Economy*, Toronto edition, p. 573; Ashley edition, p. 560.
32. James Mill, *Elements of Political Economy*, third edition,

(London: Henry G. Bohn, 1844), pp. 228, 231, 237, 241; John Stuart Mill, *Principles of Political Economy*, Toronto edition, pp. 572–573; Ashley edition, pp. 558–559; John Stuart Mill, *Collected Works*, Vol. IV: *Essays on Economics and Society*, edited by J.M. Robson (Toronto: University of Toronto Press, 1967), pp. 17–18, 42.

33. James Mill argued that "annual purchases and sales" will "always balance" in his *Commerce Defended*, p. 82; J.R. McCulloch declared that there cannot "be any *selling* without an equal *buying*" (*Edinburgh Review*, March 1821, p. 108); Robert Torrens regarded supply and demand as "convertible" terms (*Edinburgh Review*, October 1819, p. 470).

34. Adam Smith, *The Wealth of Nations*, p. 322; [James Mill], "Lord Lauderdale on Public Wealth," *The Literary Journal*, July 1804, p. 12; James Mill, *Commerce Defended*, pp. 70, 71, 74, 78.

35. Jean-Baptiste Say, *Traité d'économie politique*, 1803 edition, Vol. II, p. 178; David Ricardo, *The Works and Correspondence of David Ricardo*, Vol. VIII, p. 277; ibid., Vol. II, p. 306; Robert Torrens, *An Essay on the Production of Wealth* (London: Longman, Hurst, Rees, Orme, and Brown, 1821), pp. 391, 392, 396; John Ramsey McCulloch, *Principles of Political Economy*, fifth edition (Edinburgh: Adam and Charles Black, 1864), p. 145; James Mill, *Commerce Defended*, p. 85; James Mill, *Elements of Political Economy*, pp. 234–235, 240, 241; Harriet Martineau, *The Moral of Many Fables* (London: Charles Fox, 1834), p. 128.

36. According to Malthus, the secular growth of the economy "is absolutely unlimited" (letter in David Ricardo, *The Works and Correspondence of David Ricardo*, Vol. VI, p. 318). Despite his attack on Say's Law, "the question of a glut is exclusively whether it may be general as well as particular and not whether it may be permanent as well as

temporary." T.R. Malthus, *Definitions in Political Economy* (London: John Murray, 1827), p. 62. Sismondi likewise had a theory of short-run aggregate disequilibrium, but denied secular stagnation. According to Sismondi, the "natural path of nations" is "the progressive increase of their prosperity, the increase and consequence of their demand for new products and of the means of paying for them." J.C.L. Simonde de Sismondi, *Nouveaux Principes d'économie politique*, third edition (Geneva-Paris: Edition Jeheber, 1953), Vol. II, p. 308. Similar ideas are found in other critics of Say's Law. See James Maitland, 8th Earl of Lauderdale, *An Inquiry into the Nature and Origin of Public Wealth* (London: T. Cadell and W. Davies, 1805 [originally 1767], p. 229; Thomas Chalmers, *On Political Economy* (Glasgow: William Collins, 1832), pp. 96, 104–105,158.

37. J.C.L. Simonde de Sismondi, *Nouveaux Principes d'économie politique*, Vol. I, p. 118; James Maitland, 8th Earl of Lauderdale, *Nature and Origin of Public Wealth*, pp. 3–4, 212; Thomas Chalmers, *On Political Economy*, p. 158.

38. J.C.L. Simonde de Sismondi, *Nouveaux Principes d'économie politique*, Vol. I, pp. 71–75.

39. Ibid., p. 110.

40. Ibid., pp. 250–251.

41. T.R. Malthus, letter to Ricardo, David Ricardo, *The Works and Correspondence of David Ricardo*, Vol. IX, p. 20.

42. Robert L. Heilbroner, *The Worldly Philosophers*, third edition (New York: Simon & Schuster, 1967), p. 91.

43. John Stuart Mill, *Principles of Political Economy*, Toronto edition, p. 573; Ashley edition, p. 559.

44. David Ricardo, *The Works and Correspondence of David Ricardo*, Vol. II, p. 306.

45. Ibid., Vol. VIII, p. 277.

46. [J.R. McCulloch,] "The Opinions of Messrs. SAY,

SISMONDI, and MALTHUS on the Effects of Machinery, and Accumulation, Stated and Examined," *Edinburgh Review*, March 1821, pp. 106–107.

47. J.C.L. Simonde de Sismondi, *Nouveaux Principes d'économie politique*, Vol. II, p. 253.

48. David Ricardo, *The Works and Correspondence of David Ricardo*, Vol. I, pp. 382–383; ibid., Vol. VI, p. 109.

49. J.C.L. Simonde de Sismondi, *Études sur l'économie politique* (Paris: Treuttel et Würtz, 1838), Vol. II, p. 381.

50. See note 37, for examples.

51. T.R. Malthus, letter to Ricardo, David Ricardo, *The Works and Correspondence of David Ricardo*, Vol. VI, p. 21.

52. J.C.L. Simonde [de Sismondi], *De la Richesse commerciale* (Geneva: J. J. Paschoud, 1803), Vol. I, pp. 99–108.

53. [Robert Torrens,] "Mr. Owen's Plans for Relieving the National Distress," *Edinburgh Review*, October 1819, p. 473. Since there has been some controversy over the identity of the author of this anonymous article, the reasons for believing that it was Robert Torrens are discussed in my *Say's Law: An Historical Analysis* (Princeton: Princeton University Press, 1972), p. 11n.

54. J.R. McCulloch, *Principles of Political Economy*, fifth edition, p. 149.

55. David Ricardo, *The Works and Correspondence of David Ricardo*, Vol. II, p. 390.

56. J.R. McCulloch, *Principles of Political Economy*, p. 144.

57. Ibid., p. 145; John Stuart Mill, *Principles of Political Economy*, Toronto edition, p. 575; Ashley edition, p. 561.

58. John Stuart Mill, *Collected Works*, Vol. IV, p. 17.

59. J.R. McCulloch, *Principles of Political Economy*, p. 145.

60. James Mill, *Elements of Political Economy*, p. 145.

61. [Samuel Bailey,] *An Inquiry into Those Principles Respecting the Nature of Demand and the Necessity of Consumption Lately Advocated by Mr. Malthus* (London: R. Hunter, 1821). Bailey's authorship of this anonymous

pamphlet is indicated in my "Samuel Bailey Revisited," *Economica*, November 1970, pp. 402–408.

62. T.R. Malthus, *Definitions in Political Economy*, pp. 62–63.
63. See, for example, Don Patinkin, *Money, Interest and Prices*, second edition (New York: Harper & Row, 1965), p. 364; Mark Blaug, *Economic Theory in Retrospect* (Homewood: Richard D. Irwin, 1962), p. 140; Mark Blaug, *Ricardian Economics* (New Haven: Yale University Press, 1958), p. 93.
64. T.R. Malthus, *Definitions in Political Economy*, p. 62.
65. David Ricardo, *The Works and Correspondence of David Ricardo*, Vol. IX, pp. 15, 131.
66. Jean-Baptiste Say, *Œuvres diverses de J.-B. Say*, p. 505.
67. See J.C.L. Simonde de Sismondi, *Political Economy and the Philosophy of Government* (London: John Chapman, 1847), p. 449.
68. Jean-Baptiste Say, *Traité d'économie politique*, fifth edition (Paris: Chez Rapilly, 1826), Vol. I, pp. 194–195.
69. Ibid., p. 195.
70. Jean-Baptiste Say, *Cours complet d'économie politique pratique*, second edition, Vol. I (Paris: Guillaumin, Libraire, 1840), Part III, Chapter III.
71. ". . . products in general can be multiplied and purchased by one another until a limit which no one knows precisely how to determine, and which depends on the local circumstances of each country; beyond that limit, certain products become too expensive for the utility which they have to indemnify their consumers for what is required to obtain them." ibid., pp. 346–347.
72. John Stuart Mill, *Principles of Political Economy*, Toronto edition, pp. 574–576; Ashley edition, pp. 560–562; John Stuart Mill, *Collected Works*, Vol. IV, pp. 16–17.
73. John Stuart Mill, *Principles of Political Economy*, Toronto edition, pp. 571–572; Ashley edition, pp. 557–558; John Stuart Mill, *Collected Works*, Vol. IV, pp. 16–17.

74. John Stuart Mill, *Essays on Some Unsettled Questions of Political Economy* (London: John W. Parker, 1844), p. 69.
75. John Stuart Mill, "War Expenditure," *Collected Works*, Vol. IV, p. 16.
76. John Stuart Mill, *Essays on Some Unsettled Questions in Political Economy*, p. 70.
77. John Stuart Mill, *Principles of Political Economy*, Toronto edition, p. 574; Ashley edition, p. 561.
78. Jean-Baptiste Say, *Letters to Thomas Robert Malthus* (London: George Hardings Bookshop, Ltd., 1936 [originally London, 1821]), pp. 45n–46n; Robert Torrens, *An Essay on the Production of Wealth*, pp. 421–422; Adam Smith, *The Wealth of Nations*, p. 407; George Poulett Scrope; *Principles of Political Economy* (London: Longman, Rees, Orme, Brown, Green & Longman, 1833), pp. 214–215.
79. John Stuart Mill, *Principles of Political Economy*, Toronto edition, p. 747; Ashley edition, p. 740.
80. James Maitland, 8th Earl of Lauderdale, *Nature and Origin of Public Wealth*, pp. 227–228; J.C.L. Simonde de Sismondi, *Nouveaux Principes d'économie politique*, Vol. I, pp. 247–248. This is more implicit in T.R. Malthus, *Principles of Political Economy*, second edition (New York: Augustus M. Kelley, 1951 [originally 1836]), pp. 328, 351–352; Thomas Chalmers, *On Political Economy*, p. 136.
81. J.C.L. Simonde de Sismondi, *Nouveaux Principes d'économie politique*, Vol. I, p. 248.
82. David Ricardo, *The Works and Correspondence of David Ricardo*, Vol. II, p. 338.
83. Jean-Baptiste Say, *A Treatise on Political Economy*, p. 143; James Mill, *Commerce Defended*, p. 88.
84. The Earl of Lauderdale, *Three Letters to the Duke of Wellington* (London: John Murray, 1829), p. 134; J.C.L. Simonde de Sismondi, *Nouveaux Principes d'économie*

politique, Vol. I, pp. 328–329; ibid., Vol. II, pp. 193, 308.

85. [James Mill,] "Lord Lauderdale on Public Wealth," *The Literary Journal*, Vol. VI, No. 1 (July 1804), p. 14.

86. [J.R. McCulloch,] "The Opinions of Messrs. SAY, SISMONDI, and MALTHUS on the Effects of Machinery, and Accumulation, Stated and Examined," *Edinburgh Review*, March 1821, p. 108.

87. James Mill, *Commerce Defended*, p. 82.

88. John Stuart Mill, "War Expenditure," *Collected Works*, Vol. IV, pp. 15–16; John Stuart Mill, *Essays on Some Unsettled Questions of Political Economy*, p. 69. To Say, the very definition of "production" or of "product" included sale at cost-covering prices. See Jean-Baptiste Say, *Traité d'économie politique*, fifth edition, Vol. I, p. 195; Jean-Baptiste Say, *Cours complet d'économie politique pratique*, second edition, pp. 347–348; Jean-Baptiste Say, *Œuvres diverses de J.-B. Say*, p. 513.

89. Ricardo's preoccupation with an "invariable measure of value" was an attempt to analyze a change in the relative value of goods in such a way as to discover which one had "really" changed—that is, where the change had *originated* in some change of production cost (David Ricardo, *The Works and Correspondence of David Ricardo*, Vol. I, pp. 17–18). Malthus approached monetary theory in the same way: money supply changes were not an "original cause" or the "mainspring" of the real phenomena (*Edinburgh Review*, February 1811, pp. 343, 359), though they might be part of the "necessary consequences" of changes in real variables (*Definitions in Political Economy*, p. 66).

90. See the first essay, "Social Philosophy of Classical Economists."

91. Adam Smith, *The Wealth of Nations*, pp. 398–399; David Ricardo, *The Works and Correspondence of David Ricardo*, Vol. III, p. 145; John Stuart Mill, *Principles of Political Economy*, Toronto edition, pp. 4–5, 7, 71–72,

505–506, 592; Ashley edition, pp. 2–3, 5–6, 72–73, 487–488, 579.

92. Adam Smith, *The Wealth of Nations*, pp. 334, 335; David Ricardo, *The Works and Correspondence of David Ricardo*, Vol. III, pp. 273, 286; John Stuart Mill, *Principles of Political Economy*, Toronto edition, pp. 508–509; Ashley edition, pp. 489–490.

93. Adam Smith, *The Wealth of Nations*, p. 407.

94. Adam Smith, *The Wealth of Nations*, p. 337; David Ricardo, *The Works and Correspondence of David Ricardo*, Vol. I, pp. 363–364; ibid., Vol. III, pp. 25–26, 89, 90, 91, 92, 137, 143, 150, 341, 374, 375, 376; John Stuart Mill, *Principles of Political Economy*, Toronto edition, p. 655; Ashley edition, p. 645; John Stuart Mill, *Collected Works*, Vol. IV, p. 98.

95. Adam Smith, *The Wealth of Nations*, pp. 336, 339; David Ricardo, *The Works and Correspondence of David Ricardo*, Vol. I, p. 363; ibid., Vol. III, pp. 25–26, 143, 150, 374–375; ibid., Vol. VI, pp. 94–95, 103, 104, 108, 110; ibid., Vol. VII, p. 197; John Stuart Mill, *Collected Works*, Vol. IV, pp. 102, 300–302.

96. Jean-Baptiste Say, "Catechism of Political Economy," reprinted in Kelley edition of *Letters to Mr. Malthus* (New York: Augustus M. Kelley, 1967), p. 104.

97. Jean-Baptiste Say, *A Treatise on Political Economy*, p. 138.

98. J.R. McCulloch, *Principles of Political Economy*, fifth edition, p. 157.

99. J.C.L. Simonde de Sismondi, *Nouveaux Principes d'économie politique*, Vol. I, p. 278; idem., *Political Economy* (New York: Augustus M. Kelley, 1966), p. 79. This reprint of an encyclopedia article by Sismondi should not be confused with *Political Economy and the Philosophy of Government* cited elsewhere.

100. J.C.L. Simonde de Sismondi, *Nouveaux Principes d'économie politique*, Vol. II, p. 2. See also J.C.L. Simonde

[de Sismondi], *Richesse commerciale*, Vol. I, p. 33n.

101. Thomas Chalmers, *On Political Economy*, p. 16.
102. J.C.L. Simonde de Sismondi, *Nouveaux Principes d'économie politique*, Vol. I, p. 118.
103. James Maitland, 8th Earl of Lauderdale, *Nature and Origin of Public Wealth*, p. 212.
104. Thomas Chalmers, *On Political Economy*, p. 158.
105. Thomas Robert Malthus, *Principles of Political Economy*, second edition, p. 324n; T.R. Malthus, *Definitions in Political Economy*, pp. 54, 60n.
106. Adam Smith, *The Wealth of Nations*, p. 407; Jean-Baptiste Say, *Letters to Thomas Robert Malthus*, pp. 45n–46n; J.C.L. Simonde de Sismondi, *Nouveaux Principes d'économie politique*, Vol. II, pp. 83, 84.
107. Thomas Chalmers, *On Political Economy*, pp. 184–185.
108. David Hume, "Of Interest," *Writings on Economics*, ed. Eugen Rotwein (Madison: University of Wisconsin Press, 1970), pp. 47, 51, 56, 57; Adam Smith, *The Wealth of Nations*, p. 337; David Ricardo, *The Works and Correspondence of David Ricardo*, Vol. I, pp. 363–364; ibid., Vol. III, pp. 25–26, 89, 90, 91, 92, 137, 143, 150, 341, 374–375, 376; John Stuart Mill, *Collected Works*, Vol. IV, p. 98.
109. David Hume, *Writings on Economics*, p. 57; David Ricardo, *The Works and Correspondence of David Ricardo*, Vol. I, pp. 297–298; John Stuart Mill, *Collected Works*, Vol. IV, p. 97; John Stuart Mill, *Principles of Political Economy*, Toronto edition, pp. 655–656, 657, 678n–679n; Ashley edition, pp. 646, 647, 670n.
110. John Stuart Mill, *Collected Works*, Vol. IV, pp. 189, 190, 197; Henry Thornton, *An Enquiry into the Nature and Effects of the Paper Credit of Great Britain*, ed. F. A. v. Hayek (New York: Augustus Kelley, 1965), pp. 236, 237, 238, 239, 250.
111. David Hume, *Writings on Economics*, pp. 37, 38, 40,

91–92, 93–94; Adam Smith, *The Wealth of Nations*, p. 304; John Stuart Mill, *Principles of Political Economy*, Toronto edition, pp. 563–564; Ashley edition, p. 550.

112. David Ricardo, *The Works and Correspondence of David Ricardo,* Vol. III, p. 94.

113. Ibid., p. 245.

114. John Stuart Mill, *Principles of Political Economy*, Toronto edition, pp. 654–655; Ashley edition, pp. 644–645.

115. Ibid., Toronto edition, p. 656; Ashley edition, p. 644.

116. Ibid., Toronto edition, pp. 654–655, 678n; Ashley edition, pp. 644–645, 670.

117. David Hume, *Writings on Economics*, p. 57; John Stuart Mill, *Principles of Political Economy*, Toronto edition, pp. 655–656; Ashley edition, pp. 645–646.

118. Henry Thornton, *Paper Credit of Great Britain*, p. 152.

119. Ibid.

120. Ibid. See also p. 97.

121. Ibid., p. 250.

122. Ibid., pp. 255–256.

123. Ibid., p. 256.

124. See Ricardo's "Notes on Bentham's 'Sur Les Prix'," David Ricardo, *The Works and Correspondence of David Ricardo*, Vol. III, pp. 298–299.

125. Ibid., p. 304. See also pp. 317, 325, 329, 330.

126. Ibid., pp. 318–319.

127. Ibid., p. 324.

128. Ibid., p. 334.

129. Ibid., pp. 47–127; cf. Henry Thornton, *Paper Credit of Great Britain*, pp. 143, 151, 353; [T.R. Malthus,] "Pamphlets on the Bullion Question," *Edinburgh Review*, August 1811, pp. 448–470; David Ricardo, *The Works and Correspondence of David Ricardo*, Vol. VI, pp. 21–42.

130. David Hume, *Writings on Economics*, pp. 42–44; Adam Smith, *The Wealth of Nations*, pp. 306–308; Henry Thornton, *Paper Credit of Great Britain*, pp. 233, 263, 267;

[T.R. Malthus,] "Tooke—on High and Low Prices," *Quarterly Review*, April 1823, p. 223; David Ricardo, *The Works and Correspondence of David Ricardo*, Vol. III, p. 90; Nassau W. Senior, *Three Lectures on the Cost of Obtaining Money* (London: John Murray, 1830) pp. 57, 79, 80; Nassau W. Senior, *Three Lectures on the Value of Money* (London: B. Fellowes, 1840), pp. 14, 16, 26; John Stuart Mill, *Principles of Political Economy*, Toronto edition, p. 516; Ashley edition, p. 498; Alfred Marshall, *Official Papers* (London: Macmillan & Co., 1926), pp. 267–268; Alfred Marshall, *Money Credit & Commerce* (New York: Augustus Kelley, 1965), p. 45; Knut Wicksell, *Lectures on Political Economy* (London: Routledge & Kegan Paul, 1962), Vol. II, pp. 59–67, 150; Irving Fisher, *The Purchasing Power of Money* (New York: Augustus M. Kelley, 1963), pp. 164, 270; Milton Friedman, *The Optimum Quantity of Money* (Chicago: Aldine Publishing Company, 1969), p. 62.

131. See John Maynard Keynes, *The General Theory of Employment, Interest and Money* (New York: Harcourt, Brace & Co., 1936), pp. 209, 289, 296.

132. See notes 76, 77, and 78 above.

133. Robert Torrens, *An Essay on the Production of Wealth*, pp. 419–422.

134. J.-B. Say, *Letters to Thomas Robert Malthus*, pp. 45n–46n.

135. Knut Wicksell, *Lectures on Political Economy*, Vol. II, pp. 159–160.

136. John Stuart Mill, writing more than forty years after Thornton's *Paper Credit of Great Britain*, described this work as "even now the clearest exposition" on the subject in the English language. John Stuart Mill, *Principles of Political Economy*, Toronto edition, p. 531n; Ashley edition, p. 515n. See also [T.R. Malthus,] "Depreciation of Paper Money," *Edinburgh Review*, February 1811, p. 340; J.C.L. Simonde de Sismondi, *Nouveaux Principes*

d'économie politique, Vol. II, p. 83.

137. Henry Thornton, *Paper Credit of Great Britain*, p. 97.

138. Ibid., p. 100.

139. David Ricardo, *The Works and Correspondence of David Ricardo*, Vol. III, p. 365.

140. Ibid., Vol. I, p. 298.

141. John Stuart Mill, *Principles of Political Economy*, Toronto edition, p. 654; Ashley edition, p. 644.

142. Robert Torrens, *An Essay on the Production of Wealth*, p. 422.

143. Ibid., p. 424.

144. J.R. McCulloch, *Principles of Political Economy*, fifth edition, p. 158.

145. Henry Thornton, *Paper Credit of Great Britain*, pp. 119n, 264, 265; [T.R. Malthus,] "Depreciation of Paper Money," *Edinburgh Review*, February 1811, p. 341.

146. This is the theme of Ricardo's pamphlet *The High Price of Bullion: A Proof of the Depreciation of Bank Notes*; see David Ricardo, *The Works and Correspondence of David Ricardo*, Vol. III, pp. 47–127. See also John Stuart Mill, *Principles of Political Economy*, Toronto edition, pp. 644–646; Ashley edition, pp. 634–636.

147. Adam Smith, *The Wealth of Nations*, pp. 276, 280–281, 284; David Ricardo, *The Works and Correspondence of David Ricardo*, Vol. IV, pp. 43–114; ibid., Vol. IV, p. 69; ibid., Vol. VII, p. 151; ibid., Vol. VIII, p. 295; Robert Torrens, *An Essay on the Production of Wealth*, pp. 320–321; John Stuart Mill, *Principles of Political Economy*, Toronto edition, p. 642; Ashley edition, p. 632; John Stuart Mill, *Collected Works*, Vol. IV, p. 82.

148. David Ricardo, *The Works and Correspondence of David Ricardo*, Vol. III, pp. 318–319; ibid., Vol. VI, p. 233.

149. [T.R. Malthus,] "Depreciation of Paper Currency," *Edinburgh Review*, February 1811, p. 264; Henry Thornton, *Paper Credit of Great Britain*, p. 239; Robert

Torrens, *An Essay on the Production of Wealth*, p. 326.

150. David Ricardo, *The Works and Correspondence of David Ricardo*, Vol. III, p. 94.
151. Jean-Baptiste Say, *Letters to Thomas Robert Malthus*, pp. 45n–46n.
152. David Ricardo, *The Works and Correspondence of David Ricardo*, Vol. IX, p. 25.
153. David Ricardo, *The Works and Correspondence of David Ricardo*, Vol. VIII, p. 316.
154. Henry Thornton, *Paper Credit of Great Britain*, pp. 118–119.
155. David Ricardo, *The Works and Correspondence of David Ricardo*, Vol. VIII, pp. 132–133.
156. Adam Smith, *The Wealth of Nations*, p. 879.
157. Ibid., p. 880.
158. David Ricardo, *The Works and Correspondence of David Ricardo*, Vol. I, p. 247.
159. Ibid., Vol. IV, pp. 186–187.
160. Ibid., p. 187.
161. Ibid, p. 187; ibid., Vol. I, pp. 247–248.
162. Ibid., Vol. IV, p. 186; Adam Smith, *The Wealth of Nations*, p. 878.
163. David Ricardo, *The Works and Correspondence of David Ricardo*, Vol. IV, p. 197.
164. The Earl of Lauderdale, *Three Letters*, pp. 32, 33, 34, 44, 45, 80n.
165. Ibid., p. 33.
166. Ibid., pp. 31, 33, 39, 77, 82, 125, 126.
167. Adam Smith, *The Wealth of Nations*, p. 868; David Ricardo, *The Works and Correspondence of David Ricardo*, Vol. I, p. 249; ibid., Vol. IV, pp. 194, 195.
168. Adam Smith, *The Wealth of Nations*, pp. 868, 873; David Ricardo, *The Works and Correspondence of David Ricardo*, Vol. IV, pp. 193, 198.
169. The Earl of Lauderdale, *Observations on The Review of His*

Inquiry into the Nature and Origin of Public Wealth, Published in the VIIIth Number of the Edinburgh Review (Edinburgh: A.C.H. Constable & Co., 1804), pp. 75–76.

170. James Maitland, 8th Earl of Lauderdale, *Nature and Origin of Public Wealth*, p. 232.

171. Ibid., pp. 245, 254, 267; The Earl of Lauderdale, *Three Letters*, pp. 7, 10, 68, 79, 84, 108.

172. [James Mill,] "Lauderdale on Public Wealth," *Literary Journal*, Vol. IV, No. 1 (July 1804), p. 14.

173. James Maitland, 8th Earl of Lauderdale, *Nature and Origin of Public Wealth*, p. 245.

174. Despite Frank Albert Fetter, "Lauderdale's Oversaving Theory," *American Economic Review*, June 1945, p. 281.

175. According to Lauderdale, "nothing is found more nearly commensurate than the expenditure and revenue of every society" (*Nature and Origin of Public Wealth*, p. 229). The proposition that "the revenue and expenditure of all societies must be equivalent, if left to the natural course of things," was regarded as "so generally admitted as to require no illustration" (*Three Letters*, p. 121).

176. James Maitland, 8th Earl of Lauderdale, *Nature and Origin of Public Wealth*, pp. 252, 257, 263, 274.

177. See John Stuart Mill, *Principles of Political Economy*, Toronto edition, pp. 738–739; Ashley edition, pp. 731–732.

178. William Blake, *Observations on the Effects Produced by the Expenditure of Government During the Restriction of Cash Payments* (London: John Murray, 1823), p. 62.

179. Ibid., pp. 63, 120.

180. David Ricardo, *The Works and Correspondence of David Ricardo*, Vol. IV, pp. 323–356; James Mill, *Elements of Political Economy*, third edition (London: Henry G. Bohn, 1844), p. 237 (1829 edition., p. 231); [John Stuart Mill,] "War Expenditure," *Collected Works*, Vol. IV: *Essays on Economics and Society*, pp. 3–22.

181. John Stuart Mill, *Essays on Some Unsettled Questions of*

Political Economy, pp. 67–72.   Cf. William Blake, *Observations*, pp. 54, 62.

182. Jean-Baptiste Say, *A Treatise on Political Economy*, p. 137.

Classical Microeconomics

1.   David Ricardo, *The Works and Correspondence of David Ricardo* edited by Piero Sraffa, Vol. I: *Principles of Political Economy and Taxation* (Cambridge: Cambridge University Press, 1951), p. 5; ibid., Vol. VIII (Cambridge: Cambridge University Press, 1952), p. 278.

2.   ". . . the whole quantity of work bestowed on land . . . extracts from the soil a gradually diminishing proportionate return." [Sir Edward West,] *Essay on the Application of Capital to Land* (London: P. Underwood, 1815), p. 15; see also, pp. 29, 36, 44; John Stuart Mill, *Principles of Political Economy*, Ashley edition, pp. 177, 178, 185, 427; Toronto edition, pp. 174, 175, 181, 182, 421.

3.   [Sir Edward West,] *Essay on the Application of Capital to Land*, pp. 12, 15, 38; David Ricardo, *The Works and Correspondence of David Ricardo*, Vol. I, p. 72.

4.   John Stuart Mill, *Principles of Political Economy*, Ashley edition, p. 427; Toronto edition, p. 421.

5.   [Sir Edward West,] *An Essay on the Application of Capital to Land*, pp. 19, 23–24; Thomas Robert Malthus, *An Inquiry into the Nature and Progress of Rent* (Baltimore: Johns Hopkins Press, 1903), pp. 36, 38; Thomas Robert Malthus, *Principles of Political Economy*, second edition (London: John Murray, 1836), pp. 195–196; David Ricardo, *The Works and Correspondence of David Ricardo*, Vol. I, p. 120; John Ramsey McCulloch, *Principles of Political Economy* (Edinburgh: Adam and Charles Black, 1864), p. 414.

6.   [Sir Edward West,] *Essay on the Application of Capital to*

Land, p. 37; John Stuart Mill, *Principles of Political Economy*, Ashley edition, p. 185; Toronto edition, p. 182.

7. John Stuart Mill, loc. cit.; T.R. Malthus, *An Inquiry into the Nature and Progress of Rent*, p. 38.

8. David Ricardo, *The Works and Correspondence of David Ricardo*, Vol. I, p. 73; J.R. McCulloch, *Principles of Political Economy*, pp. 424–425.

9. John Stuart Mill, *Principles of Political Economy*, Ashley edition, p. 177; Toronto edition, p. 174.

10. David Ricardo, *The Works and Correspondence of David Ricardo*, Vol. I, p. 67.

11. Ibid., p. 71.

12. Ibid., pp. 261n–262n; see also Adam Smith, *An Inquiry into the Nature and Causes of the Wealth of Nations* (New York: Modern Library, 1937), pp. 144–145.

13. David Ricardo, *The Works and Correspondence of David Ricardo*, Vol. I, p. 73; J.R. McCulloch, *Principles of Political Economy*, pp. 424–425; John Stuart Mill, *Principles of Political Economy*, Ashley edition, pp. 476–477; Toronto edition, pp. 494–496.

14. David Ricardo, *The Works and Correspondence of David Ricardo*, Vol. I, p. 71.

15. Adam Smith, *The Wealth of Nations*, p. 147; [Sir Edward West,] *Essay on the Application of Capital to Land*, pp. 13, 14; T.R. Malthus, *Nature and Progress of Rent*, pp. 21, 23; David Ricardo, *The Works and Correspondence of David Ricardo*, Vol. I, p. 70; J.R. McCulloch, *Principles of Political Economy*, p. 422; John Stuart Mill, *Principles of Political Economy*, Ashley edition, p. 433; Toronto edition, p. 428.

16. [Sir Edward West,] *Essay on the Application of Capital to Land*, p. 14n.

17. Ibid., p. 14.

18. Loc. cit.

19. David Ricardo, *The Works and Correspondence of David*

Ricardo, Vol. I, p. 328.

20. John Stuart Mill, *Principles of Political Economy*, Ashley edition, p. 427; Toronto edition, p. 421.

21. Adam Smith, *The Wealth of Nations*, p. 145; David Ricardo, *The Works and Correspondence of David Ricardo*, Vol. I, pp. 67–68, 327–337.

22. Adam Smith, *The Wealth of Nations*, pp. 150, 151, 152, 159.

23. Ibid., p. 145.

24. Ibid., pp. 49, 50. See also p. 248.

25. David Ricardo, *The Works and Correspondence of David Ricardo*, Vol. I, p. 329.

26. Adam Smith, *The Wealth of Nations*, pp. 145–146.

27. John Stuart Mill, *Principles of Political Economy*, Ashley edition, p. 476; Toronto edition, p. 494.

28. Ibid., Ashley edition, p. 477; Toronto edition, p. 495.

29. Loc. cit.

30. Modern "rent control" laws are often based on a similar assumption, that the supply of dwelling units is relatively fixed, at least in the short run—often ignoring the auxiliary services (heat, repair, hot water, painting, etc.) which are also included in rental payments and whose supply is *not* fixed, even in the short run.

31. J.R. McCulloch, *Principles of Political Economy*, p. 423.

32. Henry George, *Progress and Poverty* (New York: Modern Library, no date), Book VIII, Chapter III; George Bernard Shaw, ed. *Fabian Essays in Socialism* (Garden City: Doubleday & Co., no date), pp. 41–42.

33. [Sir Edward West,] *Essay on the Application of Capital to Land*, pp. 12, 37; T.R. Malthus, *Nature and Progress of Rent*, pp. 33, 38; John Stuart Mill, *Principles of Political Economy*, Ashley edition, pp. 185–186; Toronto edition, p. 183.

34. David Ricardo, *The Works and Correspondence of David Ricardo*, Vol. I, pp. 94–95.

35. Ibid., p. 120.
36. [Sir Edward West,] *Essay on the Application of Capital to Land*, p. 18.
37. Ibid., p. 24.
38. Ibid., p. 21; David Ricardo, *The Works and Correspondence of David Ricardo*, Vol. I, pp. 289–290. See also John Stuart Mill, *Principles of Political Economy*, Ashley edition, pp. 726–727; Toronto edition, pp. 734–735.
39. Adam Smith, *The Wealth of Nations*, p. 87.
40. [Sir Edward West,] *Essay on the Application of Capital to Land*, p. 21; David Ricardo, *The Works and Correspondence of David Ricardo*, Vol. I, pp. 288–289.
41. David Ricardo, *The Works and Correspondence of David Ricardo*, Vol. I, p. 289.
42. Adam Smith, *The Wealth of Nations*, pp. 92–93.
43. Ibid., p. 339; David Ricardo, *The Works and Correspondence of David Ricardo*, Vol. III, pp. 25–26, 150, 374–375.
44. [Samuel Bailey,] *An Inquiry into Those Principles Respecting the Nature of Demand and the Necessity of Consumption Lately Advocated by Mr. Malthus* (London: R. Hunter, 1821), pp. 10–13; J.A. Schumpeter, *History of Economic Analysis* (New York: Oxford University Press, 1954), pp. 651–652.
45. T.R. Malthus, "An Essay on the Principle of Population" [first edition], *On Population*, edited by Gertrude Himmelfarb (New York: Random House, 1960), p. 17. See also p. 52.
46. Ibid., p. 57. This was repeated in later editions as well. See, for example, T.R. Malthus, *An Essay on the Principle of Population* (London: J. M. Dent & Sons, 1961), Vol. II, pp. 4–5.
47. T.R. Malthus, "An Essay on the Principle of Population," *On Population*, pp. 15, 57, 162, 165n, 353, 444, 470–471.
48. Ibid., p. 29.

49. Ibid., p. 37; T.R. Malthus, "A Letter to Samuel Whitbread, Esq., M.P.," *An Introduction to Malthus*, edited by D. V. Glass (London: Frank Cass and Co., 1959), p. 186.

50. T.R. Malthus, "An Essay on the Principle of Population," *On Population*, edited by Gertrude Himmelfarb, pp. 591–592.

51. Ibid., pp. 165, 337–338; T.R. Malthus, "A Summary View of the Principle of Population," *Introduction to Malthus*, edited by D. V. Glass, p. 143.

52. Malthus quoted in Nassau William Senior, *Two Lectures on Population* (London: Saunders and Otley, 1829), p. 61.

53. J.C.L. Simonde de Sismondi, *Nouveaux Principes d'économie politique*, Vol. II, third edition (Geneva- Paris: Edition Jeheber, 1953), p. 182; Richard Whately, *Introductory Lectures on Political Economy*, second edition (London: B. Fellows, 1832), pp. 248–250; Nassau William Senior, *Two Lectures on Population*, pp. 36, 56, 58, 77.

54. Malthus quoted in Senior, *Two Lectures on Population*, p. 60.

55. Ibid., p. 61.

56. T.R. Malthus, *Principles of Political Economy*, second edition, p. 226.

57. T.R. Malthus, "An Essay on the Principle of Population," *On Population*, edited by Gertrude Himmelfarb, p. 454.

58. T.R. Malthus, "A Summary View of the Principle of Population," *An Introduction to Malthus*, edited by D. V. Glass, p. 143.

59. John Stuart Mill, *Principles of Political Economy*, Ashley edition, p. 161; Toronto edition, p. 159.

60. Ibid., Ashley edition, p. 157; Toronto edition, pp. 154, 155.

61. Ibid., Ashley edition, p. 161; Toronto edition, p. 159.

62. Ibid., Ashley edition, p. 359; Toronto edition, pp. 353–354.

63. John Stuart Mill, *Collected Works of John Stuart Mill*, Vol. IV: *Essays on Economics and Society*, edited by J.M.

Robson (Toronto: University of Toronto Press, 1967), p. 449.

64. John Stuart Mill, *A System of Logic: Ratiocinative and Inductive* (London: Longmans, Green and Co., Ltd., 1959), p. 543; ibid. (Toronto: University of Toronto Press, 1974), p. 829.

65. T.R. Malthus, "An Essay on the Principle of Population," *On Population*, edited by Gertrude Himmelfarb, p. 17.

66. Ibid., pp. 16, 163.

67. Ibid., p. 151.

68. Ibid., p. 212.

69. Adam Smith, *The Wealth of Nations*, p. 56.

70. John Stuart Mill, *Collected Works*, Vol. IV, p. 400; John Stuart Mill, *Principles of Political Economy*, Ashley edition, p. 449; Toronto edition, p. 468.

71. Adam Smith, *The Wealth of Nations*, p. lviii.

72. Ibid., p. 30.

73. Ibid., p. 31.

74. Ibid., p. 33.

75. Ibid., pp. 30, 33, 78, 159, 247, 248.

76. See David Ricardo, *The Works and Correspondence of David Ricardo*, Vol. I, pp. 14, 17–18, 29, 43–44.

77. John Stuart Mill, *Principles of Political Economy*, Ashley edition, p. 566; Toronto edition, pp. 578–579.

78. T.R. Malthus, *Principles of Political Economy*, second edition, p. 82. See also T.R. Malthus, *Definitions in Political Economy* (London: John Murray, 1827), p. 210n.

79. T.R. Malthus, *Definitions in Political Economy*, p. 52.

80. Loc. cit.

81. Karl Marx and Frederick Engels, *Selected Correspondence* (New York: International Publishers, 1942), p. 232.

82. Ibid., p. 246.

83. Karl Marx, *Capital: A Critique of Political Economy*, Vol. I (Chicago: Charles H. Kerr & Co., 1906), p. 45.

84. "The nonsense about the necessity of proving the concept

of value arises from the complete ignorance both of the subject dealt with and of the method of science." Karl Marx and Frederick Engels, *Selected Correspondence*, p. 246.

85. "Every child knows that a country which ceased to work, I will not say for a year, but for a few weeks, would die. Every child knows too that the mass of products corresponding to the different needs require different and quantitatively determined masses of the total labour of society. That this necessity of distributing social labour in definite proportions cannot be done away with . . . is self-evident." Loc. cit.

86. T.R. Malthus, *The Measure of Value* (New York: Kelley & Millman, 1957), p. 16; T.R. Malthus, *Principles of Political Economy*, second edition, pp. 94–95; David Ricardo, *The Works and Correspondence of David Ricardo*, Vol. I, pp. 43–44; John Stuart Mill, *Principles of Political Economy*, Ashley edition, p. 566; Toronto edition, p. 579.

87. [Samuel Bailey,] *A Critical Dissertation on the Nature, Measures, and Causes of Value* (London: R. Hunter, 1825), p. 55.

88. Ibid., p. 127n.

89. [Samuel Bailey,] *A Critical Dissertation on the Nature, Measures, and Causes of Value*, pp. 185ff; [Samuel Bailey,] *Observations on Certain Verbal Disputes in Political Economy* (London: R. Hunter, 1821), pp. 80ff; David Ricardo, *The Works and Correspondence of David Ricardo*, Vol. I, p. 74; John Stuart Mill, *Principles of Political Economy*, Ashley edition, p. 471; Toronto edition, p. 490.

90. T.R. Malthus, *Principles of Political Economy*, second edition, p. 70; David Ricardo, *The Works and Correspondence of David Ricardo*, Vol. I, p. 384; John Stuart Mill, *Principles of Political Economy*, Ashley edition, p. 449; Toronto edition, p. 469.

91. [Samuel Bailey,] *A Critical Dissertation on the Nature, Measures, and Causes of Value*, p. 199; [Samuel Bailey,] *Observations on Certain Verbal Disputes in Political Economy*, p. 82.

92. John Stuart Mill, *Collected Works*, Vol. IV, p. 279.

93. David Ricardo, *The Works and Correspondence of David Ricardo*, Vol. VIII, p. 279.

94. "Wherever cost of production does *not* regulate the price there demand and supply *do* regulate it." John Stuart Mill, *Collected Works*, Vol. IV, p. 400.

95. Ibid., p. 33.

96. Loc. cit. See also ibid., Vol. V, p. 635.

97. David Ricardo, *The Works and Correspondence of David Ricardo*, Vol. I, p. 382; ibid., Vol. V, p. 129; John Stuart Mill, *Principles of Political Economy*, Ashley edition, pp. 446, 447, 449; Toronto edition, pp. 466, 467, 469.

98. David Ricardo, *The Works and Correspondence of David Ricardo*, Vol. VI, p. 129.

99. T.R. Malthus, *Principles of Political Economy*, second edition, p. 68.

100. T.R. Malthus, *Definitions in Political Economy*, p. 245.

101. T.R. Malthus, *Principles of Political Economy*, second edition, pp. 65n–66n.

102. [Samuel Bailey,] *Observations on Certain Verbal Disputes in Political Economy*, p. 65.

103. T.R. Malthus, *Principles of Political Economy*, second edition, pp. 71, 73, 74; T.R. Malthus, *The Measure of Value* (London: John Murray, 1823), pp. 17, 19.

104. T.R. Malthus, *Definitions in Political Economy*, p. 242.

105. T.R. Malthus, *Principles of Political Economy*, second edition, pp. 65n–66n, 72; T.R. Malthus, *Definitions in Political Economy*, p. 221; T.R. Malthus, *The Measure of Value*, p. 44.

106. Adam Smith, *The Wealth of Nations*, p. 28.

107. Nassau W. Senior, *An Outline of the Science of Political*

Economy (New York: Augustus M. Kelley, 1951), pp. 11–12.

108. T.R. Malthus, *Principles of Political Economy*, second edition, pp. 366, 384, 403; J.C.L. Simonde de Sismondi *Nouveaux Principes d'économie politique*, pp. 11, 254, 259. See also J.C.L. Simonde [de Sismondi], *De la Richesse commerciale* (Geneva: J.J. Paschoud, 1803), Vol. I, p. 347.

109. J.C.L. Simonde de Sismondi, *Études sur l'économie politique* (Paris: Treuttel et Würtz, 1838), Vol. II, pp. 233, 403; T.R. Malthus, "Tooke— On High and Low Prices," *Quarterly Review* (April 1823), pp. 226–227; T.R. Malthus, *Principles of Political Economy*, second edition, p. 68.

110. J.C.L. Simonde de Sismondi, *Études sur l'économie politique*, Vol. II, pp. 233, 403; T.R. Malthus, "Tooke— On High and Low Prices," *Quarterly Review* (April 1823), pp. 226–227; T.R. Malthus, *Principles of Political Economy*, second edition, p. 68.

111. David Ricardo, *The Works and Correspondence of David Ricardo*, Vol. VI, p. 167.

112. T.R. Malthus, *Principles of Political Economy*, second edition, pp. 351–352; J.C.L. Simonde de Sismondi, *Nouveaux Principes d'économie politique*, Vol. I, pp. 247–248.

113. T.R. Malthus, *Principles of Political Economy*, second edition, pp. 365, 367, 430.

114. Ibid., p. 60; see also [Samuel Bailey,] *An Inquiry into Those Principles Respecting the Nature of Demand and the Necessity of Consumption Lately Advocated by Mr. Malthus*, pp. 53, 65.

115. Say began by defining utility as the "capability of certain things to satisfy the various wants of mankind." Jean-Baptiste Say, *Treatise on Political Economy*, p. 66. Yet utility was later used to mean "objects of rational desire"

rather than "artificial wants," ibid., p. 208; see also pp. 402, 413, 414n.

116. T.R. Malthus, *Principles of Political Economy*, second edition, pp. 300, 301; T.R. Malthus, *Definitions in Political Economy*, pp. 207–208, 235.

117. T.R. Malthus, *Definitions in Political Economy*, pp. 22, 250, 251; T.R. Malthus, "Political Economy," *Quarterly Review* (January 1824), pp. 298, 304; letter to Say in Jean-Baptiste Say, *Œuvres diverses de J.-B. Say* (Paris: Guillaumin et Cie, 1848), p. 507. Say defended himself by reverting to his original definition of subjective utility, ibid., pp. 503, 504, 512; [Jean-Baptiste Say,] "Definitions in Political Economy, etc.," *Revue encyclopedique*, Vol. XXXIII (February 1827), p. 495. The basis for ascribing the latter article (identified only by initials) to Say is his stated intention to review this book in this journal. See Jean-Baptiste Say, *Œuvres diverses de J.-B. Say*, p. 506.

118. T.R. Malthus, *Principles of Political Economy*, second edition, p. 361. See also p. 302.

119. T.R. Malthus, *Definitions in Political Economy*, pp. 235, 251.

120. Ibid., p. 128.

121. Ibid., p. 117.

122. T.R. Malthus, *Principles of Political Economy*, second edition, pp. 362, 365, 388, 394, 413, 426; David Ricardo, *The Works and Correspondence of David Ricardo*, Vol. VI, p. 131; T.R. Malthus, "Political Economy," *Quarterly Review* (January 1824), p. 315.

123. [John Stuart Mill,] "Political Economy," *Westminster Review* (January 1825), p. 224; [Samuel Bailey,] *Observations on Certain Verbal Disputes in Political Economy*, pp. 22, 59.

124. T.R. Malthus, *Definitions in Political Economy*, p. 64, for example.

125. Ibid., p. 186.

126. T.R. Malthus, *Principles of Political Economy*, second edition, p. 396.

127. Ibid., p. 364.

128. T.R. Malthus, *Definitions in Political Economy*, p. 247.

129. T.R. Malthus, *Principles of Political Economy*, second edition, p. 316.

130. David Ricardo, *The Works and Correspondence of David Ricardo*, Vol. II, pp. 305, 306, 366, 413, 415; ibid., Vol. VIII, pp. 277, 334n.

131. T.R. Malthus, *Principles of Political Economy*, second edition, p. 317.

132. Jean-Baptiste Say, *Cours complet d'économie politique pratique*, second edition (Paris: Guillaumin, Libraire, 1840), Vol. I, pp. 348–349.

133. John Stuart Mill, *Principles of Political Economy*, Ashley edition, pp. 445, 446, 448; Toronto edition, pp. 465, 466, 467.

134. W. Stanley Jevons, *The Theory of Political Economy* (New York: Kelley & Millman, 1957), p. 275.

135. John Stuart Mill, *Collected Works*, Vol. IV, p. 30.

136. John Stuart Mill, *Principles of Political Economy*, Ashley edition, p. 436; Toronto edition, p. 456. Inexplicably, however, Mill has been credited with having "introduced into English economics the concept of demand as a schedule or function" because he stated that a greater quantity supplied than demanded causes prices to fall and a greater quantity demanded than supplied causes prices to rise— something that no economist had denied before him. Moreover, Mill's assertion that neither he nor anyone else had anything to add to the theory of value would seem to be the strongest refutation of this attempt to credit him with originality on this score. Cf. George J. Stigler, *Essays in the History of Economics* (Chicago: University of Chicago Press, 1965), p. 9.

137. David Ricardo, *The Works and Correspondence of David*

Ricardo, Vol. I, Chapter I.
138. Ibid., Vol. IX, pp. 127, 128.

Classical Methodology

1. Adam Smith, *An Inquiry into the Nature and Causes of the Wealth of Nations* (New York: Modern Library, 1937), pp. 30, 33.
2. Ibid.
3. Ibid. Rent was sometimes price determined (p. 56) and sometimes price determining (p. 146).
4. Ibid. "Real" meant goods and services on p. 78 but labor command on pp. 30, 33, 159, 247, 248.
5. David Ricardo, *The Works and Correspondence of David Ricardo*, ed. Piero Sraffa, Vol. I (Cambridge: Cambridge University Press, 1951), pp. 16–17, 19–20, 67–68; John Stuart Mill, *Principles of Political Economy*, edited by J.M. Robson (Toronto: University of Toronto, 1965), pp. 456, 580, 734–735 (cited hereafter as "Toronto edition"); ibid., edited by W. J. Ashley (London: Longmans, Green, and Co., 1909), pp. 436–437, 567, 726–727 (cited hereafter as "Ashley edition").
6. J.A. Schumpeter, *History of Economic Analysis* (New York: Oxford University Press, 1951), pp. 189–191 passim.
7. David Ricardo, *The Works and Correspondence of David Ricardo*, Vol. VII (Cambridge: Cambridge University Press, 1952), p. 120.
8. Richard Jones, *An Essay on the Distribution of Wealth* (London: John Murray, 1831), p. xx.
9. Ibid., p. xxxix.
10. Richard Jones, *Literary Remains*, ed. William Whewell (London: John Murray, 1859), p. 569.
11. Ibid., p. 600.

12. Ibid., p. 576.
13. Ibid., p. 570.
14. Ibid., p. 570.
15. Richard Jones, *An Essay on the Distribution of Wealth*, p. 325.
16. William Whewell, "Prefatory Notice," Richard Jones, *Literary Remains*, pp. xii–xiii.
17. Thomas Robert Malthus, *Principles of Political Economy* (New York: Augustus M. Kelley, 1951) second edition, p. 8.
18. Ibid., p. 6.
19. J.C.L. Simonde de Sismondi, *Nouveaux Principes d'économie politique*, second edition, Vol. II (Geneva-Paris: Edition Jeheber, 1953), p. 256.
20. Ibid., Vol. I, p. 234.
21. Ibid., Vol. II, p. 283; J.C.L. Simonde de Sismondi, *Études sur l'économie politique* (Paris: Treuttel et Würtz, 1837), Vol. I, pp. 85n–86n.
22. Jean–Baptiste Say, *Œuvres diverses de J.-B. Say* (Paris: Guillaumin et Cie, 1848), p. 527.
23. Ibid., p. 527.
24. Ibid., p. 505.
25. T.R. Malthus, *Principles of Political Economy*, second edition, pp. 1, 432, 434; T.R. Malthus, *Definitions in Political Economy* (London: John Murray, 1827), p. 2.
26. Jean-Baptiste Say, *A Treatise on Political Economy*, trans. Clement C. Biddle (Philadelphia: Grigg & Elliot, 1834), pp. xxviii–xxix; [Samuel Bailey,] *Observations on Certain Verbal Disputes in Political Economy* (London: R. Hunter, 1821), pp. 37, 62; Richard Jones, *Literary Remains*, p. 598; Nassau W. Senior, *Four Introductory Lectures on Political Economy* (London: Longman, Brown, Green, and Longmans, 1852), pp. 23, 33; John Stuart Mill, *Essays on Some Unsettled Questions of Political Economy* (London: John W. Parker, 1844), pp. 129–132.

27. Jean-Baptiste Say, *A Treatise on Political Economy*, p. xxvi.
28. Augustin Cournot, *Researches into the Mathematical Principles of the Theory of Wealth* (New York: Augustus M. Kelley, 1960), p. 3.
29. David Ricardo, *The Works and Correspondence of David Ricardo*, Vol. VIII (Cambridge: Cambridge University Press, 1952), p. 331.
30. Ibid., Vol. VI (Cambridge: Cambridge University Press, 1952), p. 204.
31. John Ramsey McCulloch, *A Treatise on the Circumstances Which Determine the Rate of Wages and the Condition of the Labouring Classes*, second edition (London: G. Routledge & Co., 1854), p. 8.
32. James Mill, *Elements of Political Economy*, third edition (London: Henry G. Bohn, 1844), p. 240.
33. John Stuart Mill, *Collected Works*, Vol. IV: *Essays on Economics and Society,* edited by J.M. Robson (Toronto: University of Toronto Press, 1967), p. 16.
34. Ibid.
35. Robert Torrens, *An Essay on the Production of Wealth* (London: Longman, Hurst, Rees, Orme, and Brown, 1821), p. xii; twenty-one years later, Nassau Senior noted how "far" economics was from firmly establishing its doctrines, principles, or definitions. Nassau Senior, *Four Introductory Lectures on Political Economy,* p. 53. Still another twenty years after this, John E. Cairnes was to make very similar observations contrasting the state of economics with Torrens' prediction. John E. Cairnes, *The Character and Logical Method of Political Economy* (New York: Augustus M. Kelley, 1970), p. 20.
36. David Ricardo, *The Works and Correspondence of David Ricardo*, Vol. VIII, p. 184. See also Vol. III, p. 205.
37. Ibid., Vol. VIII, p. 235.
38. Ibid., Vol. III, p. 181. See also pp. 173, 239.

39. John Stuart Mill, *Essays on Some Unsettled Questions of Political Economy*, p. 142.

40. Richard Whately, *Introductory Lectures on Political Economy*, second edition (London: B. Fellowes, 1832), p. 230.

41. Ibid., p. 235.

42. Ibid., p. 237.

43. [T.R. Malthus,] "Political Economy," *Quarterly Review*, January 1824, p. 334; J.C.L. Simonde de Sismondi, *Nouveaux Principes d'économie politique*, Vol. I, pp. 63, 69; Jean-Baptiste Say, *A Treatise on Political Economy*, pp. xl–xli.

44. Adam Smith, *The Wealth of Nations*, pp. 74–75.

45. "The natural price of labour is that price which is necessary to enable the labourers, one with another, to subsist and to perpetuate their race, without either increase or diminution." David Ricardo, *The Works and Correspondence of David Ricardo*, Vol. I, p.193; "Notwithstanding the tendency of wages to conform to their natural rate, their market rate may, in improving society, for an indefinite period be constantly above it." ibid., pp. 94–95.

46. "The principle object of the present essay is to examine the effects of one great cause." T.R. Malthus, *An Essay on Population* (London: J. M. Dent & Sons, 1960), Vol. I, p. 5.

47. J.C.L. Simonde de Sismondi, *Nouveaux Principes d'économie politique*, Vol. II, p. 115.

48. Sismondi's writings contained many mathematical models and Robinson Crusoe examples.

49. Jean-Baptiste Say, *A Treatise on Political Economy*, p. xlix. J.A. Schumpeter was later to christen this tendency among economists the Ricardian Vice. J.A. Schumpeter, *Essays of J.A. Schumpeter* (Cambridge, Mass.: Addison-Wesley Press, 1951), pp. 150, 154; J.A. Schumpeter, *History of Economic Analysis*, pp. 472–473.

50. Richard Jones, *Literary Remains*, p. 569.

51. Exceptions, modifications or "disturbing causes" were readily admitted, though sometimes the analysis then proceeded as if these admissions had not been made.

52. At least, this was the classical position by the time of John Stuart Mill, who said "it often happens that circumstances almost peculiar to the particular case or era have a far greater share in governing that one case." John Stuart Mill, *Essays on Some Unsettled Questions of Political Economy*, p. 155.

53. John Stuart Mill, *Collected Works*, Vol. IV, p. 225.

54. Ibid., p. 226.

55. John Stuart Mill, *Essays on Some Unsettled Questions of Political Economy*, p. 142.

56. John Stuart Mill, *A System of Logic Ratiocinative and Inductive* (London: Longmans, Green and Co., 1959), Book III, Chapter XI, Section III, p. 303. This will be referred to hereinafter as the Longmans edition of Mill's *A System of Logic*. The same book is also available as Volumes VII and VIII of Mill's *Collected Works*, whose pages are numbered continuously through the two volumes, which will be referred to hereinafter as the Toronto edition. Thus the above citation would also be referred to as John Stuart Mill, *A System of Logic*, Toronto edition, p. 460.

57. Ibid., Book III, Chapter X (both editions).

58. Karl Marx and Frederick Engels, *Selected Correspondence* (New York: International Publishers, 1942), p. 247.

59. Loc. cit.

60. Karl Marx, *Critique of Political Economy* (Chicago: Charles H. Kerr & Co., 1904), p. 292.

61. Ibid., pp. 292–293.

62. Karl Marx, *Theories of Surplus Value: Selections*, trans. G. A. Bonner and Emile Burns (New York: International Publishers, 1952), pp. 202, 231.

63. Karl Marx, *Capital*, Vol. III (Chicago: Charles H. Kerr &

Co., 1909), p. 38.

64. Karl Marx and Frederick Engels, *Selected Correspondence*, p. 245.

65. John Stuart Mill, *Essays on Some Unsettled Questions of Political Economy,* p. 149.

66. Ibid., p. 145.

67. J.C.L. Simonde [de Sismondi], *De la Richesse commerciale*, Vol. I (Geneva: J. J. Paschoud, 1803), pp. 100–104, 104n–108n.

68. David Ricardo, *The Works and Correspondence of David Ricardo*, Vol. I, p. 17; John Stuart Mill, *Principles of Political Economy*, Toronto edition, pp. 578–581; Ashley edition, pp. 566–568.

69. [T.R. Malthus,] "Depreciation of Paper Money," *Edinburgh Review*, February 1811, p. 343.

70. T. R. Malthus, letter to Ricardo, *The Works and Correspondence of David Ricardo*, Vol. VI, p. 41.

71. Friedrich Engels, "Socialism: Utopian and Scientific," Karl Marx and Friedrich Engels, *Basic Writings on Politics and Philosophy*, ed. Lewis S. Feuer (Garden City: Doubleday & Co., 1959), p. 85.

72. Friedrich Engels, letter to Conrad Schmidt, October 27, 1890, ibid., p. 407.

73. Ibid., p. 406; "... in all ideological domains tradition forms a great conservative force. But the transformations which this material undergoes spring from class relations, that is to say, out of the economic relations of the people who execute these transformations. And here that is sufficient." Friedrich Engels, "Ludwig Feuerbach and the End of Classical German Philosophy," ibid., pp. 240–241. Examples cited include law (pp. 235–237) and religion (pp. 237–238).

74. David Ricardo, *The Works and Correspondence of David Ricardo*, Vol. I, p. 21.

75. Ibid., p. 22.

76. Ibid., p. 30.

77. Loc. cit.

78. Ibid., p. 36.

79. Loc. cit.

80. John M. Cassels, "A Re-Interpretation of Ricardo on Value," *Essays in Economic Thought: Aristotle to Marshall*, ed. J.J. Spengler and W.R. Allen (Chicago: Rand McNally & Co., 1960), p. 433.

81. [Samuel Bailey,] *A Critical Dissertation on the Nature, Measures, and Causes of Value* (London: R. Hunter, 1825), pp. 12, 100, 121, 122, 127n, 178n, 236, 248.

82. See Thomas Sowell, "Marx's 'Increasing Misery' Doctrine," *American Economic Review*, March 1960, pp. 111–120.

83. Karl Marx, *Capital*, Vol. I, p. 14.

84. Ibid., Vol. III, p. 203.

85. Karl Marx and Frederick Engels, *Selected Correspondence*, pp. 129–133.

86. ". . . average prices do not directly coincide with the values of commodities, as Adam Smith, Ricardo, and others believe." Karl Marx, *Capital*, Vol. I, p. 185n.

87. Karl Marx, "Wage Labour and Capital," Karl Marx and Friedrich Engels, *Selected Works* (Moscow: Foreign Languages Publishing Co., 1955), Vol. I, p. 87; Karl Marx, *Writings of the Young Marx*, ed. L.D. Easton and Kurt H. Guddat (Garden City: Doubleday & Co., 1967), pp. 265–266.

88. Karl Marx, *Capital*, Vol. III, p. 223.

89. This phrase or a close paraphrase appears in T.R. Malthus, *Principles of Political Economy*, second edition, pp. 8, 11; David Ricardo, *The Works and Correspondence of David Ricardo*, Vol. VII, p. 122; ibid., Vol. VIII, p. 260; [T.R. Malthus,] "Political Economy," p. 297; Richard Jones, *Literary Remains*, pp. 575, 598, 600; Thorstein Veblen, *The Place of Science in Modern Civilization* (New York:

Augustus M. Kelley, 1961), p. 267.

90. Fritz Machlup, "Marginal Analysis and Empirical Research," *American Economic Review*, September 1946, p. 527; Milton Friedman, *Essays in Positive Economics* (Chicago: University of Chicago Press, 1962), pp. 4, 39.

91. See Thomas Sowell, "The 'Evolutionary' Economics of Thorstein Veblen," *Oxford Economic Papers*, July 1967, pp. 193n–194n.

92. John Stuart Mill, *A System of Logic*, Longmans edition, p. 594; Toronto edition, p. 910.

93. John Stuart Mill, *Essays on Some Unsettled Questions of Political Economy*, p. 160.

94. Ibid., pp. 160–164; John Stuart Mill, *A System of Logic*, Longmans edition, p. 293; Toronto edition, pp. 442–443.

95. John Stuart Mill, *A System of Logic*, Longmans edition, p. 292; Toronto edition, p. 443; John Stuart Mill, *Essays on Some Unsettled Questions of Political Economy*, p. 162.

96. Richard Whately, *Introductory Lectures on Political Economy*, second edition, pp. 249–250.

97. Nassau William Senior, *Two Lectures on Population* (London: Saunders and Otley, 1829), p. 59.

98. Ibid., p. 56.

99. Ibid., p. 57.

100. John Stuart Mill, *Principles of Political Econmy*, Ashley edition, p. 359; Toronto edition, p. 353.

101. Karl Marx, *Wage Labour and Capital* (Moscow: Foreign Languages Publishing House, 1947), p. 22: Karl Marx, *Theories of Surplus Value: Selections*, p. 186; F. Engels, *Engels on Capital*, ed. Leonard E. Mins (New York: International Publishers, 1937), p. 60; Karl Marx and Frederick Engels, *Selected Correspondence*, p. 485; Frederick Engels, *Herr Eugen Dühring's Revolution in Science* (New York: International Publishers, 1939), p. 117.

102. See, for example, Karl Marx, *Wage Labour and Capital*,

Section XIV, p. 67; Karl Marx, *Capital*, Vol. I, pp. 657–658.

103. Karl Marx, *Capital*, Vol. III, Chapter XV.

104. T.R. Malthus, letter to Ricardo, *The Works and Correspondence of David Ricardo*, Vol. VI, p. 154.

105. [T.R. Malthus,] "Political Economy," *Quarterly Review*, January 1824, p. 315.

106. T.R. Malthus, letter to Ricardo, *The Works and Correspondence of David Ricardo*, Vol. VII, p. 215. See also T.R. Malthus, *Principles of Political Economy*, second edition, p. 402; T.R. Malthus, *Definitions in Political Economy*, p. 26.

107. William Whewell, "Prefatory Notice," Richard Jones, *Literary Remains*, p. xvi.

108. John Stuart Mill, *A System of Logic*, Longmans edition, p. 584; Toronto edition, p. 895.

109. Ibid., Longmans edition, p. 579; Toronto edition, pp. 887–888.

110. Ibid., Longmans edition, p. 573; Toronto edition, p. 879.

111. Ibid., Longmans edition, p. 243; Toronto edition, p. 371.

112. Ibid., Longmans edition, p. 573; Toronto edition, p. 879.

113. John Stuart Mill, *Essays on Some Unsettled Questions of Political Economy*, pp. 138–140.

114. Ibid., p. 159.

115. Ibid., p. 115.

116. Nassau W. Senior, *Four Introductory Lectures on Political Economy*, p. 27.

117. Ibid., p. 28.

118. Richard Jones, *Distribution of Wealth*, p. xv.

119. John Stuart Mill, *A System of Logic*, Longmans edition, p. 579; Toronto edition, p. 887.

120. Ibid., Longmans edition, p. 579; Toronto edition, pp. 887–888.

121. Richard Whately, *Introductory Lectures on Political Economy*, second edition, p. 246.

122. [Samuel Bailey,] *A Critical Dissertation on the Nature, Measures, and Causes of Value*, p. xix.
123. Ibid., p. vi.
124. [Samuel Bailey,] *Observations on Certain Verbal Disputes in Political Economy*, p. 1.
125. Ibid., p. 4.
126. Ibid., p. 71.
127. T.R. Malthus, *Definitions in Political Economy*, p. vii.
128. [Samuel Bailey,] *A Critical Dissertation on the Nature, Measures, and Causes of Value*, pp. xxii–xxiii; [Samuel Bailey,] *Letter to a Political Economist* (London: R. Hunter, 1826), pp. 52, 54.
129. [Samuel Bailey,] *Observations on Certain Verbal Disputes in Political Economy*, p. 16.
130. Ibid., p. 84.
131. Richard Jones, *Literary Remains*, p. 598.
132. J.C.L. Simonde de Sismondi, *Études sur l'économie politique*, Vol. II, p. 143; see also ibid., pp. 227, 228; ibid., Vol. I, p. 115.
133. See J.C.L. Simonde [de Sismondi], *Richesse commerciale*, Vol. I, p. 105n.
134. Ibid., pp. 342–348.
135. According to James Mill, "annual purchases and sales" will "always balance" (*Commerce Defended*, p. 82). To Torrens, supply and demand were "convertible" terms (*Edinburgh Review*, October 1819, p. 470). John Stuart Mill stated that the equality of supply and demand "is not a deduction of probability," but rather "possesses all the certainty of a mathematical demonstration," because it depends on "the very meaning of the words, demand and supply" (*Westminster Review*, July 1824, p. 41).
136. Say's very definition of "production" included sale at cost-covering prices. See Jean-Baptiste Say, *Cours complet d'économie politique pratique*, second edition (Paris: Guillaumin, Libraire, 1840), Vol. I, pp. 347–348;

ibid., Vol. II, p. 209; Jean-Baptiste Say, *Traité d'économie politique*, fifth edition (Paris: Chez Rapilly, 1826), p. 195. Leaving aside those things which were "made inconsiderately" without really "producing" anything, Say concluded that "my doctrine on markets becomes complete." Jean-Baptiste Say, *Œuvres diverses de J.-B. Say*, p. 513.

137. [Samuel Bailey,] *An Inquiry into Those Principles Respecting the Nature of Demand and the Necessity of Consumption Lately Advocated by Mr. Malthus* (London: R. Hunter, 1821), p. 110.

138. T.R. Malthus, *Definitions in Political Economy*, pp. 4–5.

139. Richard Whately, *Introductory Lectures on Political Economy*, second edition, p. 241.

140. Ibid., pp. 241–243.

141. Ibid., p. 244.

142. [Samuel Bailey,] *Letter to a Political Economist*, pp. 62–63; [Samuel Bailey,] *An Inquiry into Those Principles Respecting the Nature of Demand and the Necessity of Consumption Lately Advocated by Mr. Malthus*, p. 8.

143. [Samuel Bailey,] *Observations on Certain Verbal Disputes in Political Economy*, p. 5.

144. Ibid., p. 3.

145. Ibid., p. 70.

146. Ibid., pp. 5–6.

147. David Ricardo, *The Works and Correspondence of David Ricardo*, Vol. VI, p. 295; John Stuart Mill, *Essays on Some Unsettled Questions of Political Economy*, pp. 147–148.

148. John Stuart Mill, *Essays on Some Unsettled Questions of Political Economy*, pp. 152–153, 154; John Stuart Mill, *A System of Logic*, Longmans edition, p. 592; Toronto edition, pp. 907–908.

149. John Stuart Mill, *A System of Logic*, Book III, Chapters XVII, XVIII.

150. John Stuart Mill, "Miss Martineau's Summary of Political

Economy," *Collected Works*, Vol. IV, p. 226; see also John
Stuart Mill, *A System of Logic*, Longmans edition, p. 238;
Toronto edition, p. 362.

151. J.A. Schumpeter, *Essays of J.A. Schumpeter*, p. 150.

152. J.A. Schumpeter, *History of Economic Analysis*, pp.
472–473.

153. J.A. Schumpeter, *Essays of J.A. Schumpeter*, p. 154.

154. Oskar Lange, "The Scope and Method of Economics,"
Review of Economic Studies, Vol. XIII, No. 1 (1945–1946),
pp. 19–32; Milton Friedman, "The Methodology of
Positive Economics," *Essays in Positive Economics*, pp.
3–43.

Sismondi: A Neglected Pioneer

1. William E. Rappard, *Economistes genevois du XIXe siecle*
(Geneva: Librairie Droz, 1966), p. 433; see also Michel
Lutfalla, "Sismondi: Critique de la loi des débouchés,"
Revue Économique, July 1967, p. 672. But compare
Henryk Grossman, *Simonde de Sismondi et ses théories
économiques* (Varsaviae: Universitatis Liberae Polonae,
1924), pp. 17–18.

2. Karl Marx, *Theories of Surplus Value*, Part III (Moscow:
Progress Publishers, 1971), p. 53.

3. See, for example, Malthus' letters to Ricardo in *The Works
and Correspondence of David Ricardo*, edited by Piero
Sraffa, Vol. VI (Cambridge: Cambridge University Press,
1952), pp. 111–112, 142, 155–156, 303; ibid., Vol. VII, p.
122.

4. Jean-R. de Salis, *Sismondi 1775–1842: La Vie et l'Œuvre
d'un cosmopolite philosophe* (Paris: Libraire Honoré
Champion, 1932), p. 47.

5. William E. Rappard, *Economistes genevois du XIXe siecle*,
pp. 331–332; Jean-R. de Salis, *Sismondi*, p. 48; Charles

Gide and Charles Rist, *A History of Economic Doctrines*, second edition (Boston: D.C. Heath, 1948), p. 190n. Rosa Luxemburg, *The Accumulation of Capital* (New York: Monthly Review Press, 1968), p. 190.

6. His family's name had been changed at least once before, since they were known as "Symond" when they first settled in Geneva in 1692, after fleeing political dangers in France. Jean-R. de Salis, *Sismondi,* pp. 6–7; Élie Halévy, *Sismondi* (Paris: Alcan, 1933), pp. 3–4.

7. Jean-R. de Salis, *Sismondi*, p. 46.

8. J.C.L. Simonde de Sismondi, *Nouveaux Principes d'économie politique*, third edition, Vol. I (Geneva-Paris: Edition Jeheber, 1951), pp. 33–34, 36; ibid., Vol. II (Geneva-Paris: Edition Jeheber, 1953), pp. 137, 244; idem, *Études sur l'économie politique* (Paris: Treuttel et Würtz, 1837), Vol. I, pp. vi, ix, 10.

9. Jean-R. de Salis, *Sismondi*, p. 461n.

10. J.C.L. Simonde de Sismondi, *Nouveaux Principes d'économie politique*, Vol. I, pp. 151, 158; ibid., Vol. II, p. 291; J.C.L. Simonde de Sismondi, *Études sur l'économie politique*, Vol. I, pp. 1, 5, 35, 93, 367, 377–448; J.C.L. Simonde [de Sismondi], *De la Richesse commerciale* (Geneva: J.J Paschoud, Libraire, 1803), Vol. II, pp. 350–351.

11. J.C.L. Simonde de Sismondi, *Political Economy* (New York: Augustus M. Kelley, 1966), p. 75. This is a reprint of Sismondi's encyclopedia article of the same title and not to be confused with a translation of Sismondi's essays entitled *Political Economy and the Philosophy of Government*. J.C.L. Simonde de Sismondi, *Nouveaux Principes d'économie politique*, Vol. I, p. 312; ibid., Vol. II, p. 194.

12. J.C.L. Simonde de Sismondi, *Nouveaux Principes d'économie politique*, Vol. II, p. 165.

13. Jean-R. de Salis, *Sismondi* pp. 44, 168, 172, 218–221.

14. Ibid., pp. 239–240, 462–463.
15. J.A. Schumpeter, *History of Economic Analysis* (New York: Oxford University Press, 1954), p. 493.
16. J.C.L. Simonde [de Sismondi], *Richesse commerciale*, Vol. I, p. 99.
17. Ibid., p. 101n.
18. Ibid., pp. 100–104.
19. Loc. cit.
20. Ibid., pp. 104n–108n.
21. J.C.L. Simonde de Sismondi, *Études sur l'économie politique*, Vol. II, p. 143. See also ibid., p. 227; ibid., Vol. I, p. 115.
22. Ibid., pp. 85n–86n; J.C.L. Simonde de Sismondi, *Nouveaux Principes d'économie politique*, Vol. II, p. 283.
23. J.C.L. Simonde [de Sismondi], *Richesse commerciale*, Vol. II, pp. 446–447.
24. See J.C.L. Simonde de Sismondi, *Nouveaux Principes d'économie politique*, Vol. I, pp. 96–97.
25. "A glut is an increase in the supply of a particular class of commodities, unaccompanied by a corresponding increase in the supply of those other commodities which should serve as their equivalents." [Robert Torrens,] "Mr. Owen's Plans for Relieving the National Distress," *Edinburgh Review*, Oct. 1819, p. 471. "It is not a consequence of production being too much increased, but of its being too little increased. Increase it more . . . and the surplus will immediately disappear." [J.R. McCulloch,] "The opinions of Messrs. SAY, SISMONDI, and MALTHUS, on the Effects of Machinery, and Accumulation, Stated and Examined," *Edinburgh Review*, March 1821, pp. 106–107. "But it is self-evident that this want of effectual demand, or profitable vend, would be occasioned, not by an excess, but by the deficiency of products. Increase the effective powers of industry . . . and then the interchange of one half of each against one half of the other, will replace, with a surplus, all

the ingredients of capital advanced. In every conceivable case, it is the deficiency, not the excess of products which prevents our finding a profitable vend." Robert Torrens, *An Essay on the Production of Wealth* (London: Longmans, Hurst, Rees, Orme and Brown, 1821), pp. 391–392. "It is because the production of some commodities has declined, that other commodities are superabundant." Jean-Baptiste Say, *A Treatise on Political Economy* (Philadelphia: Grigg & Elliott, 1834), p. 134.

26. T.R. Malthus, *Principles of Political Economy*, second edition (New York: Augustus M. Kelley, 1951), p. 323.

27. Robert Torrens, *An Essay on the Production of Wealth*, pp. 384 ff.

28. Useful but incomplete surveys may be found in B. J. Gordon, "Say's Law, Effective Demand, and the Contemporary British Periodicals, 1820–1850," *Economica*, Nov. 1965, pp. 438–446, and in Thomas Sowell, *Say's Law* (Princeton: Princeton University Press, 1972), Chapter IV.

29. David Ricardo, *The Works and Correspondence of David Ricardo*, ed. Piero Sraffa, Vol. VIII (Cambridge: Cambridge Univ. Press, 1952), p. 22; ibid., Vol. IX, p. 218.

30. J.C.L. Simonde de Sismondi, *Political Economy and the Philosophy of Government* (London: John Chapman, 1847), p. 448.

31. See, for example, J.C.L. Simonde de Sismondi, *Nouveaux Principes d'économie politique*, Vol. I, pp. 17, 70; ibid., Vol. II, pp. 246, 248, 275, 306.

32. David Ricardo, *The Works and Correspondence of David Ricardo*, Vol. IX, pp. 236, 243; ibid., Vol. X (Cambridge: Cambridge University Press, 1955), p. 278; Jean-Baptiste Say, *Œuvres diverses de J.-B. Say* (Paris: Guillaumin et Cie, 1848), p. 250.

33. McCulloch dismissed Sismondi as "too much of a sentimentalist to make a good political economist" (*The

Works and Correspondence of David Ricardo, Vol. VIII, p. 25) and Ricardo saw in Sismondi's work only "a very poor performance" (ibid., p. 57).

34. Jean-R. de Salis, *Sismondi*, p. 423.
35. J.C.L. Simonde de Sismondi, *Political Economy and the Philosophy of Government*, p. 449.
36. Jean-Baptiste Say, *Traité d'économie politique,* fifth edition (Paris: Chez Rapilly, 1826), Vol. I, pp. 194–196.
37. Ibid., pp. 194–195.
38. Jean-Baptiste Say, *Œuvres diverses de J.-B. Say*, pp. 503, 505. A letter from Say to Thomas Tooke also stated that "the method of investigation" of Ricardo, McCulloch, and others was producing "a science of adepts" and of "vain subtleties." ibid., p. 527. In an earlier letter to Tooke, Say declared that "many of your compatriots" would "reduce economic questions" to "obscure metaphysics," that they were "founding their arguments on abstract principles rather than on observed facts . . . ." ibid., p. 525.
39. Sismondi, *Political Economy and the Philosophy of Government*, p. 447.
40. Jean-Baptiste Say, *Cours complete d'économie politique pratique*, second edition (Paris: Guillaumin, Libraire, 1840), Vol. I, Part III, Chapter III. Cf. J.C.L. Simonde de Sismondi, *Nouveaux Principes d'économie politique*, Vol. I, Book II, Chapter III.
41. Paul Lambert noted the Say-Malthus correspondence of 1827, but attributed Say's change of mind to the exchange with Malthus, even though (i) Say *began* the exchange by mentioning his change of mind, (ii) the changes were already at this point incorporated in the 1826 edition of the *Traité*, and (iii) similar changes were mentioned in letters to Tooke in 1826, quoted in note 38 above. See Paul Lambert, "The Law of Markets Prior to Jean-Baptiste Say and the Say-Malthus Debate," *International Economic Papers*, No. 6 (1956), p. 17.

42. J.C.L. Simonde de Sismondi, *Nouveaux Principes d'économie politique*, Vol. II, p. 304; ibid., Vol. II, p. 364.

43. ". . . each transference of merchandise supposes an equal transference of money, equal in value and in the opposite direction . . . ." J.C.L. Simonde [de Sismondi], *Richesse commerciale*, Vol. I, p. 127.

44. Ibid., pp. 84–85.

45. Ibid., p. 90.

46. "Thus, the nation, when it forms manufacturing establishments, does not diminish its consumption; it consumes, in a productive manner, what it formerly consumed unproductively." J.C.L. Simonde de Sismondi, *Political Economy*, pp. 27–28.

47. J.C.L. Simonde [de Sismondi], *Richesse commerciale*, Vol. I, p. 111.

48. "*Consumption is the measure of reproduction*, since production which remained unconsumed would degenerate into superfluity, without utility, without value, and from that point advances would cease to be made for their cultivation." [Pierre Francois Joachim Henri Le Mercier de la Rivière,] *L'Ordre naturel et essentiel des societes politiques* (London: Jean Nourse, 1767), Vol. II, p. 250; see also ibid., pp. 138–139, 249–251.

49. James Mill, *Commerce Defended* (London, C. & R. Baldwin, 1808), pp. 81, 83; Jean-Baptiste Say, *A Treatise on Political Economy*, p. 170; John Stuart Mill, *Principles of Political Economy*, ed. W. J. Ashley (London: Longman, Green and Co., 1909), pp. 557–558; ibid. (Toronto: University of Toronto Press, 1965), pp. 571–572.

50. James Mill, *Commerce Defended*, pp. 75, 77; Jean-Baptiste Say, *A Treatise on Political Economy*, p. 137; Nassau W. Senior, *Three Lectures on the Rate of Wages* (London: John Murray, 1831), p. 49; James Mill, *Elements of Political Economy*, third edition (London: Henry G. Bohn, 1844), pp. 226–227; John R. McCulloch, *Principles of Political*

Economy, fifth edition (Edinburgh: Adam and Charles Black, 1864), p. 157.

51. Robert Torrens, *An Essay on the Distribution of Wealth*, p. 370; J.R. McCulloch, *Principles of Political Economy*, p. 156; David Ricardo, *The Works and Correspondence of David Ricardo*, Vol. II, pp. 303, 314.

52. "Political Economy you think is an enquiry into the nature and causes of wealth—I think it should rather be called an enquiry into the laws which determine the division of the produce of industry amongst the classes who concur in its formation. No law can be laid down respecting quantity, but a tolerably correct one can be laid down respecting proportions." David Ricardo, *The Works and Correspondence of David Ricardo*, Vol. VIII, p. 278.

53. J.C.L. Simonde [de Sismondi,] *Richesse commerciale*, Vol. I, p. 103.

54. Ibid., p. 105n.

55. Loc. cit.

56. Ibid., pp. 82, 99–104, 105n.

57. Ibid., pp. 101–102.

58. Ibid., pp. 99–104; J.C.L. Simonde de Sismondi, *Nouveaux Principes d'économie politique*, Vol. I, pp. 96–97.

59. J.C.L. Simonde [de Sismondi], *Richesse commerciale*, Vol. I, p. 101; J.C.L. Simonde de Sismondi, *Nouveaux Principes d'économie politique*, Vol. I, pp. 96–97.

60. J.C.L. Simonde [de Sismondi], *Richesse commerciale*, Vol. I, p. 105n–108n, 215n–216n.

61. J.C.L. Simonde [de Sismondi], *Richesse commerciale*, Vol. I, pp. 347–348; J.C.L. Simonde de Sismondi, *Nouveaux Principes d'économie politique*, Vol. I, p. 238.

62. J.C.L. Simonde de Sismondi, *Études sur l'économie politique*, Vol. II, p. 381.

63. J.C.L. Simonde de Sismondi, *Nouveaux Principes d'économie politique*, Vol. I, pp. 75, 251; ibid., Vol. II, pp. 259–260.

64. J.C.L. Simonde de Sismondi, *Nouveaux Principes d'économie politique*, Vol. I, pp. 76, 251.
65. Ibid., p. 251.
66. Ibid., pp. 114–115.
67. J.C.L. Simonde de Sismondi, *Political Economy*, p. 73; J.C.L. Simonde de Sismondi, *Nouveaux Principes d'économie politique,* Vol. I, p. 330.
68. As claimed by Henryk Grossman (*Simonde de Sismondi et ses theories économiques*, pp. 35, 42, 50, 65, 72) and Rosa Luxemburg (*The Accumulation of Capital*, p. 213).
69. J.C.L. Simonde de Sismondi, *Nouveaux Principes d'économie politique*, Vol. I, p. 260.
70. Ibid., Vol. II, p. 304. The same expression is repeated in J.C.L. Simonde de Sismondi, *Études sur l'économie politique*, Vol. I, p. 112; ibid., Vol. II, p. 364.
71. J.C.L. Simonde de Sismondi, *Nouveaux Principes d'économie politique*, Vol. I, p. 332; J.C.L. Simonde de Sismondi, *Political Economy*, p. 74.
72. J.C.L. Simonde de Sismondi, *Nouveaux Principes d'économie politique*, Vol. II, p. 203. See also ibid., Vol. I, pp. 330–331.
73. Ibid., p. 330; See also ibid., Vol. II, p. 232.
74. Ibid., Vol. II, p. 309.
75. Ibid., p. 228.
76. Ibid., Vol. I, p. 332.
77. Ibid., p. 17.
78. Ibid., Vol. II, Book VII, Chapter IX.
79. Ibid., Vol. I, p. 342.
80. J.C.L. Simonde [de Sismondi], *Richesse commerciale*, Vol. I, pp. 63, 64, 139, 145; J.C.L. Simonde de Sismondi, *Political Economy*, pp. 60, 86; J.C.L. Simonde de Sismondi, *Nouveaux Principes d'économie politique*, Vol. I, pp. 25, 114–115, 234, 235; ibid., Vol. II, pp. 148, 253, 269, 284, 303. The term "equilibrium" is applied specifically to aggregate income in J.C.L. Simonde [de

Sismondi], *Richesse commerciale*, Vol. I, p. 139; J.C.L. Simonde de Sismondi, *Nouveaux Principes d'économie politique*, Vol. II, pp. 148, 253, 269.

81. J.C.L. Simonde de Sismondi, *Nouveaux Principes d'économie politique*, Vol. II, p. 253.

82. J.C.L. Simonde de Sismondi, *Études sur l'économie politique*, Vol. I, pp. 96–97.

83. J.C.L. Simonde de Sismondi, *Nouveaux Principes d'économie politique,* Vol. II, p. 247.

84. Ibid., p. 308.

85. For example, Henryk Grossman, *Simonde de Sismondi et ses théories économiques*, p. 42 and of course John Stuart Mill, *Principles of Political Economy*, Toronto edition, pp. 574–576; Ashley edition, pp. 560–562.

86. J.C.L. Simonde de Sismondi, *Nouveaux Principes d'économie politique*, Vol. I, p. 256.

87. Ibid., pp. 254–255.

88. Ibid., p. 255.

89. Ibid., p. 131. See also ibid., pp. 254, 296.

90. Ibid., pp. 296–297. See also ibid., pp. 254–255.

91. J.C.L. Simonde de Sismondi, *Political Economy*, p. 72.

92. J.C.L. Simonde de Sismondi, *Nouveaux Principes d'économie politique*, Vol. II, p. 148.

93. Ibid., p. 118.

94. Ibid., p. 121.

95. Ibid., Vol. II, p. 82.

96. Ibid., p. 83; J.C.L. Simonde de Sismondi, *Études sur l'économie politique*, Vol. II, p. 394.

97. J.C.L. Simonde de Sismondi, *Nouveaux Principes d'économie politique*, Vol. II, p. 84.

98. Ibid., pp. 83–84.

99. As is done with J.C.L. Simonde de Sismondi, "Two Papers on Demand," *International Economic Papers*, No. 7 (1957), pp. 7–39.

100. J.C.L. Simonde de Sismondi, *Études sur l'économie*

politique, Vol. I, p. 139.

101. J.C.L. Simonde de Sismondi, *Political Economy*, pp. 21, 26, 27, 32, 33, 34, 35, 39, 66, 77, 82, 94, 96, 97, 99, 100, 101, 107, 111, 114, 130.
102. Ibid., pp. 82, 83, 84.
103. J.C.L. Simonde [de Sismondi], *Richesse commerciale*, Vol. I, pp. 105n, 345.
104. J.C.L. Simonde de Sismondi, *Nouveaux Principes d'économie politique*, Vol. I, p. 95.
105. Ibid., pp. 95–96, 102, 104, 108, 112.
106. Ibid., p. 103.
107. J.C.L. Simonde de Sismondi, *Études sur l'économie politique,* Vol. I, pp. 122–123.
108. J.C.L. Simonde de Sismondi, *Nouveaux Principes d'économie politique*, Vol. I, p. 103.
109. Loc. cit.
110. Loc. cit.
111. Loc. cit.
112. Cf. Henryk Grossman, *Sismondi et ses théories économiques,* pp. 58, 77; Michel Lutfall, "Sismondi: Critique de la loi des débouchés," *Revue Économique*, July 1967, pp. 668, 672.
113. J.C.L. Simonde de Sismondi, *Political Economy*, p. 82.
114. J.C.L. Simonde de Sismondi, *Nouveaux Principes d'économie politique*, Vol. I, p. 103.
115. Ibid., pp. 276–277; ibid., Vol. II, pp. 251–252.
116. J.C.L. Simonde [de Sismondi], *Richesse commerciale*, Vol. I, pp. 84–85; J.C.L. Simonde de Sismondi, *Études sur l'économie politique*, Vol. II, pp. 448–449.
117. Nassau W. Senior, *Two Lectures on Population* (London: Saunders and Otley, 1829), pp. 36, 56, 58, 77; Richard Whately, *Introductory Lectures on Political Economy* (London: B. Fellowes, 1832), pp. 248–250.
118. Mark Blaug, *Ricardian Economics: A Historical Study* (New Haven: Yale University Press, 1958), p. 111.

119. J.C.L. Simonde de Sismondi, *Nouveaux Principes d'économie politique*, Vol. II, p. 182.
120. Loc. cit.
121. Loc. cit.
122. Ibid., Vol. I, p. 97.
123. Ibid., Vol. II, p. 181.
124. Ibid., p. 184.
125. Ibid., p. 171.
126. Ibid., Vol. I, p. 21.
127. Ibid., Vol. II, pp. 175, 229–230.
128. Ibid., Vol. I, p. 26.
129. Ibid., pp. 105, 246, 254; ibid., Vol. II, p. 203.
130. Ibid., Vol. II, p. 192. See also ibid., p. 172; ibid., Vol. I, p. 319.
131. J.C.L. Simonde de Sismondi, Review of two books by John Barton, *Annales de Législation et d'Économie Politique*, November 1822, p. 101.
132. Ibid., p. 93.
133. Ibid., pp. 101–102.
134. Ibid., pp. 97–98, 101.
135. Ibid., pp. 110–111.
136. J.C.L. Simonde de Sismondi, *Nouveaux Principes d'économie politique*, Vol. II, p. 204.
137. Ibid., pp. 209–224.
138. Ibid., Vol. I, pp. 31, 66; J.C.L. Simonde de Sismondi, *Études sur l'économie politique*, Vol. I, p. 118; ibid., Vol. II, p. 121.
139. J.C.L. Simonde de Sismondi, *Nouveaux Principes d'économie politique*, Vol. I, pp. 29, 31, 68–69.
140. Ibid., p. 64.
141. Ibid., p. 63.
142. Loc. cit.
143. Ibid., p. 69.
144. Ibid., Vol. II, pp. 147, 250, 251, 275.
145. See, for example, Jean-R. de Salis, *Sismondi*, p. 73.

146. J.C.L. Simonde de Sismondi, *Nouveaux Principes d'économie politique*, Vol. II, p. 115.
147. Ibid., p. 279.
148. Ibid., Vol. I, p. 109.
149. Ibid., Vol. II, p. 279.
150. Ibid., Vol. I, pp. 71, 73; J.C.L. Simonde de Sismondi, *Études sur l'économie politique*, Vol. I, p. 121.
151. J.C.L. Simonde [de Sismondi], *Richesse commerciale*, Vol. I, pp. 100–104, 104n–108n, 215n–216n; J.C.L. Simonde de Sismondi, *Nouveaux Principes*, Vol. I, pp. 115–116; ibid., Vol. II, pp. 82–83, 217–218; J.C.L. Simonde de Sismondi, *Études sur l'économie politique*, Vol. I, pp. 81n–91n.
152. J.C.L. Simonde de Sismondi, *Nouveaux Principes d'économie politique*, Vol. I, p. 89.
153. Ibid., p. 96.
154. Ibid., Vol. II, p. 249.
155. Ibid., Vol. I, p. 57.
156. Ibid., pp. 115, 259; ibid., Vol. II, p. 274.
157. Ibid., Vol. I, pp. 234, 235; ibid., Vol. II, p. 147.
158. Ibid., Vol. II, p. 256.
159. Ibid., p. 147.
160. Ibid., Vol. I, pp. 37, 38, 39, 69; ibid., Vol. II, pp. 168, 250.
161. David Ricardo, *The Works and Correspondence of David Ricardo*, Vol. VIII (Cambridge: Cambridge University Press, 1952), p. 184.
162. J.C.L. Simonde de Sismondi, *A History of the Fall of the Roman Empire* (London: Longman, Rees, Orme, Brown, Green & Longman, 1834), p. 3; J.C.L. Simonde de Sismondi, *Nouveaux Principes d'économie politique*, Vol. I, p. 37. See also ibid., p. 68; ibid., Vol. II, p. 108.
163. J.C.L. Simonde [de Sismondi], *Richesse commerciale*, Vol. I, p. ix; J.C.L. Simonde de Sismondi, *Nouveaux Principes d'économie politique* Vol. I, p. 69; J.C.L. Simonde de Sismondi, *Études sur l'économie politique*, Vol. I, p. iv.
164. J.C.L. Simonde [de Sismondi], *Richesse commerciale*, Vol.

I, p. xvi; J.C.L. Simonde de Sismondi, *Études sur l'économie politique,* Vol. I, p. 133.

165. J.C.L. Simonde de Sismondi, Review of two books by John Barton, *Annales de Législation et d'Économie Politique,* November 1822, p. 83.

166. J.C.L. Simonde de Sismondi, *Nouveaux Principes d'économie politique,* Vol. I, p. 64; J.C.L. Simonde de Sismondi, *A History of the Fall of the Roman Empire,* pp. 7, 8.

167. J.C.L. Simonde de Sismondi, *Études sur les constitutions des peuples libres* (Bruxelles: H. Dumont, Libraire-Editeur, 1836), pp. i-ii; J.C.L. Simonde de Sismondi, *A History of the Fall of the Roman Empire,* p. 1.

168. J.C.L. Simonde de Sismondi, *Nouveaux Principes d'économie politique,* Vol. I, p. 18.

169. Ibid., Vol. II, p. 262.

170. J.C.L. Simonde de Sismondi, *Études sur l'économie politique,* Vol. I, p. 133.

171. J.C.L. Simonde [de Sismondi], *Richesse commerciale,* Vol. I, p. i.

172. J.C.L. Simonde de Sismondi, *Études sur les constitutions des peuples libres,* p. 31.

173. J.C.L. Simonde [de Sismondi], *Richesse commerciale,* Vol. I, p. xiv.

174. The physiocrats had an implicit notion of equilibrium income, since they mentioned the reduction in output which would follow unsold goods; but they had no *theory* of equilibrium income determination.   Lauderdale had a theory of equilibrium investment in 1804; but in his system, fluctuations in investment did not imply fluctuations in aggregate output, but only in its division between consumption and investment.

175. J.C.L. Simonde de Sismondi, *Nouveaux Principes d'économie politique,* Vol. I, p. 116.

176. David Ricardo, *The Works and Correspondence of David*

Ricardo, Vol. I (Cambridge: Cambridge University Press, 1951), p. 382; ibid., Vol. VI (Cambridge: Cambridge University Press, 1952), p. 129; John Stuart Mill, *Principles of Political Economy*, Ashley edition, p. 446; Toronto edition, p. 465.

177. James Mill, *Commerce Defended*, p. 82; [J.R. McCulloch,] "Effects of Machinery and Accumulation," *Edinburgh Review*, March 1821, p. 108; [Robert Torrens,] "Mr. Owen's Plans for Relieving the National Distress," *Edinburgh Review*, October 1819, p. 470.

178. J.C.L. Simonde de Sismondi, *Nouveaux Principes d'économie politique*, Vol. II, p. 254.

179. T.R. Malthus, *Principles of Political Economy*, second edition, pp. 61–69.

180. J.C.L. Simonde de Sismondi, *Nouveaux Principes d'économie politique*, Vol. II, p. 289; J.C.L. Simonde de Sismondi, *Études sur l'économie politique*, Vol. II, p. 336.

181. J.C.L. Simonde de Sismondi, *Nouveaux Principes d'économie politique*, Vol. I, p. 17.

182. David Ricardo, *The Works and Correspondence of David Ricardo*, Vol. VI, pp. 111–112, 142, 155–156; ibid., Vol. VII, p. 122.

183. For example, the central importance of the "proletarians," an increasing concentration of capital, recurring business cycles, technological unemployment, economic dynamics, and the recurring theme of poverty in the midst of plenty.

184. On grounds that a study of Sismondi would have to come *after* a discussion of competition and credit. Karl Marx, *Theories of Surplus Value*, Part III (Moscow: Progress Publishers, 1971), p. 53.

185. See V. I. Lenin, *A Characterization of Economic Romanticism: Sismondi and Our Native Sismondists* (Moscow: Foreign Languages Publishing House, 1951); Henryk Grossman, *Sismondi et ses théories économiques*, p. 76; Rosa Luxemburg, *The Accumulation of Capital*, pp.

173–218.

186. J.C.L. Simonde de Sismondi, *Études sur l'économie politique*, Vol. I, p. 81n.

The Enigma of John Stuart Mill

1. "It would seem that at least in his native country, during the period between the two great wars, Mill was regarded as one of those outmoded figures of the recent past whose ideas have ceased to be interesting because they have become commonplace. Most of the battles he fought had been won and to many who knew his name he probably appeared as a somewhat dim figure whose *On Liberty* they had been made to read at school but whose 'Victorian' outlook had lost most of its appeal. There was, perhaps, also some suspicion that his reputation had been somewhat exaggerated and that he had not been a great original genius but rather an honest, hardworking, and lucid expositor of ideas that other and greater minds had originated. He even came to be regarded, very unjustly, as the last of the 'orthodox' tradition in economics and politics. In fact, however, few men have done more to create the intellectual climate in which what he stood for was finally taken for granted." Friedrich A. Hayek, "Introduction," *Collected Works of John Stuart Mill*, Vol. XII: *The Earlier Letters of John Stuart Mill: 1812–1848*, edited by Francis E. Mineka (Toronto: University of Toronto Press, 1963), pp. xv–xvi.

2. See, for example, Friedrich Hayek, *John Stuart Mill and Harriet Taylor: Their Correspondence and Subsequent Marriage* (Chicago: University of Chicago Press, 1951), Chapters IV and VIII.

3. John Stuart Mill, *The Earlier Letters of John Stuart Mill*, edited by Francis E. Mineka, p. 3.

4. David Ricardo, *The Works and Correspondence of David*

Ricardo, edited by Piero Sraffa (Cambridge: Cambridge University Press, 1952), Vol. IX, p. 44.

5. Ibid., pp. 385–387.

6. John Stuart Mill, *Autobiography* (London: Oxford University Press, 1949), p. 45 (hereinafter referred to as *Autobiography*, Oxford edition); John Stuart Mill, *Collected Works of John Stuart Mill*, Vol. I: *Autobiography and Literary Essays*, edited by John M. Robson and Jack Stillinger (Toronto: University of Toronto Press, 1981), p. 55 (hereinafter referred to as *Autobiography*, Toronto edition).

7. John Stuart Mill, *Autobiography*, Oxford edition, p. 44; Toronto edition, p. 53.

8. Ibid., Toronto edition, p. 139; Oxford edition, p. 115.

9. Ibid., Toronto edition, p. 175; Oxford edition, p. 143.

10. Ibid., Toronto edition, p. 149; Oxford edition, p. 123.

11. Ibid., Toronto edition, p. 139; Oxford edition, p. 114.

12. Ibid., Toronto edition, p. 193; Oxford edition, p. 156.

13. Ibid., Toronto edition, p. 197; Oxford edition, p. 160.

14. In a letter to Justice Oliver Wendell Holmes in September 1924, Harold J. Laski said of John Stuart Mill and Harriet Taylor, "I believe that he was literally the only person who was in the least impressed by her. Mrs. Grote said briefly that she was a stupid woman; Bain said she had a knack of repeating prettily what J.S.M. said and that he told her it was wonderful... . If she was what he thought, someone else at least should have given us indications." Mark de Wolfe Howe, editor, *Holmes-Laski Letters: The Correspondence of Mr. Justice Holmes and Harold J. Laski, 1916–1935* (Cambridge, Massachusetts: Harvard University Press, 1953), pp. 675–676. Thomas Carlyle, who knew the Taylors socially, said of Harriet: "She was full of unwise intellect, asking and re-asking stupid questions." Michael St. John Packe, *The Life of John Stuart Mill* (New York: The Macmillan Company, 1954), p. 315.

15. See, for example, Friedrich Hayek, *John Stuart Mill and Harriet Taylor*, pp. 96, 99–100, 137, 144, 153, 155, 188, 210.
16. John Stuart Mill, *Collected Works*, Vol. XVIII: *Essays on Politics and Society* (Toronto: University of Toronto Press, 1977), p. 216.
17. See, for example, *The Complete Works of Harriet Taylor Mill*, edited by Jo Ellen Jacobs and Paula Harms Payne (Bloomington: Indiana University Press, 1998).
18. Michael St. John Packe, *The Life of John Stuart Mill*, pp. 306–308.
19. Ibid., pp. 309–310.
20. John Stuart Mill, *Collected Works of John Stuart Mill*: Vol. XV: *The Later Letters of John Stuart Mill: 1849–1873*, edited by Francis E. Mineka and Dwight N. Lindsey (Toronto: University of Toronto Press, 1972), pp. 726–727.
21. "The Political Economy . . . was commenced in the autumn of 1845, and was ready for press before the end of 1847. In this period of a little more than two years there was an interval of six months during which the work was laid aside, while I was writing articles." John Stuart Mill, *Autobiography*, Toronto edition, p. 243; Oxford edition, p. 199.
22. Michael St. John Packe, *The Life of John Stuart Mill*, p. 397.
23. See "Classical Macroeconomics" and "Sismondi: A Neglected Pioneer" in this volume.
24. David Ricardo, *The Works and Correspondence of David Ricardo*, Vol. I, p. 306.
25. John Stuart Mill, *Principles of Political Economy*, Toronto edition, p. 573; Ashley edition, p. 559.
26. Jean-Baptiste Say, *Traité d'économie politique*, fifth edition (Paris: Chez Rapilly, 1826), Vol. I, pp. 194–195; Jean-Baptiste Say, *Cours complet d'économie politique pratique* second edition (Paris: Guillaumin, Libraire,

1840), Vol. I, Part III, Chapter III.

27.   John Stuart Mill, *Principles of Political Economy*, Ashley edition, p. 561; Toronto edition, p. 575.

28.   Malthus said, "the question of a glut is exclusively whether it may be general as well as particular and not whether it may be permanent as well as temporary." T.R. Malthus, *Definitions in Political Economy* (London: John Murray, 1827), p. 62.

29.   See, for example, references in John Stuart Mill, *Principles of Political Economy*, Toronto edition, pp. 1126, 1142–1144; Ashley edition, pp. 1009, 1012. Although Malthus and Sismondi are mentioned in discussions of the general glut controversy, nothing that they actually said is quoted.

30.   J.A. Schumpeter, *History of Economic Analysis* (New York: Oxford University Press, 1959), p. 530.

31.   John Stuart Mill, *Essays on Some Unsettled Questions of Political Economy* (London: John W. Parker, 1844), p. 50; John Stuart Mill, "Essays on Some Unsettled Questions of Political Economy," *Collected Works*, Vol. IV: *Essays on Economics and Society* (Toronto: University of Toronto Press, 1967), p. 264.

32.   John Stuart Mill, *Principles of Political Economy*, Toronto edition, p. xci; Ashley edition, p. xxvii.

33.   John Stuart Mill, *The Collected Works of John Stuart Mill*, Vol. XIII, p. 642.

34.   Ibid., p. 731.

35.   John Stuart Mill, *The Later Letters of John Stuart Mill*, p. 37.

36.   John Stuart Mill, *Autobiography*, Toronto edition, p. 241; Oxford edition, pp. 198–199.

37.   John Stuart Mill, *The Earlier Letters of John Stuart Mill: 1812–1848*, p. 231.

38.   John Stuart Mill, *Essays on Some Unsettled Questions of Political Economy*, p. 74; John Stuart Mill, "Essays on

Some Unsettled Questions of Political Economy," *Collected Works*, Vol. IV, p. 278.

39. John Stuart Mill, *Collected Works of John Stuart Mill*, Vol. XII: *The Earlier Letters of John Stuart Mill: 1812–1848*, edited by Francis E. Mineka (Toronto: University of Toronto Press, 1963), p. 236.

40. John Maynard Keynes, *The General Theory of Employment, Interest and Money* (New York: Harcourt, Brace and Co., no date), pp. 18–20.

41. "Classical Macroeconomics" and "Sismondi: A Neglected Pioneer" in this volume.

42. James Maitland, 8th Earl of Lauderdale, *The Nature and Origin of Public Wealth* (New York: Augustus M. Kelley, 1962), p. 220.

43. Ibid., p. 221.

44. The Earl of Lauderale, *Three Letters to the Duke of Wellington* (New York: Augustus M. Kelley, 1965), p. 120.

45. Ibid., p. 121.

46. Thomas Chalmers, *On Political Economy* (Glasgow: William Collins, 1832), p. 116.

47. J.C.L. Sismonde de Sismondi, *Nouveaux Principes d'économie politique*, third edition (Genéve-Paris: Edition Jeheber, 1951), p. 248.

48. John Stuart Mill, *Principles of Political Economy*, Ashley edition, p. 731; Toronto edition, pp. 738–739.

49. John Stuart Mill, *Principles of Political Economy*, Ashley edition, p. 731; Toronto edition, pp. 739–740.

50. See Thomas Sowell, "Samuel Bailey Revisited," *Economica*, November 1970, pp. 401–408.

51. [Samuel Bailey,] *An Inquiry into Those Principles Respecting the Nature of Demand and the Necessity of Consumption Lately Advocated by Mr. Malthus* (London: R. Hunter, 1821), p. 2.

52. Ibid., p. 19.

53. [John Stuart Mill,] "War Expenditure," *Westminster*

Review, July 1824, pp. 40, 47, 48; John Stuart Mill, "War Expenditure," *Collected Works*, Vol. IV: *Essays on Economics and Society*, edited by John M. Robson (Toronto: University of Toronto Press, 1967), pp. 15, 21, 22.

54. John Stuart Mill, *Principles of Political Economy*, Ashley edition, p. 740; Toronto edition, p. 747.

55. [John Stuart Mill,] "Miss Martineuau's Summary of Political Economy," *Monthly Repository*, Vol. VII (1834), pp. 319–320.

56. John Stuart Mill, "On Liberty," *Essays on Politics and Society*, edited by J. M. Robson (Toronto: University of Toronto Press, 1977), p. 228.

57. Ibid., p. 228n.

58. Ibid., p. 240.

59. Ibid., p. 219.

60. Ibid., p. 272.

61. Ibid., pp. 222–223.

62. Ibid., p. 217.

63. Ibid., p. 220.

64. Ibid., p. 220.

65. Ibid., p. 241.

66. Ibid., p. 223.

67. Ibid., p. 270.

68. Ibid., p. 262.

69. Ibid., p. 267.

70. John Stuart Mill, "De Tocqueville on Democracy in America [I]," ibid., p. 86.

71. John Stuart Mill, "Civilization," ibid., p. 128.

72. John Stuart Mill, "On Liberty," ibid., p. 269.

73. John Stuart Mill, "Civilization," ibid., p. 139.

74. John Stuart Mill, "Civilization," ibid., p. 121.

75. John Stuart Mill, "De Tocqueville on Democracy in America," ibid., p. 86.

76. John Stuart Mill, "On Liberty," ibid., p. 222.

77. John Stuart Mill, letter to Alexander Bain, August 6, 1859, *Collected Works of John Stuart Mill*, Vol. XV: *The Later Letters of John Stuart Mill*, edited by Francis E. Mineka and Dwight N. Lindley (Toronto: University of Toronto Press, 1972), p. 631.

78. Friedrich Hayek, *John Stuart Mill and Harriet Taylor*, p. 191.

79. Ibid., p. 92.

80. John Stuart Mill, *Earlier Letters*, p. 731.

81. [Samuel Bailey,] *An Inquiry into Those Principles Respecting the Nature of Demand and the Necessity of Consumption Lately Advocated by Mr. Malthus* (London: R. Hunter, 1821). Although both this monograph and Bailey's *Critical Dissertation*, which also searchingly critiqued Richardian economics, were anonymous, Bailey's authorship of the latter is widely accepted. My own research led to the conclusion that the *Inquiry* was also Bailey's work. See Thomas Sowell, "Samuel Bailey Revisited," *Economica*, November 1970, pp. 402–408.

82. Karl Marx, *Theories of Surplus Value: Selections* (New York: International Publishers, 1952), p. 375.

83. John Stuart Mill, *Principles of Political Economy*, Ashley edition, p. 199; Toronto edition, p. 199.

84. Ibid., Ashley edition, p. 200; Toronto edition., p. 199.

85. Loc. cit.

86. Ibid., Ashley edition, p. 200; Toronto edition, pp. 199–200.

87. Ibid., Ashley edition, p. 200; Toronto edition, p. 200.

88. Ibid., Ashley edition, pp. 200–201; Toronto edition, p. 200.

89. John Stuart Mill, "Rationale of Representation," *Collected Works of John Stuart Mill*, Vol. XVIII: *Essays on Politics and Society*, edited by J.M. Robson (Toronto: University of Toronto Press, 1977), pp. 41–42.

90. Ibid., pp. 42–43.

91. John Stuart Mill, *Autobiography*, Toronto edition, p. 251.

No comparable passage was found in the Oxford edition.

92. George J. Stigler, *Essays on the History of Economics* (Chicago: University of Chicago Press, 1965), p. 7.

93. Ibid., p. 9.

94. [John Stuart Mill,] "The Quarterly Review—Political Economy," *Westminster Review*, January 1825, p. 218; John Stuart Mill, *Essays on Economics and Society*, p. 30.

95. John Stuart Mill, *Principles of Political Economy*, Ashley edition, p. 436; Toronto edition, p. 456.

96. Adam Smith, *The Wealth of Nations* (New York: The Modern Library, 1937), pp. 56–57; John Stuart Mill, *Principles of Political Economy*, Ashley edition, p. 448; Toronto edition, pp. 467–468.

97. Jean-Baptiste Say, *Traité d'économie politique* (Paris: Deterville, 1803), Vol. II, p. 58.

98. George J. Stigler, *Essays in the History of Economics*, p. 69.

99. Stigler, op. cit., p. 8.

100. Adam Smith, *The Wealth of Nations,* pp. 152, 159.

101. Jean-Baptiste Say, *Cours complet d'économie politique pratique*, second edition (Paris: Guillaumin, Libraire, 1840), Vol. I, Part III, Chapter III. Cf J.C.L. Simonde de Sismondi, *Nouveaux Principes d'économie politique* (Geneva-Paris: Edition Jeheber, 1951), Vol. I, Book II, Chapter III.

102. Robert Torrens, *An Essay on the Production of Wealth* (London: Longmans, Hurst, Rees, Orme and Brown, 1821), pp. 414, 419–420, 424; George Poulett Scrope, *Principles of Political Economy* (London: Longman, Rees, Orme, Brown, Green & Longman, 1833), pp. 214–215.

103. George J. Stigler, *Essays on the History of Economics*, p. 14.

104. W. Stanley Jevons, *The Theory of Political Economy* (New York: Kelley & Millman, 1957), pp. 275–277.

105. George J. Stigler, *Essays on the History of Economics*, p.

15.

106. J.A. Schumpeter, *History of Economic Analysis*, p. 529.
107. Ibid., p. 528.

The Mysteries of Marxian Economics

1.   Joseph A. Schumpeter, *History of Economic Analysis* (New York: Oxford University Press, 1959), p. 392.
2.   A landmark in this peculiar approach was Paul A. Samuelson, "Wages and Interest: A Modern Dissection of Marxian Economic Models," *American Economics Review*, December 1957, pp. 884–992. Other distinguished economists have managed to tie Samuelson's record for zero citations from Marx in a scholarly exposition of Marxian economics. For example: Martin Bronfenbrenner, "*Das Kapital* for the Modern Man," *Science & Society*, Fall 1965, pp. 419–438; William Fellner, *Modern Economic Analysis* (New York: McGraw-Hill, Inc., 1960), pp. 121–141. Others who came close to these performances in ignoring Marx while discussing "Marxism" include Fred M. Gottheil, "Increasing Misery of the Proletariat," *Canadian Journal of Economics and Political Science*, February 1962, pp. 103–113.
3.   Georg Wilhelm Friedrich Hegel, *The Philosophy of History*, translated by J. Sibree (New York: Dover Publications, Inc., 1956), pp. 410–411.
4.   Karl Marx, *Capital: A Critique of Political Economy*, Vol. I, translated by Edward Aveling (Chicago: Charles H. Kerr & Co., 1906), p. 823.
5.   For example, Shlomo Avineri, *The Social and Political Thought of Karl Marx* (Cambridge: Cambridge University Press, 1968), pp. 6, 65, 66, 69–70, 72, 86, 95, 143, 144, 155, 178n–179n, 229, 235; Joseph A. Schumpeter, *Capitalism, Socialism, and Democracy* (New York: Harper

& Row, 1950), pp. 11, 38n; David McLellan, *Engels* (Glasgow: Fontana/Collins, 1977), pp. 69, 70–71, 73; John Weeks, *Capital and Exploitation* (Princeton: Princeton University Press, 1981), pp. 8, 26, 28, 36, 41, 53, 57, 61, 62, 93, 94.

6.   In addition to various collections of their letters, see Saul K. Padover, *Karl Marx* (New York: New American Library, 1980), p. 190.

7.   Robert Payne, *Marx* (New York: Simon and Schuster, 1968), p. 260. See also Frederick Engels, *Herr Eugen Dühring's Revolution in Science* [*Anti-Dühring*] (New York: International Publishers, 1939), p. 13; Karl Marx, *Capital: A Critique of Political Economy*, Vol. II, translated by Ernest Untermann (Chicago: Charles H. Kerr, 1913), pp. 7–8.

8.   See Frederick Engels, *Herr Eugen Dühring's Revolution in Science* [*Anti-Dühring*], p. 13.

9.   Karl Marx, *Capital*, Volume I (Chicago: Charles H. Kerr & Co., 1919), pp. 24–25; Karl Marx, *Critique of Political Economy* (Chicago: Charles H. Kerr & Co., 1904), pp. 292–294; Karl Marx and Frederick Engels, *Selected Correspondence*, translated by Dona Torr (New York: International Publishers, 1942), p. 496.

10.   See, for example, Friedrich Engels, "Ludwig Feuerbach and the End of Classical German Philosophy," Karl Marx and Friedrich Engels, *Basic Writings on Politics and Philosophy*, edited by Lewis S. Feuer (Anchor Books, 1959), p. 219; Frederick Engels, *Herr Eugen Dühring's Revolution in Science* [*Anti-Dühring*], p. 117; Karl Marx and Frederick Engels, *Selected Correspondence*, translated by Dona Torr, p. 485n; Karl Marx, "Wage Labour and Capital," Karl Marx and Friedrich Engels, *Selected Works*, Volume I (Moscow: Foreign Languages Publishing House, 1955), p. 83; Karl Marx, *Grundrisse*, translated by Martin Nicolaus (New York: Vintage Books, 1973), pp. 548–549;

Frederick Engels, *Engels on Capital*, translated & edited by Leonard E. Mins (New York: International Publishers Co., Inc., 1937), p. 60; Karl Marx, *Capital*, Volume I, pp. 71, 77, 124, 128, 132, 139, 146, 162, 837; ibid., Volume II, pp. 36, 51, 59, 112, 120, 130, 431.

11. Karl Marx, *Capital*, Vol. I, pp. 238, 244n, 425n, 443n, 574, 618–619. See also Frederick Engels, *Engels on Capital*, ed., Leonard E. Mins, pp. 126–127.

12. Karl Marx, *Capital*, Vol. I, p. 244n.

13. Karl Marx and Frederick Engels, *Selected Correspondence*, translated by Dona Torr, p. 220. See also Frederick Engels, *Engels on Capital*, translated and edited by Leonard E. Mins, p. 125.

14. Compare Eugen von Böhm-Bawerk, *Karl Marx and the Close of His System*, translated by Alice M. Macdonald (New York: The MacMillan Co., 1898); Karl Marx, *Theories of Surplus Value: Selections* (New York: International Publishers, 1952), pp. 133, 212, 214, 221, 232, 250, 282. See also Karl Marx and Frederick Engels, *Selected Correspondence*, p. 243.

15. Karl Marx, *Capital*, Vol. III, p. 38.

16. Ibid., p. 203.

17. Karl Marx and Frederick Engels, *Selected Correspondence*, p. 130.

18. David Ricardo, *The Works and Correspondence of David Ricardo*, ed. Piero Sraffa, Vol. I: *Principles of Political Economy and Taxation* (Cambridge: Cambridge University Press, 1951), p. 50.

19. John Stuart Mill, *Essays on Some Unsettled Questions of Political Economy* (London: John W. Parker, 1844), p. 96.

20. Karl Marx, *Theories of Surplus Value: Selections*, p. 320.

21. David Ricardo, *The Works and Correspondence of David Ricardo*, Vol. II, pp. 249–250.

22. Karl Marx and Frederick Engels, *Collected Works* (New York: International Publishers, 1976), Vol. VI , p. 426.

23. Karl Marx and Friedrich Engels, "Manifesto of the Communist Party," Karl Marx and Friedrich Engels, *Basic Writings on Politics and Philosophy*, p. 19; Karl Marx, *The Poverty of Philosophy* (New York: International Publishers, 1963), p. 51.

24. Karl Marx, *The Poverty of Philosophy*, p. 51n.

25. Karl Marx, "Critique of the Gotha Proramme," Karl Marx and Friedrich Engels, *Basic Writings on Politics and Philosophy*, p. 124.

26. Karl Marx, "Wage Labour and Capital," Karl Marx and Friedrich Engels, *Selected Works*, Vol. I, p. 83.

27. Karl Marx, *Theories of Surplus Value: Selections*, p. 186.

28. Karl Marx, *Capital*, Vol. I, p. 399.

29. Ibid., p. 396.

30. Ibid., p. 708.

31. Ibid., pp. 708–709.

32. Ibid., p. 534.

33. Karl Marx and Frederick Engels, *Selected Correspondence*, pp. 129–131.

34. Karl Marx, *Capital*, Vol. III, pp. 182–185.

35. Karl Marx and Frederick Engels, *Selected Correspondence*, pp. 106, 232, 246; Karl Marx, *Capital*, Vol. I, p. 45.

36. Karl Marx, *Capital*, Vol. III, p. 1026.

37. Karl Marx and Frederick Engels, *Selected Correspondence*, p. 246.

38. Karl Marx, *The Poverty of Philosophy*, pp. 60–61.

39. Karl Marx, *A Contribution to the Critique of Political Economy* (Chicago: Charles H. Kerr & Co., 1904), p. 107.

40. Frederick Engels, "Preface to the First German Edition," Karl Marx, *The Poverty of Philosophy*, pp. 18, 19.

41. David Ricardo, *The Works and Correspondence of David Ricardo,* Vol. VIII, p. 277.

42. Frederick Engels, "Outlines of a Critique of Political Economy," Karl Marx, *Economic and Philosophic Manuscripts of 1844* (Moscow: Foreign Languages

Publishing House, 1961), p. 195. It should be noted here that Engels, like the Ricardians before him, defined demand as quantity demanded, not the schedule concept of demand used today.

43. Ibid., pp. 195–196.
44. Ibid., p. 196.
45. The interpretation of ever-deepening crises is found in Paul Sweezy, *The Theory of Capitalist Development* (New York: Monthly Review Press, 1956), p. 190 and in other economists who have relied on Sweezy, rather than on reading Marx.
46. Karl Marx and Friedrich Engels, "Manifesto of the Communist Party," *Basic Writings on Politics and Philosophy*, edited by L.S. Feuer, p. 10.
47. For example, Martin Bronfenbrenner cited Sweezy, who in turn cited a number of other economists—but not including Karl Marx. See Martin Bronfenbrenner, "*Das Kapital* for the Modern Man," *Science & Society*, Fall 1965, p. 419; Paul Sweezy, *The Theory of Capitalist Development*, Chapter XI.
48. Paul Sweezy, *The Theory of Capitalist Development*, Chapter XI.
49. Karl Marx, *Capital*, Vol. III, p. 568.
50. Karl Marx, *Grundrisse*, p. 750.
51. Friedrich Engels, "Letters on Historical Materialism," Karl Marx and Friedrich Engels, *Basic Writings on Politics and Philosophy*, p. 401.
52. Karl Marx, *Capital*, Vol. III, p. 292.
53. Karl Marx, *Theories of Surplus Value: Selections*, p. 373n.
54. Joseph A. Schumpeter, *History of Economic Analysis*, p. 438n.
55. Karl Marx, *Capital*, Vol. I, p. 837.
56. See, for example, Paul Sweezy, *The Theory of Capitalist Development*, Chapter XI.
57. G.W.F. Hegel, "The Doctrine of Essence," *Hegel*

Selections, edited by J. Lowenberg (Chicago: Charles Scribner's Sons, 1939), p. 119.

58. Quoted in Herbert Marcuse, *Reason and Revolution*, second edition (New York: The Humanities Press, 1954), p. 124.

59. Karl Marx, *Capital*, Vol. I, p. 837.

60. Paul Sweezy, *The Theory of Capitalist Development*, p. 176.

61. Karl Marx, *Capital*, Vol. III, p. 359.

62. Karl Marx and Frederick Engels, *Selected Correspondence*, p. 205.

63. Ibid., p. 54.

64. Frederick Engels, Paul and Laura Lafargue, *Correspondence* translated by Yvonne Kapp (Moscow: Foreign Languages Publishing House, 1959), Vol. I, p. 134.

65. "The manuscript next following in the order of time is that of Volume III. It was written for the greater part in 1864 and 1865. After this manuscript had been completed in its essential parts, Marx undertook the elaboration of Volume I, which was published in 1867." Friedrich Engels, "Preface," Karl Marx, *Capital*, Vol. II, p. 9.

66. Karl Marx, *Grundrisse*, p. 412.

67. Ibid., p. 413. See also Karl Marx, *Theories of Surplus Value: Selections*, p. 368.

68. Karl Marx, "Wage Labour and Capital," Karl Marx and Friedrich Engels, *Selected Works*, Vol. I, p. 86.

69. Karl Marx, *Economic and Philosophic Manuscripts of 1844*, p. 128. See also ibid., p. 119.

70. Karl Marx, *Theories of Surplus Value: Selections*, p. 396.

71. Ibid., p. 393.

72. Ibid., p. 379.

73. Ibid., p. 371.

74. Ibid., pp. 203, 369.

75. Ibid., p. 369.

76. Karl Marx, *Capital*, Vol. III, p. 979n.

77. Karl Marx, *A Contribution to the Critique of Political Economy*, p. 232.
78. Karl Marx, *Theories of Surplus Value: Selections*, p. 370.
79. Ibid., p. 408.
80. David Ricardo, *The Works and Correspondence of David Ricardo*, Vol. II, p. 306; John Stuart Mill, *Principles of Political Economy*, edited by W. J. Ashley (London: Longman, Green, and Co., 1909), p. 559.
81. James Mill, *Elements of Political Economy*, third edition (London: Henry G. Bohn, 1844), pp. 228, 231, 237, 241; John Stuart Mill, *Principles of Political Economy* (London: Longmans, Green, and Co., 1909) p. 559; ibid. (Toronto: University of Toronto Press, 1965), p. 579; John Stuart Mill, *Collected Works* (Toronto: University of Toronto, 1967), Vol. IV, pp. 17–18, 42.
82. Karl Marx, *Capital*, Vol. I, p. 132.
83. Karl Marx, *Theories of Surplus Value*, translated by Jack Cohen and S.W. Ryaznaskaya (Moscow: Progress Publishers, 1971), Part III, p. 102. This is the only reference to this particular edition in this essay. All subsequent citations of *Theories of Surplus Value* refer to the edition already referred in previous notes in this essay, an edition more widely available, even though it consists only of selections, obviously not including the cited passage from the complete translation.
84. These and other quotes from Sismondi are my translations. J.C.L. Simonde de Sismondi, *Nouveaux Principes d'économie politique* (Geneva-Paris: Edition Jeheber, 1953), Vol. II, p. 247.
85. J.C.L. Simonde de Sismondi, *Études sur l'économie politique* (Paris: Treuttel et Würtz, Libraires, 1837), Vol. I, pp. 96–97.
86. J.C.L. Simonde de Sismondi, *Nouveaux Principes d'économie politique*, Vol. I, p. 251. See also *Études sur l'économie politique*, Vol. I, p. 120; ibid., Vol. II, p. 249.

87. In addition to calling the working class the "proletariat," decades before Marx, Sismondi also argued that the difficulties of forecasting insured aggregate disequilibrium, postulated an increasing concentration of capital, recurring business cycles, and technological unemployment, as well as using economic dynamics, and having a recurring theme of poverty in the midst of plenty.

88. Karl Marx, *Capital*, Vol. II, Chapter XX.

89. Ibid., Chapter XXI.

90. ". . . the increase of wealth . . . implied in capitalist production." Karl Marx, *Capital*, Vol. I, p. 337.

91. Karl Marx, *Capital*, Vol. II, p. 86.

92. Ibid., pp. 86–87.

93. Ibid., p. 378.

94. Page 126 of this present book.

95. J.C.L. Simonde de Sismondi, *Nouveaux Principes d'économie politique*, Vol. II, p. 148.

96. Karl Marx, *Theories of Surplus Value: Selections*, p. 387.

97. Ibid., p. 393.

98. Karl Marx, *Capital*, Vol. I, p. 155n.

99. Karl Marx, *Theories of Surplus Value: Selections*, p. 380.

100. Ibid.

101. Karl Marx, *Theories of Surplus Value: Selections*, p. 379.

102. Ibid. The distinction between those factors which made crises possible and those that actually precipitated crises was made repeatedly by Marx. See Karl Marx, *Theories of Surplus Value: Selections*, pp. 331, 383–384; Karl Marx, *Capital*, Vol. I, p. 328.

103. Karl Marx, *Capital*, Vol. I, p. 154.

104. Ibid., p. 155.

105. Karl Marx, *Theories of Surplus Value: Selections*, p. 386.

106. Ibid., p. 389.

107. Karl Marx, *Capital*, Vol. III, p. 543. See also ibid., p. 602; Karl Marx, *A Contribution to the Critique of Political Economy*, p. 193.

108. Karl Marx, *Theories of Surplus Value: Selections*, p. 392.
109. Ibid., p. 393.
110. Ibid., pp. 390–391.
111. Ibid., p. 401.
112. Ibid., p. 408.
113. Robert Torrens, *An Essay on the Production of Wealth* (London: Longman, Hurst, Rees, Orme and Brown, 1821), p. 414.
114. Ibid., p. 424.
115. Karl Marx, *Grundrisse*, p. 621.
116. Karl Marx, *Capital*, Vol. I, p. 26n. See also ibid., p. 495; Karl Marx, "On Proudhon," Karl Marx and Friedrich Engels, *Selected Works*, Vol. I, p. 391.
117. Karl Marx, *Capital*, Vol. I, p. 31; Frederick Engels, *The Condition of the Working-Class in England in 1844* (London: George Allen & Unwin Ltd., 1952), p. x.
118. Karl Marx, *Capital*, Vol. I, p. 694. See also ibid., p. 699.
119. Karl Marx and Frederick Engels, *Selected Correspondence*, p. 422. See also Frederick Engels, *The Condition of the Working-Class in England in 1844*, pp. x–xi.
120. Frederick Engels, "An Outline of a Critique of Political Economy," Karl Marx, *Economic and Philosophic Manuscripts of 1844*, p. 195.
121. Karl Marx, *Capital*, Vol. II, p. 211.
122. Karl Marx, *Capital*, Vol. III, pp. 574n–575n; Frederick Engels, "Preface to the First German Edition," Karl Marx, *The Poverty of Philosophy*, p. 20n; Frederick Engels, *The Condition of the Working-Class in England in 1844*, p. xvi.
123. For example: "The calculations given in the text are intended merely as illustrations. We have in fact assumed that prices=values. We shall, however, see, in Volume III, that even in the case of average prices the assumption cannot be made in this very simple manner." (Karl Marx, *Capital*, Vol. I, p. 244n.) In another footnote, Marx declared, "average prices do not coincide with the values of

commodities, as Adam Smith, Ricardo, and others believe." (ibid., p. 185n).

124. Frederick Engels, *Engels on Capital*, edited and translated by Leonard E. Mins, pp. 125–127.

125. Karl Marx and Frederick Engels, *Selected Correspondence*, p. 219.

126. V.I. Lenin, "The Fight to Overcome the Fuel Crisis," "The Role and Functions of Trade Unions Under the New Economic Policy," "Five Years of the Russian Revolution and the Prospects of the World Revolution," and "Ninth Congress of the Russian Communist Party (Bolsheviks)," all quoted from the 1951 edition of *Selected Works* by V. I. Lenin, published in Moscow by the Foreign Languages Publishing House.

127. Edmund Wilson, *To the Finland Station* (New York: Harcourt, Brace and Co., 1940), p. 292.

128. See, for example, Karl Marx and Frederick Engels, *Selected Correspondence*, pp. 226–227; Karl Marx, *Capital*, Vol. II, pp. 23, 24, 25; Friedrich Engels, "Socialism: Utopian and Scientific," Karl Marx and Friedrich Engels, *Basic Writings on Politics and Philosophy,* edited by Lewis S. Feuer, pp. 89–90; Karl Marx, *Grundrisse*, translated by Martin Nicolaus, p. 684.

129. Paul A. Samuelson, "Wages and Interest: A Modern Dissection of Marxian Economic Models," *American Economic Review*, December 1957, p. 911.

Thoughts on the History of Economics

1. For examples of the devious tactics of Marx and Engels, see Thomas Sowell, *Marxism: Philosophy and Economics* (New York: William Morrow, 1985), pp. 171, 172, 176, 177, 179–180.

2. David Ricardo, *The Works and Correspondence of David*

Ricardo, edited by Piero Sraffa (Cambridge: Cambridge University Press, 1952), Vol. VII, p. 372.

3. Karl Marx, *Theories of Surplus Value: Selections* (New York: International Publishers, 1952), pp. 202–203.

4. As noted in the essay on John Stuart Mill, Mill himself pointed out that *On Liberty* was not about freedom from government. It was about freedom from social pressures— and more specifically, about freedom from social pressures for an intellectual elite who not only had the right, but the duty, to exert their own moral hegemony over the rest of society.

5. Adam Smith, *The Wealth of Nations* (New York: Modern Library, 1937), p. 423.

6. This latter phenomenon is explored at length in my *A Conflict of Visions* (New York: Basic Books, 2002).

7. Karl Marx and Frederick Engels, *Selected Correspondence* (New York: International Publishers, 1942), pp. 106, 232, 246; Karl Marx, *Capital: A Critique of Political Economy*, Vol. I (Chicago: Charles H. Kerr, 1906), p. 45.

8. Milton Friedman, *A Theory of the Consumption Function* (Princeton: Princeton University Press, 1957).

9. Joseph A. Schumpeter, *Capitalism, Socialism and Democracy* (New York: Harper and Brothers, 1950), p. 313.

10. Karl Marx, "The Civil War in France," Karl Marx and Friedrich Engels, *Basic Writings on Politics and Philosophy*, edited by Lewis S. Feuer (New York: Anchor Books, 1959), pp. 521, 525, 527, 528. Marxian views on the need for democratic rights in the "dictatorship of the proletariat" are discussed in my *Marxism: Philosophy and Economics* (New York: William Morrow, 1985), pp. 143–151.

11. John Maynard Keynes, *The General Theory of Employment, Interest and Money* (New York: Harcourt, Brace and Co. [1936]), p. 383.

12. Karl Marx, "The Eighteenth Brumaire of Louis Bonaparte," Karl Marx and Friedrich Engels, *Selected Works* (Moscow: Foreign Languages Publishing House, 1955), Vol. I, p. 272.

13. Ibid., p. 247.

14. See Thomas Sowell, *Marxism: Philosophy and Economics*, Chapter IV.

15. John Stuart Mill, *A System of Logic* (London: Longmans, Green and Co., Ltd., 1959), p. 605. See also pp. 604, 610.

16. Karl Marx and Frederick Engels, *Selected Correspondence*, p. 159.

17. See, for example, Thomas Sowell, "Assumptions versus History in Ethnic Education," *Teachers College Record*, Vol. 83, No. 1 (Fall 1981), pp. 42–44.

18. J.A. Schumpeter, *History of Economic Analysis* (New York: Oxford University Press, 1951), p. 302.

19. George J. Stigler, *Essays in the History of Economics* (Chicago: University of Chicago Press, 1965), pp. 20–22, passim.

20. For a detailed account of that controversy, see Thomas Sowell, *Say's Law: An Historical Analysis* (Princeton: Princeton University Press, 1972), Chapters I–IV.

21. J.A. Schumpeter, *History of Economic Analysis*, p. 494.

22. Schumpeter made a distinction between economists who used arithmetic or even algebraic examples as a "restatement in algebraic form of some result of non-mathematical reasoning" as distinguished from a situation where "the reasoning that produces this result is explicitly mathematical." J.A. Schumpeter, *History of Economic Analysis*, pp. 954–955. However the extensive and systematic progression of algebraic equations to derive economic results in *Richesse commerciale* not only did so but did so earlier than the work of others credited with being pioneers in mathematical economics. See J.C.L. Simonde [de Sismondi], *De la Richesse commerciale*, Vol. I (Genéve: Chez J.J. Paschoud, Libraire, 1803), pp.

105n–108n, 215n–216n.

23. David Ricardo, *The Works and Correspondence of David Ricardo*, Vol. VIII, p. 278.

24. See, for example, David Ricardo, *The Works and Correspondence of David Ricardo*, Vol. VI, pp. 111–112, 142, 155–156, 303; ibid., Vol. VII, p. 122.

25. See, for example, Thomas Sowell, *Say's Law*, p. 221n.

26. Augustin Cournot, *Researches into the Mathematical Principles of The Theory of Wealth* (New York: Augustus M. Kelley, 1960), pp. 51–52. See Figure 1 in the back of the book for the graph.

27. Ibid., pp. 52–53.

28. Ibid., pp. 59-60.

29. Ibid., p. 140.

30. Irving Fisher, "Foreword," ibid., p. xi.

31. John Stuart Mill, for example, carried on correspondence in French.

32. George J. Stigler, *Essays in the History of Economics*, pp. 13–15.

33. Thomas Kuhn, *The Structure of Scientific Revolutions* (Chicago: University of Chicago Press, 1970), p. 17.

INDEX

Abstraction, 2, 79, 80, 81, 82, 85, 86, 87–88, 89, 102, 103, 109, 120, 122–123, 242 (note 51)
Agriculture, 8, 22, 49, 50–56, 63, 66, 76, 123
Allen, William R., ix
Allocation of resources, 9, 43, 48, 50, 85, 163–165, 172, 183
Anachronistic Interpretations, vii, 26, 49
Appearance (see Dialectics)
Aristocracy, 6, 8
Assumptions, 42, 44, 46, 47, 48, 51, 55, 56, 58, 63, 83, 86, 88, 90, 95, 96, 101–102, 153, 158, 175, 179, 181–182, 183, 190

Bagehot, Walter, 18
Bailey, Samuel, 67, 68, 71, 77, 90, 97–98, 99, 141, 147, 269 (note 81)
    demand 71
    Say's Law 98, 141
    supply and demand 68, 71, 141
    value 67–68, 90
    words 97–98
Barton, John, 121–122
Beard, Charles E., 195
Behavioral Theories, (see also Mathematics, identities), 4, 10, 11, 24, 32, 43, 59, 62, 110–111, 126
Bentham, Jeremy, 38, 130, 131, 132
Blake, William, 45, 47
Boisguillebert, Pierre le Pesant, Sieur de, 2
Bonaparte, Napoleon, 15, 45, 106, 110
Bosanquet, James Whatman, 79
Businessmen (see Capitalists)

Cairnes, John Elliot, 8
Capital, 25, 32, 33, 35, 40, 43, 44, 45, 46, 55, 56, 73, 77, 94, 115, 117, 123, 139, 142, 184
Capitalists, 6, 8–9, 14, 184–185
Causation (see also Methodology), 88–97
 changes vs. states of being 89, 90–92, 95
 intentions 194
 mutual determination 35
 reciprocal interactions 35, 89, 95
 sequential causation 35, 88, 89, 96, 101–102
 simultaneous determination 88, 89
 tendencies 60–61, 89, 92–95, 120
Chalmers, Thomas, 18, 29, 33, 36, 127, 140
 growth 33
 money 29, 36
 saving 33, 36
Change (see Causation, changes versus states of being)
Charity, 17–18
Circular Flow, 29, 74, 110, 114
Classes, 5, 7, 8, 10, 11–12, 14, 19, 20, 121, 192
 aristocracy 6, 8
 capitalists 8–16
 harmony 4, 10–11, 12, 13–14
 landlords 9–10, 17, 18, 50, 54, 76, 81, 127
 workers 5, 7, 11, 13, 18, 18–19, 22–23, 26–27, 27–28, 51, 52, 55, 56, 58, 59, 61, 74, 91, 94, 111, 112, 113, 115, 116, 117, 118, 119, 121, 122, 123, 184–185, 192
Classical Economics
 defined 1–4
 era 3
 versus "vulgar economics" 2, 12
Cobbett, William, 18
Combination Laws, 18
Comparative Statics (see Statics and Dynamics)
Competition (see Monopoly)
Comte, August, 138

Condorcet, Marquis de, 20
Conservatism, 4–16, 18, 19, 20, 60, 102–103, 189, 243 (note 73)
Consumption, 22, 24, 25, 110
      aggregate demand 24, 41, 46, 254 (note 48)
      consumption demand 25, 44, 45
Controversies (see Polemics)
Corn Laws, 10, 19, 54, 101
Costa, Elizabeth, ix
Cost-covering Prices (see Demand, cost-covering prices)
Costs, 52, 55, 76–77, 114
      cost functions 55, 63
      ex ante 29, 114
      ex post 29, 114
      marginal costs 55
      supply-determining 71
      value determining 52, 68, 69, 71, 77
Cournot, Antoine Augustin, 82, 198, 200

Deductive Reasoning (see Methodology, inductive and deductive
      reasoning)
Definitions (see Methodology)
Demand, 63–64
      aggregate 24, 25, 26–27, 29, 32, 43, 46, 67, 74, 166
      consumption demand 25
      cost-covering prices 25, 29
      effective demand 64, 75
      investment demand 24–25, 110
      quantity demanded 29, 64, 73, 76, 125, 275 (note 42)
      schedule 70–71, 72–73, 125–126
      utility 64, 75, 115, 184
Dialectics (see also Hegel; Marx), 89, 157–158, 182
      appearance 87, 88, 159, 170, 171
      essence 88, 159, 170, 171
      interaction 89
      internal conflicts 93–94, 169–170, 171
      metamorphosis 94, 158, 166, 171

  method of thinking 157–158

  processes 158, 166

  successive approximations 158, 159, 181–182

Diminishing Returns, 3, 48–63, 76, 85

  analytical 48, 49, 54–55, 56

  historical 48, 49, 54–55, 56, 58, 76, 102

  population 76

  rent 51–52, 76

Disproportionality, 27, 28, 40, 107–108, 116, 135, 164–166, 172, 173, 183, 184, 251 (note 25)

Distribution (see Income, functional distribution, personal distribution)

Division of Labor, 13

Dynamics (see Statics and Dynamics)

Economic Growth, 22, 25, 27, 33–34, 46–47, 48, 76, 175

  causes 22, 33

  consequences 22–23

  growth models 30, 104, 106, 110–113, 125, 198

  technology 33, 46, 49, 56, 63, 65, 73, 127, 139, 140, 163

Edgeworth, F.Y., 200

Education, 13, 15, 17, 18, 19, 22, 105, 117, 188–189

Empiricism (see Methodology, empiricism, inductive and deductive reasoning)

Employment and Unemployment, 108, 121, 122, 127

  employment 43, 122

  unemployment 28, 42, 127

Engels, Friedrich, 89, 91, 94, 156, 157, 158, 159, 160, 161, 163, 164, 165, 166, 167, 168, 169, 171, 172, 180, 181, 182, 183, 184, 185, 192, 194

  Capital 85, 91, 158, 182

  crisis theory 166–169

  Hegelian dialectics 89, 93–94

Equilibrium, 20, 24

Equilibrium Income, 24–25, 27–29, 30, 31, 67, 74, 104, 107, 108, 111, 114–119, 125, 135, 150–151, 193

  disequilibrium 24–25, 28–29

reproduction 24–25, 67, 75, 110, 114, 175, 254 (note 48)
    secular stagnation 27, 30, 46, 107, 116–117
Essence (see Dialectics)
Ex Ante and *Ex Post*, 24, 27, 29, 33, 34, 98, 174
Externalities, 8, 11, 13

Factor Payments, 26, 29, 114
Facts (see Methodology, empiricism, inductive and deductive
    reasoning)
Fiscal Policy, 34, 42–46
    deficit spending 43–44, 46
    national debt 43–44, 127
    sinking fund 16, 44–45, 139
    spending 44
    taxation 6, 9, 13, 16, 42–45, 54, 139–140
Fischer, Irving, 39
Food, 57–59, 63, 76, 190–191
Forced Saving, 42, 45
Friedman, Milton, 39, 103, 191
Functional Distribution (see Income, functional distribution)

Galbraith, John Kenneth, 103
General Gluts (see Gluts, general)
George, Henry, 54
Gluts, 22, 30, 114, 116, 138–139, 173
    disproportionality 27, 28, 40, 116, 166, 168, 172, 251 (note 25)
    general 22, 26, 27, 28–29, 30, 34, 114, 173, 179, 251 (note 25)
    partial 26, 114, 173, 179
Godwin, William, 20
Gold, 5, 6, 35, 41–42, 65, 193
Government, 4, 5, 7, 14–15, 16, 41, 42–46, 60, 106, 115, 116,
    129, 139–140, 143, 144, 149, 164, 192
    controls 13, 14, 20, 41
    spending 9, 13, 45–46
    taxation 6, 9, 13, 16, 42–45, 54, 139–140

Growth
      economic growth 22–23, 25, 27, 30, 33–34, 46–47, 48,
           56, 63, 73, 76, 104, 106, 110–113, 124, 127,
           139, 140, 163, 175, 198
      growth vs. development 161

Harmony, 4, 10–11, 12, 13–14
Hegel, G.W.F. (see also Dialectics), 156, 157–159, 181
      contradiction 169–170, 171
      negation 169, 170
History
      Marx's theory of history 89, 90, 91, 185, 194–195,
           243 (note 73)
      J.S. Mill's theory of history 194–195
History of Ideas, vii, 20, 175, 187, 189, 190, 201
      anachronistic history vii, 26, 49
      controversies vii, 190–193
      evolution of economics vii, 187, 191, 198–201
      influence of events 187, 193–197
      interpreters vii, 1, 26, 30, 34, 35, 38, 42, 46, 47, 70, 80,
           88, 94, 106, 115, 159–162, 167, 169, 171, 181,
           183, 184, 187, 275 (note 47)
Hoarding (see Money)
Hobson, John A., 103
Hoover Institution, vii, ix
Hume, David, 2, 21, 37, 39

Identities (see Mathematics, identities)
Imperialism, 5–7, 106
Income
      aggregate 27–29, 31, 67, 74, 104, 107–108, 111, 114–119,
           125, 135, 193, 255 (note 52)
      functional distribution 11, 48, 65, 67
      per capita income 65
      personal distribution 11, 12, 147–148

Inductive Reasoning (see Methodology, inductive and deductive reasoning)
Interest Rates, 35–36, 37, 40, 42, 56–57
International Trade and Payments, 5, 30, 37, 41, 54, 65, 106, 110
    balance of trade 30, 106
    gold 5
    purchasing power parity 41
Interpreters (see Anachronistic Interpretations; History of Ideas, interpreters)
Investment, 24–25, 28, 33, 44–46, 54, 73, 100, 113, 115, 118–119

Jevons, William Stanley, 76, 151, 152, 196, 197, 200
Jones, Richard, 80, 81, 85, 91, 96, 98
Justice, 10

Keynes, John Maynard, 2, 3, 25, 34, 35, 39, 42, 43, 104, 119, 125, 139, 190, 191, 193, 194, 195, 196, 198, 199, 201
    on Malthus 104, 198
    price flexibility 42
    quantity theory of money 2–3, 38–39
    role of ideas 193–194
Kuhn, Thomas, 201

Labor, 11, 18–19, 22, 55–56, 63, 76, 123, 184
Labor Command, 60, 65, 66–67, 74, 119
Labor Theory of Value (see Value)
Laissez-Faire, 4, 15, 19, 20, 35, 42–43, 116, 192
Landlords, 9–10, 17, 18, 50, 54, 76, 81, 127
Lange, Oskar, 103
Lauderdale, Earl of, 18, 29, 33, 36, 43, 44, 45, 46, 47, 73, 107, 116, 127, 139–140, 147, 226 (note 175)
    aggregate demand 45, 226 (note 175), 261 (note 174)
    fiscal policy 44–45, 46
    growth 45

    investment 44–45, 46, 261 (note 174)
    money 29, 36
    national debt 44, 127
    period analysis 129, 140
    saving 33, 34, 45
    secular stagnation 46, 107
    sinking fund 44–45, 139
Law of Diminishing Returns (see Diminishing Returns)
Laws of Production, 147–148
Lenin, V.I., 185, 192
Liu, Na, ix
Long Run and Short Run, 23, 30, 31, 33, 34–35, 36, 37, 38, 45,
    46, 47, 48, 59

McCulloch, John Ramsey, 3, 18, 21, 28, 34, 40, 50, 54, 77, 108
Macroeconomics, 22–47, 72–73, 73–74, 75, 164, 165
    economic growth 22–23
    equilibrium income 24–25, 27–29, 30, 31, 67, 74, 104,
        108, 111, 114–119, 125, 135, 150–151, 193
Maize, 54n
Malthus, Thomas Robert, vii, 2, 3, 4, 12, 18, 19, 20, 25, 27, 28,
    29, 30, 31, 32, 33, 36, 38, 39, 42, 46, 51, 57, 58, 59, 60,
    61, 62, 66, 67, 68, 69, 70, 71, 72, 73, 74, 75, 76, 77, 79,
    82, 83, 84, 89, 91, 93, 94, 97, 98, 104, 107, 108, 109,
    114, 116, 119, 120, 121, 126, 127, 135, 136, 137, 138,
    139, 147, 150, 151, 166, 183, 193, 198, 199
    aggregate demand 67, 74
    aggregate equilibrium income 28, 74, 193
    cost 29
    demand 29, 70–71, 150
    diminishing returns 3, 57, 76
    dynamics 28, 30–31, 32
    employment 28
    equilibrium aggregate income 28, 67
    investment 28
    labor command 66–67, 74, 75

    market clearing 46

    money 27, 29, 36, 39, 89

    originality 104, 127

    population theory 4, 20, 22, 48, 57–63, 76, 84, 93, 120–
        121, 127

    reproduction 67, 75

    saving 28, 33, 42, 46, 73

    Say's Law 75

    secular stagnation 30, 43, 107, 265 (note 28)

    social philosophy 1–21

    tendencies 60–61, 93, 120

    utility 73

    value 74

    "value of the whole produce" 74

    wages 42

Marcet, Jane, 3, 12

Markets, 1, 13–15, 189

Market clearing versus output sustainability, 46, 111, 114, 141

Marshall, Alfred, 39, 129, 200

Martineau, Harriet, 3, 12

Marx, Karl (see also Dialectics; Hegel), vii, 3, 4, 12, 56, 67, 77,
    87, 88, 90, 91, 93, 94, 103, 104, 127, 137, 138,147, 155–186,
    187, 188, 189, 191, 192, 194, 195, 199, 280 (note 1)

    abstraction 2, 87–88, 103

    allocation and distribution 9, 163–165, 172, 183

    "breakdown" theory 169, 171, 172, 176, 184

    Capital 2, 88, 91, 155, 156, 158, 159, 172, 182–183,
        184, 276 (note 65)

    classical economics 2

    "crises" 165–181, 184, 194, 275 (note 45), 278 (note 102)

    dictatorship of the proletariat 192, 281 (note 10)

    Engels' role 85, 156, 158, 161, 166–168, 182

    Hegelian concepts 89, 93–94, 156–159, 169–171, 181–182

    historic role 155, 185–186

    history, theory of 89, 90, 91, 194–195, 243 (note 73)

    increasing misery of the proletariat 94, 160–162, 168–169

    interpreters of Marx 88, 155, 156, 159, 162, 169, 171,

181, 182–183, 184, 275 (note 47)
"law of value" 91, 163–165
metamorphosis 94, 158, 161, 171
money 175, 176, 177, 178–180
profits 56–57, 94, 163
reciprocal interaction 89
Ricardian concepts 159–162, 181
Say's Law 173–174, 183
science 87
Sismondi 127, 174–175, 262 (notes 183, 184)
successive approximations 88, 158, 181–182
Sweezy, Paul 171
tendencies 94
value 67, 91, 168, 159, 163–165, 279 (note 123)
vulgar economics 2, 12, 87, 88
wages 159, 160
workers 81, 94, 100, 159–162, 167, 168–169, 185, 192, 194
Mathematics, 30, 32, 79, 82, 94, 96–97, 99, 106, 153, 175, 188,
190, 191, 198, 200, 282 (note 22)
conceptual clarity 82
identities 11, 24, 32, 34, 40, 98, 119
models 30, 104, 106, 111–113, 125, 198, 282 (note 22)
rigor 190, 191, 200
use in economics 30, 82, 98, 123, 124, 198, 282 (note 22)
Measures of Value, 65–68, 89, 90, 191
Menger, Carl, 152, 196, 197
Mercantilism, 5–6, 29, 34, 35, 47, 193, 207 (note 45)
Mercier de la Rivière, Pierre François Joachim Henri Le, 24–25
Metamorphosis, 94, 158, 161, 170, 171
Methodology (see also Causation), 4, 31, 79–103
abstraction 2, 79, 81, 82, 85, 86, 87–88, 89, 102, 109,
122–123, 242 (note 51)
assumptions 88
changes vs. states of being 89, 90–92, 95
complexity 87
definitions 79, 81, 82, 86, 97–99, 106–107
empiricism 59, 60, 61, 62, 63, 82, 83, 84, 86–87, 93,

100, 120, 122

   experiments 80, 87, 96, 100, 124

   inductive and deductive reasoning 85, 86–88, 95–96, 98, 103

   mathematics 79, 82, 96–97, 99, 191, 280 (note 22)

   rigor 82–83, 84, 106, 124, 127, 190, 199, 200

   science 79, 80–88, 95–96, 100, 190, 201, 240 (note 35)

   scope 83–84, 85–86, 101

   successive approximations 88, 96, 158, 159, 181–182, 190, 240 (note 35)

   tendencies 60–61, 89, 92–95, 120

   theory 82, 84, 86, 123

Microeconomics, 22, 48–78, 164

Mill, James, 3, 7, 15, 18, 19, 21, 23, 24, 25, 34, 45, 46, 77, 98, 130, 131, 138, 139, 199

   economic growth 33–34, 45

   India 131, 134

   Say's Law 23, 24, 25, 34

Mill, John Stuart, vii, 2, 3, 6, 8, 9, 10, 11, 12, 13, 14, 15, 18, 19, 20, 21, 24, 25, 28, 31, 32, 33, 34, 37, 39, 40, 45, 46, 50, 52, 53, 54, 61, 62, 66, 67, 68, 69, 76, 79, 84, 86, 87, 88, 91, 92, 93, 95, 96, 98, 100, 125, 129–154, 159, 166, 178, 187, 188, 189, 190, 191, 194, 195, 199, 200, 283 (note 31)

   demand 32, 76, 135, 150

   equilibrium aggregate income 28, 135, 150–151

   intellectuals 145–146, 195

   inconsistencies 31–32, 33, 147–149

   laws 148–149

   laws of production 147–148

   life and times 130–134

   loyalty 132, 138, 139, 188

   Marx, Karl 137–138, 189

   methodology 79, 84, 86–87, 88, 91–92, 95–96, 96–97, 100–101, 146, 242 (note 52)

   Mill, James 132, 138–139

   misinterpretations of others 32, 46, 75–76, 135, 140, 141, 142, 147, 150, 151–152, 188, 189, 199

   money 32, 37, 39, 40, 146

music 132
On Liberty 134, 143–146, 188, 280 (note 4)
originality 45–46, 104, 149–151, 153, 237 (note 136)
population theory 61–62, 93, 134, 191
reputation 129, 130, 146, 153–154, 191, 263 (note 1)
rent 150
Ricardo, David 131–132, 138, 146, 152, 153, 188
saving 33, 45
Say's Law 28, 31–32, 34, 134, 135–142
sinking fund 16, 44–45
socialism 129, 137, 138
stationary state 140–141
supply and demand 68–69
Taylor, Harriet 132–134, 146, 149, 264 (note 14)
theory of history 194–195
value 66, 76, 134
writing of *Principles of Political Economy* 134, 135, 136–137, 152, 265 (note 21)
Models
growth models 30, 104, 106, 110–113, 125, 198, 282 (note 22)
mathematical models 30, 104, 106, 111–113, 125, 198, 282 (note 22)
Ricardian models 102
Robinson Crusoe models 28, 115, 117, 123
Money, 6, 24, 34–42, 46–47, 66, 89, 193
demand for money 26, 32, 35, 36, 37, 39–40
effects on real variables 34, 35–36, 37, 38, 39, 41, 42, 47, 193
hoarding 26, 36, 37, 40, 42, 46, 111
inflation 41
interest rates 35–36, 37, 40, 42, 56–57
means of exchange 24, 26, 35
neutral money 35
quantity theory of money 38
"veil" 24, 27, 36, 38–39, 46, 117
velocity 2–3, 39, 40, 117
wealth 6, 24, 35

Monopoly, 13, 14, 64
Morality, 10
More, Hannah, 18
Music, 132

Nation, 5–6
National Debt, 16, 43–44, 139
Neoclassical Economics, 3, 38, 40, 79, 182–183

O'Driscoll, Gerald P., ix
Originality, 46, 104, 122, 127, 149, 187, 237 (note 4)
Overproduction, 25, 27–29, 30–31, 67, 74, 110, 114-119, 135,
        150–151, 176, 177
Owen, Robert, 20
Oxford University, 18, 21

Period Analysis (see Statics and Dynamics)
Petty, Sir William, 2
Phillips Curve, 190, 201
Physiocrats, 24–25, 110, 125, 189, 261 (note 174)
Place, Frances, 18, 19
Polemics, vii, 34 , 35, 38, 46, 83, 108, 188–189, 190–193
Politics, 9, 14, 187
Population, 3, 4, 6, 20, 22, 48, 56, 57–63, 76, 93, 94, 115, 119,
        120–121, 127, 134, 191
Poverty, 11, 12, 18, 19, 20, 59–60, 62, 63, 101, 119
Practicality, 31, 79, 81, 83, 84, 85, 86, 91, 101, 109, 123, 136,
        147, 148, 149, 193
"Productive" versus "Unproductive," 22, 110, 254 (note 46)
Profits, 42, 48, 50, 51, 52, 53, 54–57, 75, 76, 94, 115–116, 141
Proletarians
        Marx 161, 162, 168–169, 185, 194
        Sismondi 121, 122, 127
Purchasing Power,

domestic 24–29, 42, 45–46, 66–67, 110, 166
international 41

Quantity Theory of Money, 2, 4, 38–40

Real Variables, 34, 35–36, 37, 38, 41, 42, 47, 66, 79
Reform, 19–20
Rent, 3, 50–54, 55, 80–81, 229 (note 30)
    defined 50
    no-rent land 50–51, 52, 191
    price-determined 52, 53
    price-determining 52–53, 150
Reproduction, 24–25, 67, 75, 110, 114, 175, 254 (note 48)
Revenue, 112, 118–119, 121, 123
Revolution, 15, 162, 167, 168–169, 185, 192
Ricardo, David, vii, 2, 3, 7, 8, 11, 13, 15, 16, 17, 18, 19, 20, 21,
    23, 28, 30, 33, 35, 37, 38, 39, 40, 42, 43, 44, 45, 46, 48,
    50, 51, 52, 53, 54, 55, 56, 66, 67, 68, 69, 77, 79, 80, 81,
    82, 83, 84, 85, 88, 89, 90, 94, 101, 102, 104, 105, 108,
    109, 111, 116, 123, 124, 125, 127, 128, 131, 132, 135,
    136, 138, 139, 146, 153, 155, 156, 157, 159, 160, 163,
    166, 178, 181, 183, 187, 188, 197, 198, 199
    abstraction 80, 81, 82, 88, 109
    comparative statics 20, 34–35, 38, 39, 80, 89, 102, 111, 139
    demand 29, 68, 69–70
    diminishing returns 3, 50, 55, 76, 85, 102
    disproportionality 28, 135, 166
    dynamics 30–31
    equilibrium aggregate income 28, 30, 111, 135, 198,
        255 (note 52)
    growth 33
    methodology 31, 80, 101–102
    money 34–35, 40
    national debt 43–44

rent 3, 22,50–53, 81, 85, 90
parliamentary career 187–188
"Ricardian vice" 101–102, 124, 241 (note 49)
Say's Law 28
static model 22, 30
stationary state 22, 23, 55
supply and demand 68, 69–70
value 66
wages 55
Robinson Crusoe models, 28, 115, 117, 123

Samuelson, Paul A., 186
Saving, 25–26, 27, 33–34, 45
forced saving 42, 45
investment 26, 28, 45
Say, Jean Baptiste, 2, 3, 4, 11, 15, 18, 20, 21, 22, 23, 24, 25, 26,
27, 28, 31, 32, 33, 34, 36, 38, 39, 40, 42, 44, 46, 48, 49,
72, 73, 75, 82, 83, 85, 98, 100, 102, 104, 107, 108, 109,
110, 114, 116, 123, 126, 134, 135, 136, 138, 139, 147,
150, 151, 173, 183, 193, 199, 236 (note 117)
change of mind 31, 109, 135, 139, 193, 253 (note 41)
definition of "production" 31, 247 (note 136)
growth 33–34
methodology 41, 82, 253 (note 38)
money 36, 39, 42
social philosophy 11–12
tautology 34
translation 31
utility 31, 71–72, 75
Say's Law (see also Consumption; Demand, aggregate;
Disproportionality; Economic Growth; Equilibrium
Income; *Ex Ante* and *Ex Post*; Factor Payments; Gluts;
Money; Saving; Secular Growth and Stagnation) 2, 3, 4,
20, 22, 23–29, 31, 34, 36, 38, 40, 44, 46, 48, 72, 83, 98,
100, 102, 104, 107, 108, 110, 114, 123, 126, 134, 135,
138, 139, 147, 151, 173, 183, 193, 199

Samuel Bailey 98, 141
Thomas Malthus 75
Karl Marx 173–174, 183
James Mill 23, 24, 25, 34
John Stuart Mill 28, 31–32, 34, 134, 135–142
Physiocrats 24
David Ricardo 28
Say's Identity 40
J.C.L. Simonde de Sismondi 107, 117
Adam Smith 24, 25–26
Robert Torrens 34, 39, 98, 108
Schumpter, Joseph A., 101, 136, 152, 155, 156, 169, 197, 198
Science, 80–88, 100, 201, 240 (note 35)
abstraction 82, 87
methods 82
certainty 82, 83
empiricism 82, 83
mathematics 82
rigor 82
Scots and Scotland, 21, 130
Scrope, George Poulett, 32, 39, 151
Secular Growth and Stagnation, 24–25, 27, 30, 32, 43, 45, 46, 48, 91, 107, 116–117, 265 (note 28)
Self-interest, 17–18, 19, 187, 194
Simonde de Sismondi, J.C.L., 2, 4, 2, 20, 25, 27, 28, 29, 30, 31, 32, 33, 36, 46, 60, 61, 72, 73, 82, 84, 89, 98, 104–128, 135, 136, 137, 139, 140, 147, 151, 166, 174, 175, 176, 183, 187, 193, 198, 199, 200
abstractions 82, 109, 122–123
demand 29, 36, 125
destablizing responses 117, 126, 176
dynamics 30, 32, 89, 106, 110, 115, 121
empiricism 110
equilibrium aggregate income 27–29, 31, 104, 107, 108, 111, 114–119, 125, 135, 193
government 115, 116
growth model 30, 104, 106, 110–113, 125, 198, 282 (note 22)

    investment 110, 113, 115, 118–119
    life and times 104–110
    market clearing 46, 114
    mathematics 104, 106, 111–113, 123, 124, 282 (note 22)
    methodology 82, 84–85, 89, 93, 98, 106–107, 122–124
    money 36, 117, 119, 254 (note 43)
    neglected 104, 107, 110, 127, 198
    originality 104, 120, 125–126
    period analysis 30, 89, 106, 110, 111, 115, 121
    population 120–122, 127
    quality of analysis 98, 105–107, 118, 127, 199–200, 252 (note 33)
    reproduction 110, 114
    revenue 107, 112, 118–119, 121, 123
    Robinson Crusoe models 28, 115, 117, 123
    saving 33, 46, 111, 113, 140
    Say's Law 107, 117
    secular stagnation 32, 46, 107, 110, 116–117
    shut-down point 126
    utility 27–28, 114–115
Sinking Fund, 16, 44–45, 139
Slavery, 5, 6, 7, 8, 106
Smith, Adam, 3, 5, 6, 7, 8, 9, 10, 11, 13, 14, 15, 16, 17, 18, 19,
    21, 22, 24, 25, 26, 32, 33, 35, 36, 37, 39, 43, 44, 45, 51,
    52, 53, 56, 64, 65, 66, 71, 79, 84, 88, 102, 106, 122, 123,
    139, 150, 184, 187, 188, 189, 193, 197
    demand 64
    division of labor 13
    fiscal policy 43
    gluts 26
    "invisible hand" 11
    mercantilism 5–6, 9, 35
    methodology 79
    money 26, 66
    morality 10
    nation 5–6
    "real" 66, 79
    rent 52–53, 79, 150

saving 25–26, 139
Say's Law 24, 25–26
self-interest 10, 11
social philosophy 5–8, 9, 10–11, 13, 14–15, 19
sympathy 10
utility 65, 71–72, 197
value 71–72, 79
wealth 6
Social Costs (see Externalities)
Social Philosophy, 1–21
harmony 4, 10–11
landlords 9–10, 127
social conservatism 4–8
Socialism, 20, 54, 164–165, 185, 192
Soviet Union, 165, 185
Statics and Dynamics, 22, 30–34, 48, 49, 102, 139
comparative statics 20, 30, 32, 34–35, 37, 38, 39, 46, 89,
102, 111, 139, 140
dynamics 30–31, 33
period analysis 30
stationary state 22, 23, 55, 140–141, 171
Stationary State, 22, 23, 55, 140–141, 171
Statistics, 60
Stigler, George J.
history of economics 197, 201
Mill, John Stuart 150–152
Subsistence, 22, 23, 55, 58, 84, 94, 241 (note 45)
Successive Approximations, 158, 159, 181–182
Sweezy, Paul, 171

Taxes, 6, 9, 13, 16, 42–45, 54, 139–140
Taylor, Harriet, 132, 133, 134, 146, 149
Technology, 33, 46, 49, 56, 63, 65, 73, 104, 127, 139, 140, 163, 185
Tendencies, 60–61, 88–89, 92–95, 120
Thompson, Earl, ix
Thornton, Henry, 18, 37, 38, 39, 40, 42, 118, 223 (note 136)

hoarding 40
interest 37–38
quantity theory of money 40
unemployment 42
Torrens, Robert, 4, 32, 34, 39, 40, 42, 83, 98, 108, 138, 151,
179, 216 (note 53), 240 (note 35)
equilibrium aggregate income 108
forced saving 42
interest 40
money 32, 39, 151
Say's Law 34, 39, 98, 108
scientific economics 83
Translation, 31

Unemployment, 28, 42, 66, 104, 108, 127
"Unproductive" (see "Productive" and "Unproductive")
Utility, 27–28, 31, 64, 65, 71–72, 73, 75, 77, 114–115, 165, 184,
188, 196, 197, 198
equilibrium income 27–28, 31
prices 63–64, 71–72

Value, 3, 48, 63–76, 76–77, 182–183
definition of value 67, 74
labor 4, 77, 90
measure of value 65–68, 89, 90, 191
supply and demand 68–71
theory of value 48, 77
utility 63–64, 71–72, 197
Veblen, Thorstein, 91, 103
Velocity of Money, 2–3, 39, 40, 117
"Vulgar Economists," 2, 12, 87, 88

Wages, 5, 22–23, 38, 42, 48, 53, 55, 111, 113, 115, 116, 119,
121, 159–162

　　　　flexibility and rigidity 20, 102
　　　　subsistence 22–23, 55, 84, 94, 121, 241 (note 45)
　　　　trends over time 48, 241 (note 45)
War, 15–16, 44, 106, 197
Walras, Marie Ésprit Léon, 88, 200
Wealth, 5, 6, 8
West, Sir Edward, 3, 51, 52, 56
Whately, Richard, 60, 84, 92, 97, 98, 120
Whewell, William, 80, 81, 94, 95
Wicksell, Knut, 39
Wilson, Edmund, 185
Workers (see also Classes; Proletarians; Wages), 5, 7, 11, 13,
　　　　18, 19, 22–23, 26–27, 27–28, 51, 52, 55, 56, 58, 59, 61,
　　　　74, 91, 94, 111, 112, 113, 115, 116, 117, 118, 119, 121,
　　　　122, 123, 127, 161, 162, 183, 184–185, 192